Racing Post Chronicles

STRANGE STUFF

GRAHAM SHARPE

RACING POST

First published by Pitch Publishing on behalf of the *Racing Post*, 2021

Pitch Publishing
A2 Yeoman Gate
Yeoman Way
Worthing
Sussex
BN13 3QZ

www.pitchpublishing.co.uk
info@pitchpublishing.co.uk
www.racingpost.com/shop

© 2021, Graham Sharpe

All images are © Racing Post

Every effort has been made to trace the copyright. Any oversight will be rectified in future editions at the earliest opportunity by the publisher.

All rights reserved. No part of this book may be reproduced, sold or utilised in any form or transmitted in any form or by any means, electronic or mechanical, including photocopying, recording or by any information storage and retrieval system, without prior permission in writing from the Publisher.

A CIP catalogue record is available for this book from the British Library.

ISBN 9781839500800

Typesetting and origination by Pitch Publishing

Printed and bound by Replika Press

STRANGE STUFF

If this quote sums you up, you'll absolutely love this book … if it doesn't, you'll absolutely love this book for showing you what can happen when you buy in to loving horse racing:

'A sad, dyed in the wool old fart, who spends four hours at a racecourse watching horses run round in circles for the sum total of 15 minutes of action.'
Julian Muscat, father to two sons in their early 20s and a teenage step-daughter, tells *Racing Post* readers what they think of him.

Dedication
To our beautiful Kiwi-Brit granddaughter, Georgia.

CONTENTS

ALPHA-BETS	8
EVERYBODY KNOWS ... DON'T THEY?	12
YEAR WE GO ...	14
DRESSED FOR THE OCCASION	18
SAY, THERE ... QUOTABLE QUOTES	21
ODDS 'N' EVENS	34
STRANGE YEAR	38
JOCKULAR JAPES	102
TWITTERATI	115
WHAT THE DICKENS?	118
BOOKIE AND BETTING BANTER	120
INTERNATIONAL RACING	124
HORSING ABOUT	143
TRUCULENT TRAINERS	150
EARLY DAYS OF RACING	153
OF COURSE THEY DID	156
LONG SHOTS	167

BETTING STORIES	**169**
ANIMAL ANTICS	**180**
FOUR OF A KIND: MONOLULU, BERNARD, McCRIRICK, CHAPMAN ...	**184**
WHAT'S IN A NAME?	**190**
OWNERS' ODDITIES	**195**
DEAD LOSSES	**199**
ROCKING HORSES	**200**
SUPERNATURAL RACING AND BETTING MATTERS	**201**
UNEXPECTED RACING CONNECTIONS	**207**
RACING CELEBS	**209**
NATIONAL NEWS – THAT'S GRAND	**213**
SUPERSTITIONS	**220**
INTRIGUINGLY INTERESTING RACEY CHARACTERS	**222**
THE FIRST LADIES OF RACING	**252**
BIBLIOGRAPHY	**256**

ALPHA-BETS

ADELAIDE racecourse in Australia was the scene of a 1955 gamble from 33/1 to 7/2 on Thundering Legion, only for stewards to discover a battery-powered whip being carried by jockey Bill Attrill, who was taken away to be dealt with and later banned for 10 years. A substitute jockey was permitted to take over – and the horse won anyway!

BEN KEITH, of Star Sports bookmakers, summed up the essence of a true bookmaker in his comment to *Racing Post* editor Bruce Millington in a December 2019 interview: 'I've had punters go one or two million up on me before I've won the money back, because I fancy beating them.' He added: 'When you are a bookie you are the bank, and your security and radar should be on 24/7.'

CATHERINE UNSWORTH, a Liverpool doctor's wife, was the only punter at Haydock Park to back Coole to win a 15-runner handicap on 30 November 1929, so scooped a 3,410/1 payout for her two bob – 10p – winning bet.

DOROTHY PAGET, a real eccentric but mega-wealthy owner of five-time Cheltenham Gold Cup winner Golden Miller, was such an honest, heavy gambler, that her bookmaker, the eponymous William Hill, permitted her to place bets after the races had been run, as she would often sleep all day and rise at night.

EDWARD HODSON'S 5p yankee, placed on 11 February 1984, produced four winners at accumulative odds of 3,956,748/1 – but his Wolverhampton bookie had a maximum payout of £3,000 – which is the amount he was paid.

FREDDIE THE FOX was heavily backed to win the inaugural Mascot Grand National at Huntingdon racecourse in September 2001, which attracted a field of over 100 bizarrely clad clowns. Freddie bolted up, then was revealed as 24-year-old Matt Douglas, who twice competed over hurdles in the Olympics. Bookies Sportingodds.com complained, 'We've been done over for a four-figure payout.'

GHOST was the name of a racecourse bookie at the Chicago racecourse where, in 1891, popular jockey Monk Overton won all six races he contested, the first US rider to achieve such a feat. Ghost 'took on the appearance of one' it was reported, as his and other firms lost 'a combined, jaw-dropping $120,000.'

ALPHA-BETS

HUNTINGDON racecourse was the scene of betting on a most unusual race staged there in 1763 when, reported the Racing Calendar, 'a Quarter of a Mile Match was run for 100Gs between a Gentleman and a Grey Gelding with one Leg tied, and won by the former. The Horse's Leg untied in running.'

ILE DE CHYPRE, well supported from 6/1 to 4/1 to win during the 1988 Royal Ascot meeting, was clear under jockey Greville Starkey and set for victory, only to inexplicably swerve and unseat his rider. It was later alleged that criminals had targeted the horse with a 'stun-gun' to stop it winning.

J P McMANUS, bookie, owner and punter, confessed his first bet was one shilling – 5p – each-way on Orchardist, 25/1 for the 1962 Cesarewitch. The horse duly passed the post in front, but was disqualified and placed second.

KIM JONG-UN, boss of North Korea, may have been planning a betting coup, it appeared, when it was revealed in February 2020 that 'Mr Kim's secretive and impoverished state spent $75,509 (£58,000) on 12 thoroughbred Russian horses last year.' They were apparently ordered from the Altai stud farm, which had previously sold 14 to Pyongyang in 2015.

J P McManus; leading owner.

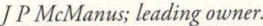

STRANGE STUFF

LINDA O'NEILL'S husband, trainer Owen, stopped her backing his two runners at Bath in August 1993. They won at 66/1 and 50/1, a 3416/1 double. 'You wouldn't be able to print what she said to me,' commented Owen.

MARIE LAZENBY ended up in hospital after winning £22 by backing Miinnehoma to win the 1994 Grand National – as the horse crossed the line she jumped for joy and cheered, upsetting her pet dog so much that it also jumped up – and bit her on the left nipple.

NEW security technology introduced by William Hill in 1992 to record bets placed by on-course punters had unexpected results when at Kempton it set off a fireworks display earlier than scheduled, and at Newbury it broadcast details of bets being taken over the course pa system.

OLIVE HARRISON, June Muggleston and Dorothy Harrison made betting history on 15 June 1967 when the trio made a book at Uttoxeter's evening meeting. The sisters already owned eight betting shops.

POSTAL ORDERS to the value of £500 were in the letter received by your author in April 1990 when he was working for William Hill – together with a letter signed 'Mr M' explaining that 'I won £475 four years ago in a bet involving two horses, but I now do not want the money. An extra £25 has been added for the trouble to which this puts you.' I sent it to a racing charity.

QUEEN MOTHER reportedly placed a bet from the cockpit of Concorde while travelling over the Irish Sea on a day trip to celebrate her 85th birthday in August 1985.

ROSS BRIERLEY introduced himself as a new columnist for the *Racing Post* on 16 February 2020, telling readers: 'They say you don't choose the betting life, the betting life chooses you. And by they, I mean me. "Congratulations, it's a gambler!" is the second least popular greeting card in the new baby section (after "Sorry! It's not yours"), but betting runs in my blood.'

SWINGER was the eyebrow-raising name of a new bet introduced by the Tote in 2008. They denied that there was any sexual connotation to the wager, which involved picking two horses to finish in the first three in any order.

TRODMORE was the entirely invented name of a fictitious racecourse which, in 1898, gullible bookies were scammed into accepting bets for, with the 'runners' and, later, results being published in racing paper *The Sportsman*. The scammers were never unmasked but made fortunes before their plot was revealed.

URQUHART was how the boy whose christian names were Tom Arkle was known at his Herefordshire Roman Catholic boarding school in 1989. That middle name was a clue to his interest in racing, which resulted in him consistently tipping winners, to the extent that when his father visited, bringing the *Sporting Life* for the boy, he was called into the office by one of the monks and asked whether he and his colleagues could be informed of the tips.

VICTOR SASSOON'S Hot Night started 9/2 second favourite for the 1927 Derby, for which the owner had backed him each-way at 1000/1 as a yearling. The horse finished runner-up, at least landing the place part of the bet at 250/1. As the wager's stake had been one penny each-way – Sir Victor feared higher stakes might jinx the horse – he collected £1 in settlement.

W F WILLIAMSON staked £10 on his Russian Hero at ante-post odds of 300/1 to win the 1949 Grand National at ante-post odds. Starting at 66/1, he duly obliged.

XENOPHOBIA is what top trainer and former England footballer Mick Channon was accused of by *Mail on Sunday* sportswriter Patrick Collins, who took exception to Mick's opinion about then-England manager Sven Goran Eriksson, calling him 'banal and risible, with a streak of xenophobia'.

YATES was the surname of lorry driver punter, Barry, who, in 1991, listened to a telephone commentary of a race in which his £2 treble's final selection won him £50. So excited was he that he forgot to put the receiver back properly – resulting in a £50+ phone bill.

ZAHIA looked set to land a gamble worth £12,500 for owner N F Gee as the 100/1 outsider came to lead the 1948 Grand National with just the last fence to clear – but jockey Eddie Reavey inexplicably took the wrong course, missing out the final fence, thus being disqualified.

EVERYBODY KNOWS ... DON'T THEY?

Everybody knows …

… that Becher's Brook on the Grand National course is named after the jockey of that name who fell into it … YET, most don't know that Captain Becher – for it was he – actually DIVED into the brook to avoid injury as other runners bore down, after his mount stopped dead, unseating him.

…. that the first Derby was run at Epsom in 1780 … NOT a bit of it – the Derby Plate, the inaugural race with such a title, was staged on the Isle of Man in 1621.

… that the term 'Sport of Kings' has always been used in the context of racing … only, since 1918, according to Gerald Hammond's 1992 *Horse Racing, A Book of Words*, in which he writes: 'only lately synonymous with horse racing. First it described war, the hunting. Its first use to describe racing does not seem to be until 1918, in a poem, "Weep for the King of Sports, the Sport of Kings".'

Becher's Brook, one of the iconic fences at Aintree.

EVERYBODY KNOWS ... DON'T THEY?

Heading towards Tattenham Corner.

... that heavily backed 1836 St Leger winner Elis was believed to be the first horse to be transported to the races, wrong-footing bookies who didn't believe the colt could make it from his Goodwood stables to Doncaster in time ... HOWEVER, it emerges that in October 1816 the Newmarket St Leger was won by 30/1 Royal Sovereign, whisked there from his Worcestershire base by owner Mr Terrett via his 'bullock float.'

... the Derby runners swing round the Tattenham Corner bend during the race ... EXCEPT that the 1929 Bloodstock Breeders Review proved that this piece of land used to be called Tottenham corner, from the name of the family owning the land, which was somehow corrupted to Tattenham, and also pointed out it is also incorrect to talk of horses 'coming round Tattenham corner as the (original) corner is on the opposite side of the course.'

... that the first evening race meeting in the UK was at Hamilton Park on 18 July 1947 ... ALTHOUGH, *The History of Horse racing in Scotland* by racing historian J Fairfax points out, 'I have records of night racing at York as early as 1784.'

... that the short-leather style of riding which revolutionised jockey styles was introduced to Britain by American rider Tod Sloan in late 1897 ... BUT NO, declares the 1927 *Bloodstock Breeders Review* in an obituary of black US jockey William Simms, who arrived in England in the mid-1890s, 'it was he who first demonstrated to English sportsmen the advantages of the crouching style of riding so brilliantly exploited by Tod Sloan a year or two later.'

YEAR WE GO ...

1504
Racing was held at Leith, Edinburgh, on a 'long stretch of bare sand', reported accounts of the Lord High Treasurer for Scotland, noting that this piece of ground was 'also notable as the grim scene of executions for piracy'.

1634
A report of a welching punter appeared in a letter, dated 20 March, and complaining that 'The Earl of Southampton, they say, hath lost a great deal of monie latelie at the Horse Races at Newmarket; but true it is, he hath licence to travel for three years and is gone in all haste to France.'

1641
Two horses taking part in a 1,000 crown-a-side race between two French noblemen were prepared on bread made with beans and aniseed, and were given between 200 and 300 fresh eggs two days before the race.

1654
Cromwell banned horse racing, fearing it might bring together crowds of people with Royalist sympathies and result in political disturbances.

1679
Believed to be the first racing form book, John Nelson of Newmarket's *Register of Horse Matches* appeared for sale.

1718
Early skulduggery at York races when 'Crutches started a very hot favourite, but jockey Thomas Black, finding his horse winning, in spite of all his efforts to stop him, with courage worthy of a better cause, threw himself off when leading at the distance post.'

1731
Probably the first race for three-year-olds attracted nine runners at Beldale in Yorkshire.

1771
'In order to save Mr Quick, Mr Castle, or any of the Ascott [sic] Confederacy the trouble and expense of training, they are desired to take notice that none of their horses will be allowed to run,' at Chester Races, 'nor will Thomas Dunn be permitted to ride,' declared the *Racing Calendar*.

1774
A winner at Chester races was called Mine-Ass-in-a-Band-Box.

1775
The Stewards of Morpeth Races in the North East 'ordered five pounds of the subscription money to be distributed amongst the prisoners in the jail, an example worthy of imitation,' declared the *Newcastle Journal*.

1788
York staged a race between two runners, set to carry 30 stones for 100 guineas.
Former MP George Baker's (any relation, one wonders?) grey horse was 1-2 favourite but was beaten by Mr Maynard's un-named bay mare.

1798
In a freak accident at Chester races, Mr Lockley's Hairbreadth bolted 'when leading near the winning posts, jumped the cords and struck his head against an officer's helmet, being killed instantaneously,' as the point of the spiked helmet entered the horse's brain.

1800
At the turn of the century, a blind Scottish jockey, Willie McGilvray, competed on a regular basis at his local racecourses. It was reported that 'as he never went upon unknown ground his lack of sight did not appear to be much detriment.'

1803
There may have been more exciting race meetings than the four day one held at Kelso, as it attracted a total of three runners and every race actually run was a walk-over.

1812
This year's 2,000 Guineas winner had a baffling-to-pronounce name of Cwrw.

1815
The Portuguese name of 1815 St Leger winner, Filho da Puta, translates as 'son of a whore'.

STRANGE STUFF

1820
Having been discovered watching trials on Newmarket Heath through a telescope, William 'Snipe' Taylor became the first 'tout' to be warned off of the Heath.

1826
The 1776 St Leger winner was un-named at the time – but 50 years later a racing historian dubbed her Allabaculla – which stuck.

1846
The weather was so foggy at Newmarket's Houghton meeting that 'men were stationed at intervals on the course to guide jockeys, and the line of the course was tracked with tan and sawdust.'

1854
Leading the fabled Charge of the Light Brigade, Lord Cardigan rode a racehorse, Roland, who had won the Wolverhampton Stakes.

1857
They staged a race at Hartlepool in September of this year, open only to riders who were 'captains of vessels'. The Mariners' Stakes saw three skippers going to post, with Captain Thomson sinking his rivals' hopes by sailing to victory on Phoenix.

1863
Lanark Silver Bell winner was named Dick Swiveller.

1898
A trial of a newly invented Starting Gate Machine was arranged at Epsom's summer meeting – and by 1901 they were being used at most meetings.

1909
Minoru, Derby winner this year, was exported to Russia only to be reportedly seized by Bolsheviks during the Revolution and executed for being an aristocrat.

1914
Connections finally realised Mr Solly Joel's Poor Boy would never win Goodwood's Stewards Cup, as he finished unplaced, having been runner-up in 1908 as a three-year-old; unplaced in 1909; runner-up again in 1910; unplaced in 1911; runner-up in both 1912 and 1913.

1944
After the racecourse had suffered from air raids, the Romanian 1,000 Guineas was finally run – and won by Bombi.

1948
Sheila's Cottage won the 1948 Grand National – but showed scant gratitude to jockey Arthur Thompson – when he visited her after the race, she bit off the top of his finger.

1983
Huntress Grace was pulled up during a Fakenham meeting in May 1983 – twice, as she took part in two races on the card.

1986
During the Christmas holiday students from Widnes Sixth Form were blamed for damaging the stuffed remains of great racehorse Brown Jack, which had been kept at the Stable Grill, Widnes, only to be found lying on the ground, minus one ear.

1993
Peter Upson-trained Mansfield House raced on an unfamiliar surface in February this year, after his horse-box crashed on the A604 near Huntingdon, and he charged off down the fast lane, somehow being caught before damaging himself.

2009
Tony McCoy received a gift from Fakenham racecourse in March this year to mark his recent achievement of 3,000 winners … an apple tree.

2021
Celerity shocked racegoers at Haydock on Friday evening, 6 August 2021, by finally shedding her maiden status at the 106th time of asking with a front-running victory under 7lb claimer Erika Parkinson.

The seven-year-old, trained by Lisa Williamson, had amassed the longest losing streak in British and Irish racing history, having failed to score in a career that began at Dundalk in April 2016.

And Jockey Gary Bardwell rode his first winner for 18 years on 8 September 2021. Having retired back in February 2003, he teamed up with Natural Colour in the St Leger Legends Classified Stakes over one mile at Doncaster, and stormed to an 11/1 victory – afterwards attributing his win to 'no sex, no drink'!

DRESSED FOR THE OCCASION

- Starter in Hong Kong during the 19th century Sir Henry May would trot up on a pony to each flag start, wearing top hat and formal dress.
- 'Love-locks flowed out from the front of his cap to frame his forehead, and he was much addicted to the wearing of frills, while bunches of ribbons adorned the tops of his boots' read a description of early 'superstar' dandy jockey Sam Chifney senior, 1753–1807.
- Riding his own horse in a late 19th-century hurdles race at Melbourne, Australia, when his jockey failed to turn up, George Owen won on Modesty, but was fined £5 for being improperly dressed in white shirt and 'shepherd's plaid trousers'.
- Top jump jockey Graham Thorner finished a race feeling somewhat exposed, remembered fellow rider, Philip Blacker, who described 'watching Graham ride a finish without his trousers. The bottom had popped early in the race and by the time he'd jumped the last he was down to jockstrap and ladies' tights.' Thorner rode Well To Do to win the 1972 Grand National and afterwards insisted on wearing the same pair of underpants every time he raced until, said fellow jockey Richard Pitman, 'He wore them until there was nothing left, just a bit of elastic round his legs. He even had to keep them on with another pair – but there was no way he'd ride without them.' As for Pitman – he always had to put his right boot on first.
- Punters are often said to have lost their shirts but in 1992 racecourse bookie Norrie Drummond of Lanarkshire accepted a bet of 50 shirts to £250 at Edinburgh for an even money chance – which was beaten.
- Trainer Martin Pipe's wife Carol was with him at Taunton in 1993 when their Elite Reg's tongue strap went missing. Carol dashed to the 'ladies', removed her tights – which were then used to hold down their runner's tongue. The horse was pulled up in the race.
- Here's an eye-witness description of owner, steward and starter Lord George Bentinck (1802–1848) at Doncaster races – 'Dressed in buckskin breeches in the hides of his own stags, with exquisitely made boots of antique colouring in top, a buff waistcoat of reddish brown, double breasted coat, ornamented with the buttons of the Jockey Club; a quiet

Carol Pipe came to the rescue of husband Martin (left) in 1993, pictured here with Peter Scudamore MBE, eight-time Champion Jockey and trainer in National Hunt racing.

beaver placed neither at right angle, nor yet at left, but in the juste milieu of gentlemanly taste, on a well-formed head of auburn hair, with large whiskers of the same colour.' Eat your heart out, Matt Chapman.

- Goodwood staged a series of meetings during the 1820s in which a weight allowance was given to riders who wore a cocked hat.

- A fraction over the weight he was set to carry to ride Langley Vale at Goodwood in September 2015, former champion jockey Seb Sanders realised drastic measures were called for – so jumped on the horse and went out to ride in stockinged feet, without boots – reportedly the first time such a thing had happened in modern British racing history.

The horse finished fourth and Sanders faced some criticism for his decision, but hit back: 'I got held up getting to Goodwood and didn't have time for a sweat, so I left the boots off to make the weight. That's all it was and I think a mountain's been made out of a molehill.'

STRANGE STUFF

In November 2014 French jockey Pierre-Charles Boudot had ridden without boots when Noir Garcon finished runner-up in a two-year-old newcomers' race in Japan, having weighed out without them to make the required 55kg weight. Boudot told the Tokyo stewards, 'We often do it in France,' but was reprimanded for his actions.

KHADIJAH UNIQUE

The 2019 Magnolia Cup, a charity race staged at the Glorious Goodwood meeting, saw a unique achievement by 18-year-old student Khadija Mellah who rode the Charlie Fellowes-trained Haverland to victory, in the process becoming the first rider to win a British race wearing a hijab.

Goodwood's 1900 July meeting saw American jockey 'Little' Johnny Reiff, nicknamed 'Knickerbocker' after the garment he wore on his nether regions, win eight races.

Khadija Mellah, the first rider to win a race wearing a hijab.

SAY, THERE ... QUOTABLE QUOTES

UNIQUE
'My name is Ross Brierley, and I hereby declare myself to be the world's only stand-up comedian, professional gambler and racing journalist.' Difficult to argue with this introduction by Brierley to his new *Racing Post* column on 16 February 2020.

V POINTLESS
'What's the point of a language that doesn't have a "V" in it?' asked Matt Chapman on the ITV4 Racing breakfast show on 29 February 2020, having been told that was the case as he tried to pronounce a name beginning with the letters 'Bh', but pronounced as a 'v' sound.

Matt Chapman, problems with pronouncing a name correctly.

STRANGE STUFF

Paul Nicholls; bang on the money.

FAT-PLUS

'We don't do thin here – we do fat with a bit of cover.' Trainer Emma Lavelle (*Racing Post,* 26 January 2020).

BEN'S BEHIND

'There are a few lads these days buying women's perfume as they think it smells better. But each to his own.' Conditional jockey, Ben Jones (*Racing Post,* 26 January 2020), adding as his earliest racing memory, 'My first pony race, when I was so far behind, I thanked them for waiting for me to cross the line.'

CHRIS THE SMASHER

Welsh National winning trainer Christian Williams – 'As long as it's not your neck or back you can usually be repaired. I didn't retire because I was injured, I just wanted to be doing a little better than I was.' Retired at 29, having 'smashed' his right shoulder 'to bits', meaning a year-long recovery, also suffered multiple fractures of the left leg, while the bones of his left arm went through the skin in a double open fracture.

PAUL'S SNIP
'Everything about Paul is bang on the money apart from one thing,' he says. 'He needs to be gelded. The sooner the better.' One of his most loyal owners, Andy Stewart, with his presumably tongue-in-cheek view of trainer Paul Nicholls (*Racing Post*, 17 February 2020).

ON THE FLAT
'I suppose we will be told no animals were harmed in the making of *Baghdad Central*, but I can't lie: when that beautiful racehorse was flattened by a car in a gratuitous scene 16 minutes in, I did not feel well disposed to this drama.' TV critic Carol Midgley (*Times Magazine*, 4 February 2020).

LAST APPEAL
'The appeal it [racing] once had as a quasi-acceptable theatre of skulduggery has significantly diminished.' Julian Muscat (*Racing Post*, 11 December 2019).

MAJESTIC LAUGH
'I told the Queen a horse racing joke and I was off and running.' Legendary portrait photographer Terry O'Neill (1938–2019) recalled how he put The Queen at her ease when he photographed her in 1992.

HUNG UP ON HORSES
'I have racehorses, but I don't want to hang out with billionaires.' Ryanair's Michael O'Leary (*Times Magazine*, 22 February 2020).

HEAVY BREATHER
Jockey Chester Williams on his funniest racecourse experience: 'A man, who must have been 14st, wanted to just finish a race. He actually pulled up with about a mile left to give himself and the horse a breather before continuing and he still fell off.' (*Racing Post*, 23 February 2020).

CORNELIUS BLOWS UP?
Once described to me by a mutual journalist friend as 'Semtex' ('on account of his explosive temper,' it was explained), BBC racing correspondent Cornelius Lysaght's almost 30-year stint with the national broadcaster was brought to a close at the beginning of 2020.

STRANGE STUFF

Cornelius Lysaght – former BBC racing correspondent.

The respected Cornelius claimed to be unaware why the decision to part company had been made, but told the *Racing Post's* Lee Mottershead: 'There have been suggestions a few of us at the BBC are victims of being white, middle aged and male. I can only assume that cannot be the case, because I think that would be against discrimination laws – and I'm sure the BBC wouldn't want to break the law.'

However, he warned: 'Racing and the mainstream media had a long affair going way back – that love affair has soured in recent years. Nobody really knows why ... racing seems to have been sucked into the view that betting is awful.'

PRESENTING SELF ASSEMBLY ED

'Racing is full of factions ... My hope is one day a private equity firm might eye up racing and think the sport is ripe to be run by one streamlined company. I'm not a business expert but it seems to me racing needs to go down that track.' ITV Racing presenter Ed Chamberlin in an interview by Lee Mottershead in the *Racing Post* of 8 February 2020, in which he recalled the opening day of his role on 1 January 2017: 'The next day we were slaughtered. I always quote Giles Smith, who wrote in *The Times* that as a presenter I was as exciting as a self-assembly chest of drawers from Ikea.'

SAY, THERE ... QUOTABLE QUOTES

COCKY COBDEN
'A cocky little ***t, whose a*** I still have to kick from time to time.' Paul Nicholls on stable jockey Harry Cobden (*Racing Post Annual 2020*).

ARE YOU SIGNING UP?
'If you choose to engage with horse racing you sign up to every clause of the contract, and that includes equine deaths.' Dave Yates (*Daily Mirror,* 20 December 2019).

TEA-ING UP IDEA
'A condition of racecourse licences will be that receptacles are provided for used tea-bags – or I may scream.' David Ashforth of the *Racing Post's* suggestion/demand of 18 December 2019 for racecourse innovations during the forthcoming decade.

RACING IS ALL ABOUT LIFE
'Racing is all about life. People want to be able to watch sport because it makes them feel good, or they want to be able to compete. This is all part of the circle of life. You can't eliminate risk in anything. There is only one thing certain for us all, that we will only get so far and our bodies will fade and we will move off this earth ... racing is a sport and horses are athletes ... athletes get injured. We're flesh and blood and there is nothing perfect about anything in life. If a horse doesn't want to race they will let you know very quickly and people who care for horses and are looking at them every day, they know when a horse is happy or sad.' An unusually frank Aidan O'Brien in a 7 July 2019 *Racing Post* interview.

NO FUDGING ISSUE
'Fudge' – Lady Cecil's answer when asked to name her guiltiest pleasure.

JOCKULAR REMARKS
'The camaraderie among pole vaulters is a joy to behold. You see it at every event and definitely tonight. Possibly the nearest thing you'll get to jump jockeys.' Tweet by Lee Mottershead of the *Racing Post* during 2019 World Athletics Championships in Doha.

LOAD OF RUBBISH
'There is a lot of rubbish among the best-bred horses. I have always said you should buy the horses you like.' Leading French trainer Jean-Claude Rouget not endearing himself to breeders in October 2019 during a *Racing Post* interview.

STRANGE STUFF

Former trainer Alan Bailey.

TWO IN ONE

Asked which was the best horse in his yard, trainer Richard Harper, whose Chapel House had just won at Hereford in April 2012, replied, 'I've just got the one horse, so he's the best and the worst.'

QUOTES

'Racing does not have the same place in society as it did. The raging love affair with the mainstream media is not even a flirtation in some ways now.' BBC Racing Correspondent Cornelius Lysaght, as his departure from the role after 18 years was announced in December 2019.

END OF THE LINE?

'I reckon most trainers will be out of business in 10 years' time. It's all work and no reward, as you can't compete with the big guys running horses that cost 300,000 guineas or more in maidens with prize money of £4000.' Retiring trainer Alan Bailey, 80 (*Racing Post,* 27 January 2020).

WHIP HAND

'The whip should be carried as an aid rather than something that needs to be applied. It would be absolutely ridiculous to take it away. I wouldn't take a horse over fences without one. Its use is something the regulator must manage alongside what the public will accept.' David Muir, 21 years into his role as racing consultant to the RSPCA (*Racing Post,* 27 January 2020).

BOG STANDARD?

'Yes, the toilet seat.' Former champion jump jockey turned TV pundit John Francome's response on being told he had become 'part of the furniture of Channel 4 Racing' in July 2006.

SAY, THERE ... QUOTABLE QUOTES

Former jockey and TV pundit John Francome.

GET STUFFED
'Not usually a sentimental man, AP [McCoy] insisted that when [talented hurdler] Get Me Out Of Here retired he would have a home forever with him and it is at McCoy Towers that he can be seen – beautifully stuffed in the corner of the hall. Alastair Down (*Racing Post* 8 March 2015).

WALK LIKE AN ...?
'My husband spent a couple of days running round after me like I was some sort of Egyptian pharaoh.' Jockey Lizzie Kelly in the *Racing Post* on 22 October 2019, having broken her right forearm, while her left collarbone had come away from the joint.

NAP OF THE DAY?
'They call me Napoleon, but I'd rather it was Wellington.' Born in Spain, French trainer Andre Fabre, who tends to keep himself to himself, to Sheikh Mohammed's racing manager of the time Anthony Stroud. The same Fabre who played serious polo in Argentina, whose Arcangues

STRANGE STUFF

Andre Fabre; Wellington or Napoleon?

was a record odds (133/1) Breeders' Cup winner and who spent three years in Berlin as the son of a diplomat.

PUN INTENDED

Trainer Robin Dickin said of his popular chaser, Thomas Crapper, that he could 'always rely on him to get me out of the sh*t.'

HIS NUMBER'S UP

'The day he mounted another horse out at exercise and knocked the rider off was the day I thought "that's enough". It wouldn't have been quite so bad but the horse he was trying to mount was a gelding.' John Holt, trainer of Number Theory, explains why he took the decision to geld the 2012 Old Newton Cup winner.

SAY, THERE ... QUOTABLE QUOTES

SPRINTING TO DERBY
'I thought then we had bought a sprinter, not a potential Derby winner.' Celebrating three-year-old gelding Wolf Hunter's 2019 Jersey Derby victory, owner David Moon reflected that when he bought him for 10,000 guineas after he'd won on the all-weather over 6f at Kempton, he'd thought that would be the horse's ultimate distance. But he then was tried and won over 7f, then 1m½f, then 1m 1f, 1m2f, and finally the traditional Derby distance of one and a half miles. Unlike most Derby races, the Jersey version is open to runners of all ages – indeed, Wolf Hunter beat five rivals including nine-year-old Aussie Lyrics, who had won the race three times previously, and 11-year-old Barwick, who had been runner-up in the Jersey Champion Hurdle on his previous outing!

CHAMPAGNE MOMENT
'I'm sitting here with a big bacon sandwich and a bottle of champagne – and I know I can do the same thing again tomorrow morning if I feel like it.' Great jump jockey John Francome explaining his decision to fellow top rider Terry Biddlecombe after earlier announcing his retirement from the saddle following a fall from The Reject at Chepstow on 9 April 1985.

GREAT BUM
'I give out a longshot play every day at Gulfstream, and when one of those wins, you walk through the stands and people are yelling, "You did great!" Then when you don't win, they call you a bum. That's the beauty of racing.' Ron Nicoletti, US handicapper and race analyst at Gulfstream Park (November 2019).

PUSH OFF
'It's very emotional for me. I feel like pushing the wife over to one side of the bed and putting him in the middle.' Owner Paul Barber after his popular chaser Denman finished runner-up in the 2011 Cheltenham Gold Cup.

FIRED UP
'One evening, for a bet, I set my boxer shorts on fire. Unfortunately, I was wearing them at the time, and the scars took weeks to heal.' The *Racing Post's* 25th anniversary bash in 2011 proved to be a red-hot event – according to Betfair media chief Tony Calvin.

BALLS-UP
Impressed by the performances of jump jockey Lucy Alexander, the late trainer Ferdy Murphy said, somewhat anatomically inaccurately, of her during 2012 – 'She's some rider – she's got balls of steel.'

STRANGE STUFF

DOPEY BAN
'Continue to lengthen the ban each year so, by the time 2025, comes around the ban for a positive cocaine test is five years or more.' *Racing Post* writer David Jennings (1 October 2019) on possible punishments for jockeys who indulge in prohibited substances.

MESSY McCOY
Having won the 2012 Cheltenham Gold Cup on Synchronised, AP McCoy rode the horse in the Grand National, only for the horse to fall at Becher's Brook, gallop on, then suffer a fatal hind-leg fracture. When he was told, said McCoy, 'I cried, to be honest. I was in a mess and plenty sore in the ambulance room, and when JP [McManus, the horse's owner] came in to see me I was still crying. I went straight home, didn't ride for days and just stayed in the house.'

HARD LUCK
'It's hard getting to the top. Once you're there it's just as hard, if not harder, to stay there.' Multiple champion jump trainer Paul Nicholls, speaking in 2012. He's still there.

Nicky Henderson has sleepless nights over Cheltenham.

SAY, THERE ... QUOTABLE QUOTES

Willie Mullins mixed emotions on celebrating a winner.

SAVAGE LOSS
'Upsides when tried to savage winner close home, just failed.' *Racing Post* comment on 33/1 shot Sir Gerry, runner-up in Newbury's September 2010 Dubai Duty Free Handicap behind 3/1 Delegator, partnered by Ted Durcan, who had previously won on Sir Gerry.

DEAD LOSS
Shortly after joining the *Sporting Life* racing paper in 1990, journalist David Ashforth was tasked with calling Gordon Richards to ask how his promising chaser Full Strength was doing. He was informed by the trainer, 'Not reet well, lad. He broke his neck at Ascot three days ago.'

MOUTHY MALE
'As he was coming to the top of the stairs, I asked him what his problem was. As he opened his mouth, I just punched him one – all that anger that came from when he dropped me.' US jockey Sophie Doyle, who had 28 wins from 249 rides in the UK in 2010, making her the leading female apprentice of that year, before deciding to move to the States in 2013, finally ran out of patience with a male jockey who kept causing dangerous in-race confrontations with her 'a few years ago' when they were both riding at an Indiana track. From that day on, declared Doyle, sister of top UK rider, James, in 2019, 'the guys in the jocks' room have respected me.'

STRANGE STUFF

SISTER SOPHIE
'I saw it on Facebook the other day, "why is it when you Google Sophie, she comes up as James Doyle's sister. Surely by now, it should just be Sophie Doyle?"' Sophie Doyle, quoted in 2019.

STOUTE FELLOW
'Well, he's come up here because he wants to be trained by a proper trainer.' Sir Michael Stoute tells Paul Hayward of *The Telegraph* in July 2019 what Henry Cecil told him after Shergar dropped his jockey and ran off one morning, ending up outside Cecil's then Warren Place yard.

LEG-ENDARY
'It is a pity his amazing legs cannot be patented.' Tribute to 19-year-old hunter chaser Culmleigh Padre in the 1992 Mackenzie & Selby annual round up of that scene. The horse had been running for an amazing 13 consecutive seasons.

SEXY FUTURE
The same volume suggested that 11-year-old. Flying Trove was now past his best and should be retired to 'hopefully be allowed to concentrate on rampant sex in future'.

FRANC-LY HOPELESS
Of Francolina, an eight-year-old mare who won a race despite being a 'remote fourth' when the three ahead all fell independently at the last at the Garnons track – it was said that she still 'only managed to hold a remounter by a length. She is basically hopeless.'

AGGRESSIVELY CRACKERS
11-year-old gelding French Aggression, readers were told, was 'a well-known lunatic' – professionals jockeys refused to ride him – who 'is as crackers at home as on the racecourse. Cares not one whit for his own safety.'

BUCK OFF
My Man Buck, 14 years old, 'cannot run very fast' and is 'usually soundly trounced', so 'would probably like to put his feet up now.'

STRANGELY EMPTY
'What always strikes me is it's a funny place when empty, stranger still when full.' Trainer Nicky Henderson on the Cheltenham Festival, after admitting that he has a sleeping tablet, prescribed by his doctor, to take each night on the run-in to the event (*Evening Standard*, 6 March 2020).

BROKEN SLUMBER
'I just slept for a week, you're that broken.' Paul Nicholls on the aftermath of the Cheltenham Festival. (*Evening Standard,* 6 March 2020).

PHOTO NEGATIVE
'It's very hard to throw your hat and your binoculars in the air when your son and your horse are down behind a screen.' Irish trainer Willie Mullins tells *Mail on Sunday* writer Oliver Holt about his feelings as he watched his horse Al Boum Photo winning the 2019 Cheltenham Gold Cup while his son Patrick and his mount, Invitation Only, had fallen. 'It was 20 minutes before I found out that Patrick was OK, but that the horse had died.'

Holt said of Mullins: 'He acts like a man who would rather die than let a boast escape his lips.'

ODDS 'N' EVENS

4 All four horses lining up for the 4.25 at Towcester in March 2011 failed to finish, leaving the race having to be voided.

6 Fred Archer rode six winners from six races at Lewes in 1882 – the second time he'd achieved the feat.

007 The number worn on training saddlecloths of New York trainer Harold James Bond's string.

8 runners lined up for the fifth race at Australian track Mackay in Queensland on 9 October 2010. All eight were trained by John Manzelmann. Not only that, he and his wife owned them all, too.

8 The number of walkovers the first equine superstar racehorse Eclipse had amongst his 18 wins from 18 races in 1769 and 1770.

9 runners contested the last race at Aussie course Dubbo in New South Wales on 20 December 2010. They overcame reported odds of 362,880/1 by finishing from 1–9 in racecard order.

11 of the 12 runners entered for the final British Group 1 race of the 2019 season, the Vertem Futurity, came from a single stable at Doncaster – that of Aidan O'Brien. Only Andrew Balding had dared to enter a two-year-old, Kameko, against the Irish battalion at the five-day stage. John Dance of the Newcastle-based sponsor, and himself a racehorse owner, didn't seem to know whether to be pleased or distraught. 'Hugely disappointing,' he harrumphed to the *Racing Post*, 'Embarrassing.'

However, he also had to admit that as a result he was getting far more publicity for his company than he otherwise might have expected.

And, er, hadn't he also entered a horse for the race which had now been scratched? Well, yes, but, of course, he'd now sold it to Hong Kong.

In the end, the race fell foul of the weather, and was eventually run at Newcastle, where it became the first Group 1 race run on an all-weather track in Britain – and was won by 11/2 chance Kameko, beating Aidan O'Brien runners into second, third and fourth positions.

13 was a number leading jockey of the 70s and 80s Eddie Hide always claimed to be wary of. This is a little odd. Yes, he broke his leg at York one Friday 13th – but his last winner came on

ODDS 'N' EVENS

Wally Pyrah; how old?

13 August 1985 – and when Morston won the 1973 Derby he was Hide's 13th mount in the race, and he carried the number 13. Mind you, the horse was then injured and never raced again.

14 The smallest-ever Derby winner, Daniel O'Rourke in 1852, stood just 14 hands and three inches high.

16 A TV documentary in 1992 showed the Queen winning the Royal Family's Derby Sweepstake on the 1991 Derby – and collecting £16 in winnings.

26 The record number of jockey championships won by Sir Gordon Richards.

33-year-old Julie Bovill from Hull won £500 at Wetherby races in 1988 – and spent the winnings on having her breasts enlarged from 34A to 34DD, it was reported.

34 The record number of Derby runners, in 1862.

42 The number of runners who set off in the 1928 Grand National, but only two completed the course.

49 Claiming to have witnessed 49 runnings of the St Leger in person, by the time racing fanatic Mr Short, the landlord of the Bowling Hand Inn in Mansfield, finally passed away in 1871 he was buried in Mansfield cemetery – on St Leger day.

STRANGE STUFF

Kameko, the only non-Aidan O'Brien trained horse to be entered in the final Group 1 race of the 2019 season.

51 years – the amount of time during which permit trainer William Francis tried unsuccessfully to win his own point-to-point Members' Race.

60 The age at which punter Jimmy Peters died in 1985 – Cardiff bookie John Lovell staged Jimmy's wake in his local betting shop.

69 Working at York racecourse on one occasion, BBC racing correspondent Cornelius Lysaght was concerned that an ice-cream van was parked in his line of sight for the next race – 'I heard myself asking colleague John Hunt if he could use his binoculars to see the price list as I fancied a 69 – rather than a 99! Private Eye enjoyed it and the Daily Star made it one of the broadcasting faux pas of the year,' he told the *Racing Post Weekender* in August 2011.

71 The age the *Racing Post* told the world, on 22 October 2019, that former bookie PR man who went on to work for the Hong Kong Jockey Club Wally Pyrah had reached. 'Well done, Wally, at least you're still older than me,' I thought … until I received a prompt from Facebook, suggesting I wish Wally Pyrah a Happy Birthday to mark reaching … 61. Vain, ageist? Who, not Wally, surely?

86 Sam Baxter, who died in 1986, was such a fan of Huntingdon racecourse that his ashes were scattered there.

130 Oxford student John Godley wrote a 130-page book, *Tell Me The Next One*, in 1950 about his well publicised ability to dream the winners of horse races.

137 Number of lay bets former champion Irish jump jockey Tom Morgan was disqualified for 18 months in October 2019, for placing over a period of ten years while 'employed' at stables where he claimed to be 'just helping out.'

145 'The Kentuky [sic] Derby decision was not a good one. It was a rough and tumble race on a wet and sloppy track, actually. A beautiful thing to watch. Only in these days of political correctness could such an overturn occur. The best horse did not win the Kentucky Derby – not even close!' Tweet on 4 May 2019 from President Trump after the long-time leader Maximum Security, a 9/2 shot, passed the post in front, ahead of second-placed Country House, a 65/1 chance, only to be controversially disqualified for drifting off a straight line earlier in the race – the first time this had happened in 145 runnings of the event.

166 The record number of runners at Windsor in November 1955.

180 The number of rides Fred Archer rode as a 15-year-old, winning 27 of them.

184 The weight in pounds (13st 2lbs) that rider Theo West of Louth carried on third-placed Cornafulla at Market Rasen in 1934.

100,001 In *The Sweeney Guide to the Irish Turf* it was claimed that the 100,000th recorded race to be run in Ireland was a maiden plate at Gowran Park on 11 August 1969, won by Strawberry Belle, trained by John Oxx. No one can now remember which was the 100,001st…

STRANGE YEAR

1 JANUARY
Known as 'Crying Jackie' for regularly bursting into tears if his horse was beaten, jockey John Mangle, who died on this date in 1831, nonetheless won five St Legers.

2 JANUARY
Despite having held a permit licence to train for 13 years, triple Grand National winner Red Rum's trainer Donald 'Ginger' McCain only landed his first winner, 3/1 San Lorenzo, at Liverpool on this date in 1965.

3 JANUARY
Jockey Adam Kirby had never seen such a thing, John Francome called it extraordinary as, on this date in 2009, six-year-old Namu stopped and relieved herself copiously, before deigning to enter the stalls at Kempton – but then romped home to win the 6f all-weather sprint.

4 JANUARY
'They told me it was not a fast-food store,' said chastened Frankie Dettori today in 1992 after being cautioned by Hong Kong stewards for chewing gum during an enquiry.

5 JANUARY
Buchan racecourse in East Gippsland, Australia, was 'decimated by bushfire' it was reported today in 2020 as bushfires raged in many parts of the country. The region's racecourse at Canni Creek had also failed to escape the effects of the inferno.

   Also on this day, in 1920, both horses contesting a Plumpton chase fell. One was remounted and went on to win. The other was caught by a spectator who rode him to the finish and was officially placed second as he – a Mr Dale – made the weight.

STRANGE YEAR

The late Ginger McCain had his first winner 13 years after first holding a permit licence.

STRANGE STUFF

Frankie Dettori: told off for chewing gum in 1992.

6 JANUARY
A post-race sample showing traces of a banned substance resulted in the disqualification of De Rigueur from a 1986 race at Ascot today in 1987. Blame for the test failure was attributed to the horse eating a pre-race Mars Bar.

7 JANUARY
Mattie Kneafsey rode Sporting Spirit to victory at Southwell today in 1994, the 16-year-old having taken the day off school to ride the 50/1 shot.

Also on this day, for the first time since he began training in 1992, Seamus Mullins sent out a horse which dead-heated today in 2020 – Inspireus sharing the honours with Touch Screen at Lingfield.

8 JANUARY
Trainer Reg Hollinshead sent out Loch Style and Taniyar to race at Southwell today in 1996 – which they did, but unfortunately each in the other's race.

9 JANUARY
Driving a Snowcat tractor over the ice and snow course at St Moritz today in 1986, a racecourse worker narrowly escaped with his life as the vehicle sank through and under the ice surface.

10 JANUARY
'The last time the Queen tapped me on the shoulder was to complain about the ride I had given one of her mum's horses,' revealed John Francome today in 2009 whilst congratulating the Injured Jockeys Fund's Serena Oxley on her OBE.

11 JANUARY
A new betting shop was officially opened at Old Bailey, London, today in 1991 by the Dean of St Paul's Cathedral.

12 JANUARY
Not a single Tote punter fancied Starmine to win at Leicester today in 1993. It started at 66/1 and had just one Tote client backed it would have returned 1530/1.

13 JANUARY
Almost universally lauded as one of America's top trainers, not all punters love Bob Baffert – one disgruntled punter set up a website page 'IHateBobBaffert', explaining, 'He's a snob. Got too much money. He's a snob. Never takes off his glasses. He's a snob.' Baffert was born today in 1953.

14 JANUARY
Explaining why it was against Jefferson Park racecourse's free admission experiment today in 1993, US magazine *The Blood-Horse* looked down its nose and sniffed, 'When there is no admission, desirable persons remain away, because they do not want to be present with the sort of people who attend only because it is free.'

15 JANUARY
The owners of Indian Arrow, who won the Lillo Lumb Chase at Wincanton today in 1998, did not receive the race trophy as the last winner of it, the Queen Mother, owner of Norman Conqueror, had mislaid it.

16 JANUARY
Raahin won a Fontwell hurdle today in 1995, in the process becoming probably the first dead horse to win a race – the ten-year-old had died for six minutes whilst under anaesthetic in February 1994, only to be revived.

17 JANUARY
After-shocks from a nearby 6.6 Richter Scale earthquake caused the press box and grandstand at Santa Anita to sway today in 1994, but 19,000 turned up to watch the racing.

18 JANUARY
Appearing on the *ITV Racing* preview programme today in 2020, moustachioed on-course bookmaker Barry 'Pino' Pinnington revealed his business slogan was: 'Increase your stash with the 'tache.'

The outcome of a 16 runner, 3m5f chase run at Navan today, also in 2020, was – first, Ask And Answer 7/1; second, Ask Mary, 7/1; third, Ask Cory, 14/1 ... well, I ask you!

19 JANUARY
Jockey Sylvester Carmouche was suspended for three months today in 1990 – he was found guilty of hiding his mount in thick fog at Delta Downs before joining in on the second circuit and romping home by 24 lengths on 23/1 Landing Officer.

20 JANUARY
Two of the greatest chasers ever, five times Cheltenham Gold Cup winner Golden Miller and triple winner of the same race Arkle, both landed their first career victories on this date – the Miller in 1931, Arkle in 1962.

21 JANUARY
'Some geese have decided to stage a sit-in,' commentator Mike Cattermole informed Kempton racegoers as the track's opening race today in 2008 was delayed while they were removed from the course.

Also, six racehorses were caught up in a major international drugs sting after over 80kg of cocaine was seized from a plane in Argentina, reported the *Racing Post* today in 2020. The horses – said not to be directly involved in the crime – were en route to British trainer, based in Singapore, James Peters.

22 JANUARY
Hugely popular, but remarkably unsuccessful horse Amrullah – 74 races without a victory – was permitted to experience uncharted territory and was led into the winner's enclosure at Kempton to mark his retirement today in 1993.

23 JANUARY
In the excitement of the victory at Lingfield today in 1993 of his horse Ann Hill – named after his wife – owner Tony Hill explained why: 'Their back ends are similar.'

24 JANUARY
Watching the racing in a betting shop in Bethnal Green, London, today in 1994, 50-year-old Terry Garrett suffered concussion when glass fell out of the TV screen and hit him on the head.

25 JANUARY
'My wife got a ride on our honeymoon,' declared Richard Dunwoody on Channel 4's *Morning Line* show today in 1997, elaborating that Carol had ridden a winner while they were in Jersey.

26 JANUARY
Amy Starkey, MD of Kempton, announced today in 2009 that a jet-ski would in future be moored in the course's lake – in response to an incident when a horse had broken loose, crashed through the rails and plunged into the water, finally being rescued.

And a meeting run today in 1847 at the Southgate course in Barnet, London, saw The Witch beat Broomstick in the final event on the card.

27 JANUARY
The Thatcher Stakes at Lingfield today in 1994 was won by jockey A Tory – bizarrely enough that same race was, in 1996, won by Carrolls Marc, the first names of Mrs Thatcher's children.

28 JANUARY
Another coincidental Lingfield winner, today in 1993, as the Albert Handicap was won by ... Albert.

STRANGE STUFF

29 JANUARY
Keen racegoer and small-stakes punter Ralph Hoare, of Gloucester, died today in 2019 – aged 110. In 2018 Ralph attended the Cheltenham Festival, seeing Native River win the Gold Cup he'd seen Arkle win three times, and where he was photographed with 91-year-younger jockey Jack Kennedy.

30 JANUARY
The only trainer whose name enabled him to double up as a London tube station, Stan Moore, saddled his first winner, Dramatic Event, today at Windsor in 1991.

31 JANUARY
Julie Krone finished second on 30/1 Quilma at Gulfstream Park today in 1991, despite having to jump a fox lying on the course sunning itself … with the trifecta for the race, which had a 46/1 winner and 31/1 third, paying a record 96,751/1 dividend.

Also today in 1840, Mr Woodham's mare, partnered by Mr Sampson, took on Mr Cave's horse, ridden by Mr Monk, at Alfriston Downs racecourse, Sussex, over a course with 40 hurdles to jump, placed 40 yards apart. The mare cruised to victory.

1 FEBRUARY
Digpast won at 10/3 at Lingfield today in 1996 – ridden by 60s band The Monkees' lead singer and heart-throb Davy Jones.

2 FEBRUARY
Skeletal remains found near Lexington, Kentucky, were said today in 1993 to be those of missing jockey James A Kratz, who vanished in 1973 after telling his wife he'd been offered $2,000 to 'stop' a horse he was riding.

3 FEBRUARY
Chris Powell bet £20 at 3/1 on Lingfield winner Halsion Chancer today in 2007 – and spent his £60 profit on a tattoo of the horse's name on his chest.

4 FEBRUARY
After his runner Toughnuttocrack finished last of 12 at Lingfield today in 1994, trainer John Panvert claimed his horse had been 'poisoned by the all-weather track'.

5 FEBRUARY
After nine years during which the going was only ever declared as 'Standard' for Lingfield's all-weather surface, today in 1998 it was given as 'Slow'.

Also today, in 2020, The *Racing Post* reported that 'betting shops in Hong Kong have been closed with immediate effect in the latest moves to combat the spread of the deadly coronavirus, which claimed its first victim in the territory on Monday.'

6 FEBRUARY
80 years old, brilliantly named trainer Noble Threewitt sent out the first two winners at Santa Anita today in 1992 – both were owned by 85-year-old W R Johnson.

7 FEBRUARY
Jockey Tony Ives was born today in 1952 – he named his Newmarket house … Linga Longa.

8 FEBRUARY
Jockey Tony Charlton effectively objected to himself after winning a race at Fontwell today in 1993. Believing he and Metal Oiseau had been beaten by Gallant Effort in a photo-finish, he lodged an objection to 'the winner', only to find out that he'd won.

9 FEBRUARY
Sir Freddie Laker, the pioneer of budget airlines, died aged 83 today in 2006. He was also a steward – not on his airline, but on the racecourse, at Brighton and Lingfield.

10 FEBRUARY
Jockey Tim Reed rode two winners at Catterick today in 1990 – where 100/1 Wrekin Melody and 20/1 Alistair's Girl resulted in a 2120/1 double.

11 FEBRUARY
Plumpton staged its first race meeting today in 1884, and Harry Eacott rode a treble – two of his wins coming on the same horse, hurdler Cowslip.

12 FEBRUARY
The most expensive horse ever at the time, $16m, four-year-old The Green Monkey was retired today in 2008, having managed a third and two fourth places. Coolmore paid that sum for him in 2006.

STRANGE STUFF

Plumpton racecourse staged its first race on 11 February 1884.

13 FEBRUARY
6/4 favourite Jive won a Sandown race today in 1959 – the 20th and final hurdles winner for his jockey, Lester Piggott.

14 FEBRUARY
Unplaced on Silver Gal at Catterick today in 1976, Val Greaves became the first 'lady rider' to compete against pros over hurdles.

15 FEBRUARY
Ben Dearg won a chase at Wolverhampton today in 1971, making modern history as the first horse returned at decimal odds – 13/10.

16 FEBRUARY
'Racing is first and cricket comes second,' said West Indies' fast bowling legend and turf obsessive/owner Michael 'Whispering Death' Holding, whose birthday is today – born 1954.

17 FEBRUARY
Fort Leney won the Leopardstown Chase today in 1968 for trainer Tom Dreaper – as he had done for the six previous consecutive years.

18 FEBRUARY
High-profile owner Alec Wildenstein, who died today in 2008, once sacked jockey Dominique Boeuf, declaring, after he was beaten on Vallee Enchantee, 'We weren't unlucky, she was ridden by an asshole who didn't follow instructions.'

19 FEBRUARY
VEGANS 'should be given their own shelf in the office fridge and a pass from work trips to the races,' declared a story on the front page of *The Times* newspaper today in 2020, quoting 'a new set of guidelines' issued to companies by the Vegan Society. Further explanation by the paper added that vegans 'should be allowed not to attend corporate events such as horse racing or team-building events that revolve around animal products such as a hog roast.'

20 FEBRUARY
Running at Sha Tin today in 1993, Beat Them Up lived up to his name by rearing up at the start and gashing jockey Lester Piggott over his left eye, putting the rider in hospital as a result.

21 FEBRUARY
On this day in 1989, after novice hurdler Hello Rocky jumped atrociously and fell at Huntingdon, jockey Barrie Wright claimed to stewards that the horse was deaf, and that this was a contributory factor.

22 FEBRUARY
With two to jump in a Stratford chase on this day in 1992, 8/11 Plat Reay was clear under Carl Llewellyn who rode him into the fence, just as there was a flash from a camera, and the horse fell. After something like this had developed it seemed likely Carl might snap, but he didn't and put everyone in the picture instead.

23 FEBRUARY
Peter Upson-trained Mansfield House raced on an unfamiliar surface today in 1993, after his horse-box crashed on the A604 near Huntingdon, and he charged off down the fast lane, somehow being caught before damaging himself.

24 FEBRUARY
Jockey Brendan Powell broke a leg at Doncaster today in 1992, declaring 'Over the years I've been very lucky.' Perhaps – if you overlook the ruptured stomach, internal bleeding, another broken leg, broken arm, broken wrist and broken collar bones he sustained during his career.

STRANGE STUFF

Michael Holding; racing comes first.

25 FEBRUARY
Jockey Richard Guest fell at Wincanton today in 1988 – his eighth fall in just five days.

26 FEBRUARY
Racing was abandoned at Catterick today in 2008, even though the runners were circling at the start, only for 75mph winds to batter the track.

27 FEBRUARY
After 25 years of unsuccessful riding, and believed to be the oldest jump rider still active, George Turner rode his first winner, Rathmichael, today at Lemalla point-to-point in Cornwall – at the age of 56.

28 FEBRUARY
Sonny Somers won over fences at Lingfield today in 1980 – registering his second success at an equine age seldom equalled and never exceeded – 18 years old.

29 FEBRUARY
A 54/1 winner at Oaklawn racecourse in Arkansas lived up to his name for those who were on Expect Money, today in 2008.

1 MARCH
'A very hard way to make easy money,' was today's response in 2000 by pro gambler Dave Nevison when asked to describe his work.

And racing first took place at High Wycombe today in 1836. The course lasted until 1844, but in March 1840 staged what may have been a unique meeting whose races were started by the firing of a cannon on West Wycombe Hill.

2 MARCH
The opening race of today's 1954 Cheltenham Festival meeting was the Birdlip Hurdle – won by Mull Sack, ridden by youngster Lester Piggott.

3 MARCH
Owner/trainer/breeder John Thorne rode his Woodland Wedding, 10/1, to a dead-heat at Warwick, today in 1974 – with that horse's sister, 20/1 Flying Timber, who he also bred.

Pro-gambler Dave Nevison; a hard way to make easy money.

STRANGE STUFF

Today in 2020, 15-year-old Sunny Ledgend, trained and owned by Andrew Martin and sent off at an unconsidered 66-1, ran his 14 Exeter rivals ragged in the 3m handicap chase under a disbelieving Richard Patrick, returning to an ovation from an equally shocked crowd and posting a Tote return of £139.90.

4 MARCH

Jason Brautigam sponsored the 'Zoe Hurworth Will You Marry Me? Stakes' at Lingfield today in 1995. She said 'Yes' ... but poignantly, the wedding never happened.

5 MARCH

Cure-All walked from Grimsby to Aintree to win the Grand National today in 1845 – then walked back with groom Kathy Crisp to be greeted by church bells on their arrival.

Also today in 2020, with its annual festival imminent, Cheltenham racecourse posted a unique public health notice, informing the public, via the British Horse racing Authority's administration site: 'Do not travel to the Festival if you have any of the following symptoms – a cough, a high temperature or shortness of breath AND you have been to or transited through the high-risk countries, or been in contact with anyone that has, in the last 14 days. To protect yourself and others, please do not travel. These measures are being taken in order for us to protect everyone's health and wellbeing during the current public health situation. Thank you for your understanding.' The announcement was made in response to the coronavirus emergency.

6 MARCH

Tony McCoy received a gift from Fakenham Racecourse today in 2009 to mark his recent achievement of 3,000 winners ... an apple tree.

7 MARCH

On this day in 1964, Arkle, 7/4, beat Mill House, 8/13, by five lengths to win his first Cheltenham Gold Cup. This race 'defies the laws of perspective; the further it recedes into history, the greater it appears,' wrote racing historian, John Randall.

8 MARCH

He'd retired six days earlier, but today in 1997 Willie Carson returned at Wolverhampton, partnering sprinter, River, against greyhound Gorgeous over 180 yards. Given a slight start to allow the horse to hit its stride, Carson's mount duly obliged to upset the odds.

9 MARCH
The Stewart Tory Chase at Wincanton today in 1989 was won by Sirrah Jay, partnered by Stewart Tory's grandson, Anthony Tory.

10 MARCH
'Don't ride the brute, he'll kill you,' top jockey Arthur Yates told amateur George Ede, who partnered Chippenham in Aintree's Sefton Chase today in 1870. Yates was right – Ede died after he and his mount fell at the water jump.

11 MARCH
7/1 shot Make A Stand won today's 1997 Champion Hurdle, to the chagrin of broadcaster John Inverdale, who had sold the 'leg' of the horse he'd once owned.

12 MARCH
Richard Mussell, a cleaner from Havant, won £567,066.25 from his five-horse accumulator at Cheltenham today in 1992.

The owner of the 2020 winner of the £325,000 G1 Paddy Power Stayers' Hurdle received the world's first moving and musical trophy also on this day. The Paddy Power Stayers' Hurdle took place on day three of the Festival, and was won by Lisnagar Oscar.

The trophy design was conceived in-house by Paddy Power staff and created by Designworks in Windsor, known for their work on the 2018 Commonwealth Games batons. The perpetual trophy's eye-catching carousel design featured six of the best multiple winners of the race – Big Buck's, Inglis Drever, Baracouda, Galmoy, Crimson Embers and Silver Bay.

13 MARCH
Sullenberger, 4/1, flew to victory at Wolverhampton today in 2009, having been named in honour of the hero pilot who brought a stricken plane in to land on the surface of the USA's Hudson River earlier in the year.

14 MARCH
Having won on Mountview in Macau today in 1992, British jockey Tony Ives tripped whilst weighing in, knocking himself out. He recovered to ride in the next, only for his mount to play up in the stalls and injure Ives' leg so severely that he couldn't ride for the rest of the day.

Cheltenham Festival 2020; just days before the UK shut down.

15 MARCH

On this day in 1984, Jenny Pitman became the first woman to train a Cheltenham Gold Cup winner as Burrough Hill Lad and Phil Tuck beat Brown Chamberlin by three lengths.

16 MARCH

In an alternative universe, Theatreworld may have become an all-time hurdling great today in 1999, as he finished second in the Champion Hurdle, having done the same in the previous two runnings of the event.

17 MARCH

An unequalled feat to this day, trainer Michael Dickinson trained the first five runners home in today's 1983 Cheltenham Gold Cup – Bregawn, Captain John, Wayward Lad, Silver Buck and Ashley House.

18 MARCH

After imbibing some pre-race Dutch courage, jockey Tommy Pickernell had to be pointed in the right direction by fellow riders, as the runners milled about before today's 1875 Grand National. Tommy sobered up enough to make Pathfinder his third winning mount in the event.

19 MARCH

So committed was trainer Arthur Stephenson to his motto – 'Little fish are sweet' – that when he won the Cheltenham Gold Cup with The Thinker, today in 1987, he was actually at Hexham racecourse.

20 MARCH

On this day in 1993, Uttoxeter became the first racecourse to offer bungee jumping – whereupon Lord Oaksey plunged 200ft head first to raise funds for the Injured Jockeys Fund.

Andrew Gemmell holds the Stayers' Hurdle trophy in 2019 after Paisley Park wins.

STRANGE STUFF

Michael Dickinson achieved the unthinkable in 1983.

21 MARCH
Having won the 471st running of what is still the world's oldest race, the ancient Kiplingcotes Derby in East Yorkshire, under jockey Sheila Ashby, today in 1997, nine-year-old mare Sunny was sadly killed when she ran into a parked car.

22 MARCH
An extraordinary field of 66 runners contested today's Grand National in 1929 – with 100/1 chance Gregalach winning.

23 MARCH
Displaying one of the most eccentric and unorthodox riding styles ever seen, Fred Hobson won today's 1877 Grand National on 15/1 Austerlitz, holding on to his saddle at every jump. He never contested the race again.

24 MARCH
Despite claiming an unexpected call of nature was to blame, jockey Fred Hutsby was disqualified and fined £265 today in 1999 after winning on 2/1 favourite Rusk at Towcester but then weighing in one and a half pounds light.

25 MARCH
Scottish jockey Willie Carson became a director of Swindon Town Football Club today in 1997 – having recently been bizarrely nominated in a newspaper lookalike competition as a dead ringer for ... actress Britt Ekland.

26 MARCH
Drakes Drum won the race before today's Grand National in 1966, a 6f sprint, after which the horse was led in by Paul McCartney, who had bought him for his father.

27 MARCH
Two-year-old filly Wear The Fox Hat was scheduled to run in the first race at Folkestone today in 1995 – until the Jockey Club demanded the horse be withdrawn unless her name was changed. It was – to Nameless – but she was then withdrawn.

28 MARCH
All White finished fifth in today's 1919 Grand National – but may have been closer to winner Poethlyn had jockey T Williams not had to stop en route for a while to be sick after earlier eating dodgy seafood.

29 MARCH
You'd 'butter' believe that 2lbs of what is more usually spread on bread, was the secret ingredient which, packed into his hooves to stop him losing his footing as snow fell, helped Grudon to victory in today's 1901 Grand National.

30 MARCH
Hops And Pops broke a leg before the start of Ascot's Golden Eagle Novice Chase in 1994, but still won the race – as the leg she broke belonged to jockey Carl Llewellyn, set to ride Ghia Gneuiagh.

31 MARCH
The betting shop at Cressy's Corner, Hounslow, became the first in the UK to have a Japanese owner, today in 1995, as it was purchased from Ken Munden.

1 APRIL
Frank Wise was no April Fool as he won the Irish National at Fairyhouse on Alike today in 1929 – wearing an artificial leg.

STRANGE STUFF

Longchamp today, a far cry from the bombed racecourse in 1943.

2 APRIL
Gerald Foljambe rode two jump winners at a Melton, Leicestershire, meeting today in 1925 – a common enough achievement – but rare for any jockey who had had a leg amputated below the knee.

3 APRIL
Jockeys Johnny Murtagh and Brian Lee suffered almost certainly unique injuries when they were struck by wires hanging down as they rode under the Grand National starting gate en route to contest a 1m6f Flat race at Aintree today in 1970.

4 APRIL
Longchamp racecourse staged a meeting today in 1943 – despite the track having been bombed by the British shortly before racing was scheduled to start.

Gianfranco Dettori being embraced by son Frankie; a far cry from his jockey days in 1970 when he was stoned at San Siro.

5 APRIL

Frankie Dettori's dad, Gianfranco, was literally stoned when riding at San Siro today in 1970 – as stones were hurled at him after his Furibondo, a complete outsider who had been disappointing last time out, beat a 1/5 favourite.

6 APRIL

Jockey Steve Williams's parallel profession paid off today in 1995 as he won for the first time as a professional boxer, beating Andy 'Mighty Atom' Roberts on points.

7 APRIL

As Mr Frisk won the Grand National in record time today in 1990, on the same date, over in the States, the Santa Anita Derby was won by Mister Frisky.

8 APRIL

Jockey Stephen Davis was fined £75 at Hereford today, in 1995, for carrying a yellow plastic bag whilst riding Arcticflow in a chase – 'to encourage the horse to put his best foot forward.' The horse was pulled up.

STRANGE STUFF

Miinnehoma wins the 1994 Grand National for owner Freddie Starr.

9 APRIL
Miinnehoma, 16/1, won the Grand National today in 1994 for comedian owner Freddie Starr, who bought the horse at auction by sticking his tongue out to make each bid.

And the first meeting took place at Pewsey Vale, Wiltshire, today in 1858. It is one of very few courses where spectators could watch the racing from canal barges.

10 APRIL
Today in, it is reported, 1408, the King of Tibetan province Gyantse decreed that 10–28 April each year should be set aside for prayer ceremonies, featuring, amongst them, horse racing.

11 APRIL
Coverdale refused during a chase at Plumpton, and was returned to the paddock – but when the other two runners also refused, Coverdale was rushed back out on course and jumped round for an unlikely victory, on this day in 1892.

12 APRIL
Commentator Mike Cattermole may have been scarred for life – having revealed today in 2009 that 'I once saw a couple engaging very intimately, shall we say, behind the weighing room at York.'

13 APRIL
Bobbyjo, 10/1 Grand National winner, today in 1999, was reportedly won by owner Robert Burke in a game of cards.

14 APRIL
The 2,000 Guineas was won today in 1812 by a horse with perhaps the most unpronounceable four-letter name in racing history – 7/1 chance Cwrw.

15 APRIL
The *Racing Post* was published for the first time today in 1986. Today in 1950 the future Queen had her first winner on the Flat – and today, in 1963, her mother had her first Plumpton winner.

16 APRIL
After his horse, Simon, refused twice at the second fence and again at the third, fourth and eighth fences at Derwent point-to-point today in 1994, Austrian jockey Hans Waltl was lapped by the rest of the runners before exasperated stewards ordered him over the course tannoy system to pull up.

17 APRIL
The ice-blue and claret wine morning suits flamboyant high society hairdresser and racehorse owner (his Ayala and Rag Trade each won the Grand National) 'Teasie Weasie' Raymond, who died today in 1992 aged 80, wore to Royal Ascot were a sensation.

18 APRIL
Between The Sticks was a 33/1 winner on his two-year-old debut at Newmarket today in 1989 – sadly, owner and England goalkeeper Peter Shilton was delayed en route and arrived too late to get a bet on.

19 APRIL
Five-year-old Ubedizzy was second at 20/1 behind Boldboy at Newmarket today in 1978, but behaved so badly after the race in the unsaddling enclosure, trying to savage his lad and anyone else within range. As a result the horse was banned from ever running again.

20 APRIL
Eleven-year-old Moorcroft Boy was the 20/1 winner of today's Scottish National in 1996 – despite having broken his neck when falling in the 1994 Becher Chase at Aintree.

21 APRIL
No Bombs failed a dope test after winning a hurdles race at Ascot today in 1979 – later blamed on consuming a Mars Bar pre-race.

22 APRIL
Mr Corker's bay mare was ridden 300 miles in three days on the course at Newmarket, winning a £100 wager today in 1754.

And a mere 118 years later, during the first race at Willington in County Durham, a horse veered off-track towards spectators, causing two to fall into the River Wear, by which the course was bounded on two sides. The pair were swept away and drowned.

23 APRIL
A sale of art held at Ludlow racecourse today in 2009 saw £95,000 raised at auction by the purchase of 13 paintings by Adolf Hitler.

24 APRIL
Racegoer Mr Cottingham ended up in hospital when today, in 1905, he was 'accidentally

STRANGE YEAR

The front page of the Racing Post *the day after Persian Punch collapsed and died at Ascot on 28 April 2004.*

jumped upon' at Market Rasen's jumps meeting and was 'recovering in the Cottage Hospital.' He later explained that he'd been 'sheltering' behind one of the obstacles, unaware of the imminent arrival of the runners and riders.

25 APRIL

Foggy's Dream finished 19th of 21 in a maiden race at Windsor today, in 1994, becoming in the process the first modern Arab racehorse to compete against thoroughbreds in Britain.

26 APRIL

Defaulter, Squire of Malton, Reindeer and Pulcherrina ran a quadruple dead-heat in the Omnibus Stakes at The Hoo today in 1851.

27 APRIL

Trainer Arthur Stephenson saddled five winners at Kelso today in 1971 – all ridden by different jockeys.

28 APRIL

One of the most affecting experiences your author ever had at a racecourse happened today in 2004 when hugely popular stayer Persian Punch collapsed and died at the end of a race at Ascot. The eerie silence which fell spontaneously over the course was extremely moving.

STRANGE STUFF

29 APRIL
'I was too small to become a window cleaner and too big to be a garden gnome,' said jockey Adrian Maguire, explaining his choice of career today, in 1994, after celebrating his 23rd birthday with a winner at Southwell.

30 APRIL
Coalminer Nathan Richards married dressmaker Elizabeth Dean today in 1894 – neither of them had the remotest connection with racing, yet their son Gordon became champion jockey 26 times.

1 MAY
Yesterday, in 1961, betting shops had been illegal. Today, in 1961, they became legal.

2 MAY
Moustachioed former bareback rodeo rider Bernie L 'Chips' Woolley Jr, with one win from 34 starters during 2009, today sent out 506/10 shot Mine That Bird, tailed off at the first turn, to win the 135th Kentucky Derby.

Clive Brittain performing one of his legendary dances in the winner's enclosure.

3 MAY
Aussie jockey Scobie Breasley fractured his skull in a fall from Sayonara at Alexandra Park, fracturing his skull, destroying his sense of balance and paralysing his eyes. Medics predicted he'd never ride again. A few months later he was back in the saddle.

4 MAY
In 1888 Tom Cannon Sr and Tom Cannon Jr rode against each other in the 1,000 Guineas and St Leger. On this day in 2019, for the first time since, father and son again contested a Classic, with dad John Egan riding unplaced outsider Garrel Glen, while son David partnered favourite Qabala, finishing third.

5 MAY
Trainer Sandy Carlos Clarke, whose Widnor won the 1957 Ascot Stakes, had also been a boxer in France, a cowboy in Texas, a commando during the war and a film actor, winning the Best Actor award in Canada in 1938. He died today in 2003.

6 MAY
Witch of the Air won at Kempton today in 1910 – owned by ailing monarch King Edward VII, who expressed his delight with what were virtually his dying words.

7 MAY
Jockey Terry Smith failed to win a walkover on his Rossa Prince, the only runner entered for a Tweseldown point-to-point race today in 1990. Smith only needed to canter the horse over the finish line to collect the prize money, but it bolted and couldn't be caught in time. Smith was also fined £25 for declaring the wrong colours.

8 MAY
Streaker Stephen Brighton, a barman, ran on to the course at Fontwell during a race today, in 1995, and was knocked flying by one of the runners, Boxing Match, helped on his way by a wallop from Laughing Gas's rider Richard Dunwoody's whip. Brighton was arrested, and reportedly taken to Littlehampton cop shop.

9 MAY
Actor and racehorse owner Albert Finney, born today in 1936, once bought all the tickets for a performance of a show he was in, so that he could go and watch his horse run. Come the day it was a non-runner.

10 MAY
The title of a ladies' race sponsored at Redcar today, in 1993, by 15 racecourse bookies sparked controversy for its title – the 'Worth Laying Handicap'.

11 MAY
Riding Mountain Kingdom at Chester today in 1989, jockey Steve 'Kentucky Kid' Cauthen suddenly felt his nearest rival snapping at his heels – literally, as Lazaz took a bite at his boot as they raced up the home straight.

12 MAY
5lb claimer Pat McCabe became the first jockey found guilty of 'irresponsible riding' today in 1994 when he was given a four-day ban at Brighton after 'winning' the Spring Handicap on Hello Mister, only to be relegated to last place.

13 MAY
A race at Salisbury was run today in 1864, only to be ordered to be re-run – as the judge wasn't in his box. They did it all again – and Vedette won it again.

14 MAY
Election won the Derby today in 1807. Despite being his first ever race he was heavily backed and started 3/1 favourite. The horse may well have been a four-year-old, as his trainer, Bird, later confessed on his death-bed two of his five Derby winners had been 'ringers'.

15 MAY
'I call it the Carlburg [his stables] shuffle,' declared trainer Clive Brittain, then 74, after winning with both Misheer and Nashmiah at a rainy York today in 2009, then breaking into a lengthy celebration dance in the winner's enclosure.

16 MAY
Many jockeys drained by making the weight will have felt like doing it since, but today, in 1793, jockey William Clift won the Derby on Waxy, then, in response to a question about the race by owner the Duke of Dorset, snapped tetchily at him: 'Hang me, you see I won, that's enough for you!'

17 MAY
Graham Rock, born today in 1954, who would become *Racing Post* editor, was agent for South African jockey Michael 'Muis' Roberts when he rang me to ask his odds of winning the 1992 British jockey championship – I told him 100/1, he bet £100, and collected £10,000 when Roberts duly obliged.

18 MAY
Having ridden his first winner, 20/1 Corking, at Bath, today in 2009, 17-year-old South Wales schoolboy David Pritchard confessed, 'I'm sitting a Spanish exam tomorrow. The headmaster thinks I'm revising.'

19 MAY
Born today in 1955, jockey Padge Gill named a fall as a highlight of his career – tumbling from Royal Appointment at the 23rd fence of the 1985 Grand National.

20 MAY
When Mornington Cannon, just 13, rode his first winner, Flint at Salisbury, today in 1887, trainer Charles Morton gave him a sovereign and suggested he should use it to buy sweets.

21 MAY
On this day in 1788, both horses in a one-mile match at York carried 30 stones with Mr Maynard's mare running (?) out the winner against Mr Baker's horse.

22 MAY
'We can but deeply deplore the blackguardism which, once a year, has been allowed to establish its saturnalia in the quiet village of Harpenden,' ranted the local paper about the annual race meeting in the Hertfordshire location, today in 1857.

23 MAY
Racing at Beverley was delayed today in 1989 while a bullock was removed from the track.

24 MAY
'A Tyson among jockeys,' 15-times champion French jump jockey Christophe Pieux was dubbed today, in 2009, by trainer Jean-Paul Gallorini, after he was carried from the paddock after winning his third Grand Steeple-Chase de Paris at Auteuil on Remember Rose, but breaking a toe and severing a tendon after hitting a rail.

STRANGE STUFF

15-times French champion jockey Christophe Pieux.

25 MAY
Five were injured at Goodwood today, in 2009, when a car being parked by a racecourse vet accelerated backwards through a protective rail, shot down a bank and collided with several cars. Racing was delayed for half an hour.

26 MAY
Ayr's clerk of the course, Katherine Self, 36, announced today in 2009 she was stepping down – to join the coastguards.

27 MAY
Hereford racecourse staff Holly Glover, Debbie Gray, Claire Miles and Diane Kennett appeared in the *Racing Post* today in 2007 – clad in hats and, apparently, nothing else, to promote the track's Ladies' Day.

28 MAY
Ascot's Grandstand was used for the first time today in 1839 – it cost 5/- (25p) to get in.

29 MAY
'All persons are desired to keep their dogs at home; and if any be found upon the Race-ground, it is hoped the populace will destroy them.' Racecard warning at Sheffield & Rotherham racecourse, staging a Silver Cup meeting today in 1777.

30 MAY
Hitler's bombs did for Torquay racecourse as the grandstand, weighing room and stabling were destroyed in an air raid today in 1943. The course never reopened.

31 MAY
Female jockey Dodie Duys and fellow rider Carl Gambadella came to blows after a hard-fought race at Suffolk Downs, USA, today in 1993. Both were suspended for 15 days.

1 JUNE
On this day in 1904, George Thursby, Derby runner-up on John O'Gaunt, became the first amateur placed in the race – a feat never since emulated.

On the same date Compton Plume was set to win a race at Redcar today in 2004, landing a £7,500 pay out for a £2, four-horse accumulator placed by Derek Mason from West London. But the horse's weight cloth fell off inside the final furlong and, although other bookies paid out to customers, Coomes, where Derek placed his bet, offered him a consolation £750. 'I'm gutted,' declared Mr Mason.

2 JUNE
'It's ironic that we're riding for a million dollars and yet we are only covered up to $100,000,' said top US jockey Gary Stevens today in 2004, as he refused to race in the Breeders' Cup, concerned about insurance.

3 JUNE
Actor Robert Morley, a huge racing fan, died aged 84 today in 1992. He had a clause written in his contracts that he would not appear in matinees on Derby days. Today was Derby day – Dr Devious won the race.

On the same date, singer and comic Des O'Connor applied for a permit to race as an amateur jockey in 1971.

4 JUNE
'For years I thought I had no hope of winning anything better than the Tradesmen's Selling Handicap at Bath,' said trainer Arthur Budgett on winning the Derby today in 1969.

5 JUNE
Two of the first three home in the Park Chase at Napier Park, Hastings, in New Zealand today in 1939 were being ridden by jockeys other than those who set out on them. Both fell and were remounted by spectators.

6 JUNE
Claude 'Punters' Pal' Duval, for many years *The Sun's* racing correspondent, born today in 1945, was once forced to run (almost) naked around Jockey Club HQ by his editor, who I'd reminded of his promise if the outcome of an appeal to the body did not go the way he'd predicted.

7 JUNE
A mounted policeman attempting to cross the track interfered with several runners in Ascot's Prince of Wales's Stakes today, in 1887, including favourite Reve D'Or, beaten by Claymore.

8 JUNE
Disaster was narrowly averted today in 2009 at Pontefract, when two large plastic cones had somehow been left on the course as the runners contested a 6f sprint – and several jockeys had to take urgent evasive action, scattering the cones, but avoiding injuries to horses or riders.

9 JUNE
Creggmore Boy finished fourth today in 1962, in a chase at Cartmel – in the process becoming the oldest recorded runner ever to race – aged 22.

10 JUNE
Harry Beasley rode Mollie to finish unplaced in the Corinthian Plate, run today in 1935 at Baldoyle, Dublin. Promising young rider Harry was just 83 at the time …

11 JUNE
New Zealand jockey Lynsey Satherley rode her 189th winner today in 2009, at Rotorua – just 15 days after giving birth to daughter Sophie Angela.

12 JUNE
The eight-race card at Canterbury Downs in the USA today in 1992 became something of a family affair, as David Essman rode two winners – but his wife, Kokie, won four of the other six.

13 JUNE
York racecourse had to send for an apiarist today, in 2009, when a huge swarm of bees arrived at the track and settled on a viewing bench overlooking the paddock area.

14 JUNE
Gary Carter landed a treble today in 1991, on Luvly Jubly at Southwell (1.30); Romany Rye at York (4.00) and Able Susan at Doncaster (8.15).

15 JUNE
Embarrassment for the Ascot racecourse 'jobsworth' doorman who today, in 1982, refused entry to the owners' and trainers' bar to legendary trainer Vincent O'Brien on the grounds that he did not show the correct badge.

16 JUNE
Greville Starkey fell inexplicably from his mount Ile de Chypre when clear in Royal Ascot's King George V Handicap today in 1988. Four months later a jury in a drug smuggling case was told Starkey tumbled as the result of a blast of high-pitched sound aimed at him and the horse from a high-tech, ultrasonic 'stun-gun'.

17 JUNE
Churchill Downs racetrack in the US was the venue for the first aeroplane flight to take place in Kentucky today, in 1910.

On this date in 2020, in an interview in *Metro* newspaper, jump jockey Brian Hughes was asked how he maintained his hunger for winners, answering: 'Maybe you need to be not quite sane.'

18 JUNE
Visiting Ascot racecourse from Southport today in 1930, a Mr Holbein was struck and killed by lightning whilst sheltering under a bookie's brolly.

19 JUNE
In an effort to retrieve the £360 entry fee for his horse Reverand Thickness, trainer Alan Bailey declared him for today's 1996 Royal Hunt Cup, despite the fact that he had been killed 13 days earlier.

20 JUNE
Royal Ascot racegoers had tried unsuccessfully to smuggle a parrot and a cat into the track – the parrot on its owner's shoulder, and the cat 'impeccably dressed with a bow tie,' revealed Marcus Armytage in the *Daily Telegraph* today, in 2009.

21 JUNE
Despite the 1/2 favourite Little Duchess obliging in the feature race, the Cavan Handicap at Irish course Cavan today, in 1879, the local paper's reporter was not over-impressed by the meeting, describing it thus: 'A wet day, knee deep in mud for horses and punters, wretched racing.'

22 JUNE
Lingfield's 3.45 race today in 2009, the Durex Pleasuremax Handicap, did not suffer from any early withdrawals.

23 JUNE
Run today in 1990 at Trim, Count Meath, winner of the International Nun Race was Scrubs, partnered by Sister Mary Joy.

24 JUNE
St Kevin won the Irish Derby today in 1885, in the process beating The Chicken – to whom he had been third the day before, and would again lose to tomorrow – into fourth.

25 JUNE
'Don't be ****ing silly, I've got to go out and earn my £14 riding fee in the next,' was the reported comment by Lester Piggott to Leopardstown's course doctor today in 1977, after being advised to forfeit his remaining mounts following a fall.

26 JUNE
Presenter of TV's popular show *Countdown*, Richard Whiteley, who died today in 2005, aged 61, was honorary Mayor of Wetwang in east Yorkshire – and named one of his racehorses Mare of Wetwang.

27 JUNE
The chattering classes paid attention to announcements made at Windsor racecourse today in 2009 hoping to find the owner of a set of false teeth found in the car park.

28 JUNE
Brothers William, Jack and Phillie Behan had all trained Irish Derby winners – but today in 1882 their brother Nicholas became the only family member to ride the winner, as Sortie won at 5/1.

29 JUNE
Despite 13/8 favourite at Catterick, Azureus, having already refused point blank to start in three of his previous races, one confident punter staked £3,000 on the horse, who once again refused to start.

30 JUNE
Jockey Willie Carson was unplaced in the third of a seven-race card at Newcastle today in 1990. But he won all of the other six races and later told your author in an interview that had the third been the final race he'd 'definitely have won'.

STRANGE STUFF

1 JULY
At Worcester's meeting today in 1904, the fourth race saw Lady Shamrock unship jockey George McCall and run into the crowd, knocking over five spectators, two of whom died as a result.

2 JULY
25 years after he had retired from the saddle, J Anderson, whose first winner came in 1906, returned today in 1947 to partner Gracious Sun to victory at Carlisle.

3 JULY
Something of an unexpected victory for two-year-old Anntelle, who won at Canterbury, Sydney, today, in 1982, at a then world record starting price of 500/1.

4 JULY
Amateur jockey Charlotte Towsley became the first British woman to ride a winner in Poland, at Warsaw, today in 2004.

5 JULY
25-year-old apprentice jockey Pietro Romero was literally set on fire in a freak sauna accident at Haydock racecourse in 2008. Fortunately, he survived bad burns to his chest and was back in the saddle by the end of August.

6 JULY
Clerk of the course at Newmarket, Nick Lees, was unable to water the course today in 1994 – after discovering that thieves had made off with recently installed sprinklers: 'We had 102 brass sprinklers – and all of them have been stolen, it's a bloody nuisance.'

7 JULY
A dead horse was ruled to have been a runner in a race at Pontefract today in 1992. Second favourite, O'Donnell's Folly, collapsed and died after the field came under orders, thus meaning officially he had to be regarded as a runner.

8 JULY
The London Philharmonic Orchestra played the William Tell Overture live during the running of the 7.20 at Kempton today in 2009 – another of racecourse supremo Amy Starkey's ideas to publicise the track and enhance attendance.

9 JULY
It was a case of 'Sweet 16' at Roscommon Racecourse today in 2019, as 16-year-old See Double You became the oldest winner in Ireland for 32 years by winning the Leo Dolan Memorial Handicap Hurdle.

10 JULY
'It's all daftness. It was getting out of hand,' declared jockey Phil Tuck, announcing today in 1988, his 32nd birthday, that he was ditching his many superstitions which included wearing the same socks and t-shirt when racing, and saluting magpies en route to courses. Tuck's decision was well received by the *Racing Post's* John Randall, who declared, 'The prevalence of superstition in the racing world is irritating, not endearing. Superstition is another word for stupidity.'

11 JULY
Legendary punter and owner Terry Ramsden fancied his 8/13 favourite Katies to win at Newmarket, so staked £70,000 on her today in 1983. She was beaten. In another indication of his love of a flutter I recall him phoning me the evening before the Grand National, in which his Mr Snugfit was running, to 'have a little wager' – £25,000 each-way! The horse ran through beaten runners to clinch fourth place and a payout for his owner.

12 JULY
US jockey Chip Termini was suspended for 30 days today in 1990 after dropping his towel when he emerged from the shower in the jockeys' room at Louisiana Downs in full view of what was then described as a 'jockette'.

13 JULY
At the second false start in the Ulster Harp Derby at Down Royal today in 1994, all of the field completed the course except for three horses quickly pulled up. At the third attempt – and minus jockey Willie Carson, who claimed he had a plane to catch – the three who had pulled up were the first three home.

14 JULY
Lester Piggott was probably the first British jockey to ride winners in two different countries on the same day, today in 1964, as he won at Saint-Cloud in France on a horse called Mexico; then at Birmingham he partnered Prince of Norway to victory.

On the same date 44 years later, a fast-thinking Betfair punter backed a 999/1 winner for a £15 stake when commentator Mike Cattermole mistook Windsor winner Make My Dream in running for also-ran Brazilian Brush, in 2008.

STRANGE STUFF

Jamie Spencer; compared horses to oranges.

15 JULY
An interesting race was staged today in 1775 at Rathkeale races in Ireland when a 'weight for inches' race was won by Lord Clanwilliams's horse Irish Hero – but history does not seem to have recorded whether it was the horse or rider, or both, being measured!

16 JULY
A coup was landed at Bath today in 1953 when good French horse Santa Amaro was substituted for moderate animal Francasal, to win, heavily backed at 10/1. The plotters were subsequently unmasked and four men jailed.

17 JULY
'Horses are like oranges – there is only so much juice you can squeeze out of them,' observed jockey Jamie Spencer today in 2009 – possibly after being pipped at the post?

18 JULY
Lester Piggott rode three winners in Slovakia today in 1993, before dashing off to Austria to partner two more that evening.

19 JULY
Jockey Richard Kingscote was pictured somewhat scantily clad in the *Racing Post* today in 2008 – showing off a remarkable number of bodily tattoos – acquired, he said, at a cost of £70 per hour.

20 JULY
Apprentice John Carr rode a dramatic finish at Catterick, putting Earth Spacer's head over the line first, today in 1989. Sadly, there was still over a mile of the 1m5f race to run. After the race, in which they eventually finished sixth, Carr said, 'I feel like putting a gun to my head.' He didn't do so, fortunately.

21 JULY
Returning to the weighing room at Windsor, having finished unplaced today in 2008, jockey Michael Hills was slapped in the face by a youth, who then ran off.

22 JULY
Trainer Jim Bolger's 'worst day' was today in 1982 – 'I took Favourite Niece to Gowran Park, I fancied her, and I backed her. She ran a poor race. When I returned home I found the stables on fire.'

23 JULY
Jump jockey Richard Johnson had to swim for his life today in 2007 when his 4x4 was swept away in floods near Worcester where he was due to ride – 'It was being carried towards the river and I had to get out through the sunroof and swim.'

24 JULY
Owner Ken Wheldon refused to accept the trophy after his Vado Via won a seller at Doncaster today in 1991 as the race sponsor had bid for his horse after the race, forcing him to stump up 8,200 guineas to retain it.

25 JULY
Turning up at a closed Chepstow racecourse at 5.30am today in 2008, acting clerk of the course

Edward Arkell had to scale a wall to get in – only for a passer-by to call the police, who turned up, giving him some explaining to do.

26 JULY
Niall 'Boots' Madden rode his first winner, Golden Hansel, at Limerick today in 1973 – his son, also Niall, was given the nickname 'Slippers'.

27 JULY
Lester Piggott put up 14lbs overweight on It's The Finish at Newcastle today in 1970 – but still romped to victory.

28 JULY
Racing was cancelled at Yarmouth today in 1994 after fire engines, called to deal with a fire at the neighbouring golf club, drove up and down the track, 'causing severe rutting to the full width of the track.'

29 JULY
Starter Peter McGouran sent the field off for Galway's Guinness Handicap today in 2004 at 5.31, four minutes early, thus voiding the race. 'He had it in his head that the start was 5.30,' was the timely but odd explanation put forward.

30 JULY
Future multiple champion jump jockey A P McCoy, riding in his first chase today in 1994, partnered No Sir Rom at Galway. They fell.

31 JULY
Comic singer, actor, and banjo/ukulele superstar of years to come George Formby had his third and final ride as a jockey today in 1920, finishing unplaced on Old Chris at Catterick.

1 AUGUST
Worcester's £4,000 Dylan Thomas Chase failed to attract a single entry today in 1994 – 'first time in living memory no horses have been entered for a race,' wrote the *Sporting Life*.

2 AUGUST
As an added attraction to the two-day fixture at Worcester (then known as Pitchcroft) beginning today in 1825 and featuring the Worcestershire Stakes and their four-mile Gold Cup, the

A scene from Laytown races.

racecard advised: 'Mr Green intends ascending in his balloon from the Saracen's Head Bowling Green on Saturday at 3 o'clock.'

3 AUGUST
Inadvertently left out of published runners for the Bradford Nursery at Thirsk today in 1985, Handspring won the race at 14/1, despite most punters having no idea he was running.

4 AUGUST
Returning from Datchet races in Buckinghamshire today in 1748, Mr Hindman was attacked by two highwaymen at the cost of his watch and three guineas.

STRANGE STUFF

5 AUGUST
John Jackson, who would become a jockey and won eight St Legers, was born today in 1839. He liked a drink, and once, in his cups, decided to fight a trainer called Sykes, only to set about a passing chimney sweep by mistake.

6 AUGUST
Former foreign secretary and racing fan, politician Robin Cook died today in 2005 aged 59, having once said all politicians 'should write a tipping column [as he did] to teach them humility.'

7 AUGUST
Riding Amantiss at Devon & Exeter racecourse today in 1986, jockey Anthony Charlton finished first – but the horse finished second, as Charlton tumbled out of the saddle virtually on the line – and the race was awarded to the runner-up – named Slip Up.

8 AUGUST
Having been found guilty of poisoning horses to stop them winning, Cambridge man Daniel Dawson was, today in 1812 … hanged.

9 AUGUST
Trainer Derek Garraton was fined £500 today in 1983 after his horse tested positive at Edinburgh in April. The horse was called Magic Mushroom.

10 AUGUST
A fire on the Newbury racecourse grass started on this day in 1905, leading to a duly settled claim of £10 from the Great Western Railway, as it was caused by 'sparks from the railway engines'.

11 AUGUST
The longest odds ever offered at an Aussie racecourse – 5000/1 about About Our Friend, who finished seventh – were quoted and layed today in 1994 to a $20 bet by bookie Mark Read at Canterbury racecourse.

12 AUGUST
I had to check when it was announced today in 1993 that the start of the forthcoming St Leger on 11 September would be brought forward by 40 minutes in order to avoid a TV clash with the World Chess Championship.

13 AUGUST
The *Racing Post* revealed today in 2008 that trainer Jamie Osborne had signed up to take a course in Mandarin Chinese to help sell bloodstock to China.

14 AUGUST
Today in 1986 Catterick staged a Christmas meeting, featuring race titles including Xmas Morning Nursery, Stuffed Turkey Handicap and Queen's Speech Stakes. Their 'real' Xmas meeting had been abandoned because of foul weather.

15 AUGUST
Having flown from Amsterdam to England without luggage to see his horse run at Newbury today in 1992, businessman Dave Spencer was strip-searched on arrival. Palacegate Episode duly won, and Spencer commented, 'They'll have a lot more to check on the way back.'

16 AUGUST
The bodies of three robbers, hanged earlier today in 1731, were cut down to enable racegoers an uninterrupted view of racing at York.

17 AUGUST
There was a 14-minute delay to racing at Irish course Laytown today in 1993 – as the judge's view of the beach course's finish line was blocked by a burger van.

18 AUGUST
Legendary jockey Lester Piggott's first win came today in 1948 when he partnered The Chase to win a Haydock selling race ... at the age of 12.

19 AUGUST
Today in 1997 the runners at Folkestone were faced with an unexpected obstacle as they were forced to swerve to avoid a caterer's car which suddenly appeared ahead of them.

20 AUGUST
A new racecourse at Wormwood Scrubs, London, was scheduled to open today in 1817 – only for an objection by the Army six days earlier to kill off the plan.

21 AUGUST
Pat Eddery finished third on Batshoof today in 1990 at York – despite the fact that Eddery reported 'a car emerged from the car park as we were cantering across the middle of the course, and missed us by an inch, no more.'

22 AUGUST
Sailor Dennis Collins was found guilty of high treason today in 1832 for the offence of throwing a stone at King William IV at Ascot races. His sentence to be 'hanged, decapitated and quartered' was commuted to transportation to Australia.

23 AUGUST
Stable staff who had complained of being charged £1 per slice of toast at Goodwood heard today in 2008 that free tea, coffee and toast would be provided for the rest of the season.

24 AUGUST
With a Russian coup resulting in their leader, Mikhail Gorbachev, being overthrown today in 1991, punters took the hint and backed topically named Goodwood runner Bold Russian in to 100/30, then cheered as Willie Carson rode him to victory.

25 AUGUST
British military forces in Tibet, today in 1909, organised a race meeting, complete with steeplechase and Army Cup, which took place in front of a bemused crowd of Nepalese and Tibetans, plus four important Lamas.

26 AUGUST
A leading amateur Flat rider in the UK, Angel Jacobs, was exposed as a pro jockey today in 1998. Originally Carlos Castro from Puerto Rico, he was already banned in the US.

27 AUGUST
Trapped in a baling machine while working at a relative's Dorset farm, today, in 2008, jockey Joe Tizzard suffered serious injuries to his scalp.

28 AUGUST
Newmarket jockey Allan Mackay was put out of action for two weeks today in 1992 after injuring his hand – whilst doing the washing up.

29 AUGUST
'Things have been a bit slow,' admitted trainer Tony McWilliams today in 2008 as his Miacarla won at 14/1 at Hamilton, finally ending his 1,983-day drought.

30 AUGUST
Small Heath racecourse in Birmingham was a little ahead of the game when today in 1880 their racecard included the Small Heath Stewards' Stakes in which both entries were ridden by female jockeys.

31 AUGUST
Legendary West Indian cricketer Sir Garry Sobers not only hit six sixes in one over, for Notts against Glamorgan, today in 1968 – the first ever to achieve the feat in first-class cricket– but a bet he'd placed earlier produced 4/1, 10/1 and 20/1 winners.

1 SEPTEMBER
Long-standing owner David Sullivan threatened to pull out of the sport today in 2008 after his Jack Junior was left several lengths behind from the off at Great Leighs after the stall malfunctioned, but he was offered no compensation by racing authorities.

2 SEPTEMBER
'PC Plod kept an eagle eye on Lester Piggott at Epsom as a safety precaution as the racecourse received a telephone call saying that an attempt would be made to kill the champion jockey,' reported the *Sporting Life* on this date in 1968. Imagine the contrast today if a similar threat were to be made against Frankie Dettori! Oh, Lester stayed calm – and rode a treble.

3 SEPTEMBER
Cnoc Na Cuille, trained by David Nicholson, won a Worcester chase at 7/2 today in 1987, ridden by, and giving a first winning ride to … Princess Anne.

4 SEPTEMBER
'He has no balls, so he definitely will,' declared trainer Tim Easterby today in 2004, asked whether his Haydock Sprint Cup winner, Somnus, would return to the race – and he did, fourth in 2005, fourth in 2006 and ninth in 2007.

5 SEPTEMBER
The four runners in a Sedgefield chase all fell or refused at the last fence today in 1989 – jockey

STRANGE STUFF

David Sullivan threatened to pull out of the sport in 2008 after the stalls malfunctioned.

Andy Orkney hauled 5/4 shot Grange Of Glory off the top of the fence, remounted and won by a distance.

6 SEPTEMBER
Today in 1832 a race meeting went ahead at Wigton in the Lake District, despite the local Board of Health objecting – 'on account of the danger of drawing together a great crowd of vagrants as usually attend places of amusement at a time when Cholera is raging.'

7 SEPTEMBER
21-year-old student James Florey was warned off by the Jockey Club for five years today in 1994 – as a result of running on to the track during a Royal Ascot race and bringing down one of the runners.

8 SEPTEMBER
'That place wanted bombing. It still amazes me how horses used to race round there, ridiculous, really. It wants to stay closed. It was dangerous, it wasn't good for horse or rider, they were always falling over.' Willie Carson on Alexandra Park racecourse, which closed today in 1970, when in 1999 plans to reopen appeared.

9 SEPTEMBER
For the first time, today in 1992, a race was run over six and a half furlongs at Doncaster – the EBF Fillies' Nursery Handicap was won by 7/1 Falsoola.

10 SEPTEMBER
Jump jockey Malcolm Batters announced his retirement today in 1981, announcing he would become a deep-sea diver.

11 SEPTEMBER
Robby Albarado was born today in 1973. Aged 12 he was riding at bush tracks in his native Louisiana. He suffered skull fractures in both 1998 and 1999, which were repaired with titanium, and went on to ride over 5,000 winners.

12 SEPTEMBER
Owner Lord Arlington thought so little of his filly Throstle that he offered to give her away. The prospective recipient failed to turn up to collect her, so today in 1894 she was allowed to contest the St Leger, despite being a 50/1 no-hoper. She won.

STRANGE STUFF

13 SEPTEMBER
With £200 of his own money on the 8/1 chance, jockey Tommy Lye rode Bonnet in today's 1842 St Leger, using severe force on her during the race, which she won. Far from being grateful, trainer Tom Dawson told Lye he would not permit him to ride any of his horses in the future. Bonnet never won again.

14 SEPTEMBER
Portland Meadows racetrack, USA, made history today in 1946, becoming the first course in the country to stage an evening meeting under lights.

15 SEPTEMBER
Steve Cauthen celebrated the thousandth win of his career today in 1979 – at Doncaster, riding Thousandfold.

16 SEPTEMBER
His jockey John Jackson declared, 'What – ride such a cripple as that?' on hearing he was to partner 200/1 Theodore today in the 23-runner 1882 St Leger, about which one bookie took a bet of '£1000 to a walking stick'. Despite reportedly being lame, the horse won amidst rumours of race fixing.

17 SEPTEMBER
Bespoke Boy jumped out of the Beverley pre-parade ring today in 2008, then charged through the enclosures, knocking over a fortunately baby-less pushchair and ending up uninjured inside the grandstand.

18 SEPTEMBER
A large dog appeared on course as odds-on Queen of Trumps was poised to win at Doncaster today in 1835, causing the horse to swerve, allowing Ainderby to win, landing a £2,000 bet for owner Frank Taylor, who sought out the canine's owner, bought the pooch and gave it a life of luxury.

19 SEPTEMBER
Michael, the husband of Jennie Clarke, owner of The Deaconess, was unhappy with the ride given to the horse today in 1995 at Nottingham, and told jockey Gary Hind so in no uncertain terms – to the point at which he was found guilty of 'improper conduct' and fined £275.

20 SEPTEMBER
Bookies had felt they were taking free money from punters backing Elis to win today's 1836 St Leger, as the horse had no chance of making it from his base in Goodwood up to Doncaster. So they were astonished when the colt arrived, having been transported some 250 miles in a van drawn by relays of post horses. This first horsebox proved effective when Elis, 7/2, romped home from 13 rivals by two lengths.

21 SEPTEMBER
Guy Harwood's 100th winner as a trainer, Springmount, partnered by jockey Jeff King today, in 1969, was also the horse who gave him his first winner.

22 SEPTEMBER
Former problem drinker Henry Cecil's prize after his Multidimensional won at Newbury today in 2007 was a case of John Smith's beer. 'I haven't touched a drop for three and a half years, I'll give it to the staff,' declared Henry.

23 SEPTEMBER
Champion US lady jockey Julie Krone whacked fellow rider Joe Bravo with her whip during and after a race at Meadowlands, New Jersey, today in 1989, earning herself a 15-day suspension.

24 SEPTEMBER
Pas De Reef fell during a Flat race at Hamilton today in 1990, after a golf ball from an adjacent course became wedged in her hoof.

25 SEPTEMBER
Laytown in Ireland holds annual races on the beach, but I think British track, Littlehampton, some few miles west of Brighton, got there first on this day in 1863 with a meeting of their own on the beach. Sadly, before this popular event could be repeated, the course, which also staged races on a more conventional grass surface, had gone out of business.

26 SEPTEMBER
Sandymount racecourse in Ireland, founded in 1665, staged its final meeting today in 1859 when the course became a track for human foot races.

27 SEPTEMBER
Mr Fraser's horse, Richmond, completed a two-day meeting at Inverness, Scotland, today in 1826,

STRANGE STUFF

Henry Cecil in 2000.

during which the horse won a Gold Cup over three miles; a one-mile handicap plate and two three-mile heats of the Ross-Shire Plate – and for good luck, finishing runner-up in the two-mile Ladies' Purse.

28 SEPTEMBER
It proved to be one of racing's most memorable and incredible days on this date in 1996, as Frankie Dettori rode his 'Magnificent Seven', booting home every one of the seven winners at Ascot today at accumulative odds of 25,095/1.

29 SEPTEMBER
Jockey W R Brockton won three of four races in which he competed at Market Rasen today in 1879 – but he rode only two horses all afternoon, winning twice on Moorhen, and finishing first and third on the impolitely and evidently inaccurately named Hopeless.

30 SEPTEMBER
Stetchworth reared and almost threw jockey Taffy Thomas at Redcar today in 1978 – they recovered to win the race, but afterwards gunshot marks were found on the horse's rump – he was apparently being shot at by youths hidden in nearby long grass.

1 OCTOBER
Today in 1825, Mr C C Cullen's Foxhunter won a steeplechase at Irish course Ballyshannon, which was run in 13 minutes over a four-mile course featuring '64 leaps, including six five-foot high walls'.

2 OCTOBER
Octogenarian Frank Hill, owner of Saysana, winner at Brighton today in 1990, was baffled by the odd looks racegoers were giving him – until someone told the 87-year-old his obituary had been printed in the *Daily Telegraph*.

3 OCTOBER
Jockey Dick Black rode King Penguin to win at Ludlow for trainer John de Moraville today in 1946 – first winner for the pair after agreeing their partnership while together as prisoners of war in a German camp.

4 OCTOBER
58th-time lucky for Alf Rubin today, in 1986, as the *Morning Star* tipster selected 4/9 Suhailie, winner of a three-runner race to break his sequence of 57 consecutive losers …

STRANGE STUFF

5 OCTOBER
Sue Causton, 35, made racing history today in 1992, becoming the first female member of a starting stalls team.

6 OCTOBER
An unknown punter flew into Hexham racecourse by helicopter today in 1989 – he staked a total of £100,000 on 4/5, 2/5, 1/4 and 1/4 losers, before flying off again.

7 OCTOBER
The Mick Channon-trained Youmzain finished second in the Prix de l'Arc de Triomphe today in 2007 – as he would do in 2008 and 2009.

8 OCTOBER
Jockey Bill Pyers rode Topyo to win today's 1967 Prix de l'Arc de Triomphe – only to end up in prison after a TV viewer recognised him as the driver of a car which collided with her vehicle 15 months earlier. Pyers was sentenced to three months in jail.

9 OCTOBER
The opening race on Worcester's card today in 1979 was to all intents and purposes unexceptional, apart from the outcome, with 33/1 Quantock Mauger winning. However, a stewards' inquiry was called and the race eventually declared void for starting 43 seconds earlier than its scheduled 2pm, thanks to the weighing room clock – by which the starter was instructed to set his watch – being 90 seconds fast.

10 OCTOBER
Barry Geraghty rode four winners at Kilbeggan today in 2008 – despite having been described as 'a cocky little bastard' by trainer Noel Meade earlier in his career.

11 OCTOBER
The three runners in a race at Wheeling Downs, Virginia, went past the winning post together today in 1945. The two 'placing judges' and the track steward each decided a different one of the three had won – so a triple dead-heat was given as the official result.

12 OCTOBER
Having ridden a winner in Edinburgh the day before, jockey Thomas Lye won the first race at Northallerton, Yorkshire, today in 1837. No planes or cars to get him there in time, then.

STRANGE YEAR

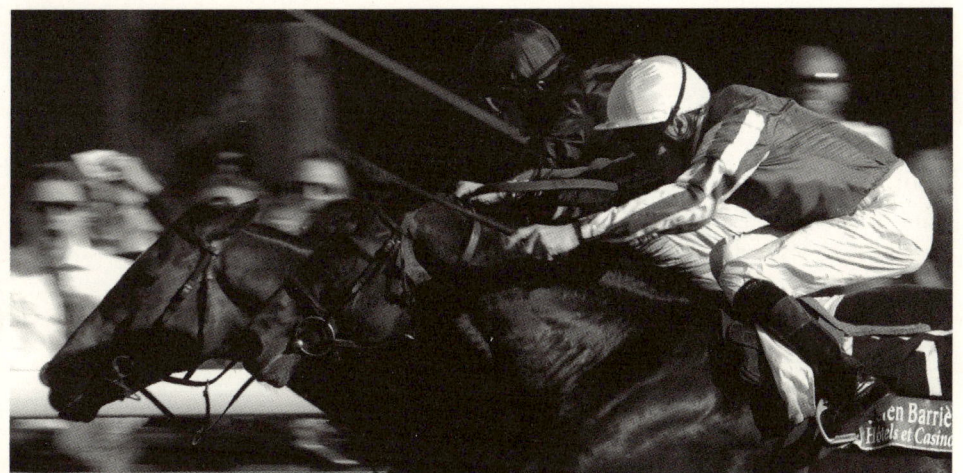

Youmzain (nearest) ridden by Johnny Murtagh was beaten by Dylan Thomas in the 2007 l'Arc de Triomphe.

13 OCTOBER
Steve Smith Eccles's riding of Green Dolphin in a Uttoxeter chase today in 1984 was rubbish, decided one punter – or else why did he throw a dustbin at them during the race? They didn't win.

14 OCTOBER
Hadn't happened before, hasn't happened since, but today in 1671 the reigning monarch, King Charles II, won the Town Plate at Newmarket.

15 OCTOBER
Absalom's Lady and Large Action were awarded a dead-heat in an Ascot hurdles race today in 1994, only for the judge, Jane Stickels, two hours later, to promote the former as outright winner by a short-head. Very few were impressed.

16 OCTOBER
Chancellor won two two-mile heats to land the inaugural Ayr Gold Cup today in 1804. On the same afternoon the horse won an event consisting of four four-mile heats, eventually finishing second, thus running a total of some 20 miles in a single afternoon, carrying 8st 10lbs. Amazingly, Chancellor won the Ayr Gold Cup again in 1805, after which the heats were scrapped.

STRANGE STUFF

17 OCTOBER
Trainer Sue Bradburne sent five horses from her Fife stables to run at Kelso today in 1992. Two were pulled up. One unseated rider at the first. Another finished last. Her best result was via Rogany, who was a non-runner.

18 OCTOBER
Three-time Grand National winner Red Rum died today in 1995. Nine years later on the same date his devoted lad Jackie Grainger died, aged 84. Rummy was buried close to Aintree's winning post.

19 OCTOBER
Super Tony won a handicap chase at Hexham on a walkover today in 1989 – the second time the horse had won this way at the track.

20 OCTOBER
Overcrowding at Worcester racecourse today in 1945 culminated in the collapse of the Tote building, injuring 25 spectators.

21 OCTOBER
With the inaugural meeting at Ashton in Lancashire two days away on this day in 1843, a crowd broke into the not-quite-finished grandstand – which promptly collapsed, causing many broken limb and bone injuries – but not enough to prevent the opening card taking place.

22 OCTOBER
A rarity, even in those days, as the judge called a four-way dead heat in a two-year-old race at Newmarket today in 1855.

23 OCTOBER
'Spillage of aviation fuel on the course' was the reason given for the abandonment of racing at Newbury today in 1992 with one race remaining, after a light aircraft crashed on to the Flat course.

24 OCTOBER
The Reverend Deric Derbyshire baptised racehorse Running Reverend in front of his congregation in Port Elizabeth, South Africa, today in 2004, before offering it as a prize in a fundraising raffle.

25 OCTOBER
Ribofilio was an unplaced favourite at Newbury today in 1968. It was his last race – having also finished as beaten favourite in the 2,000 Guineas, the (Epsom) Derby, the St Leger and the Irish Derby.

26 OCTOBER
Paul Cole-trained Run Don't Fly, a horse with £91,154 prize money to its credit, was withdrawn from Leicester's Wysall Stakes today in 1992. Not entirely surprising as race conditions, adding 1lb of weight for each £500 won in prize money, would have seen the horse carry 21st 3lbs.

27 OCTOBER
For the first time in Britain all of the runners in a race – four of them – were supplemented entries after all the entries for Doncaster's *Racing Post* Trophy were withdrawn. Steve Cauthen won today in 1990 on 2/1 favourite Peter Davies.

28 OCTOBER
Lady Winner won at Laurel, USA, today in 1989, but was then disqualified and placed last. In March 1990 the horse was reinstated as the winner by the Maryland Racing Committee, but in January 1991 was disqualified again by the Baltimore circuit court.

29 OCTOBER
Blanchard won at Newmarket today in 1886, giving multiple champion jockey Fred Archer his 2,748th winner. No one guessed it would also be his final winner. Ten days later he committed suicide, shooting himself.

30 OCTOBER
Frankie Dettori screamed 'I love America' as he rode 28/1 Wilko to win the Breeders' Cup Juvenile today in 2004 – later, Kieren Fallon won the Filly & Mare Turf, saying quietly, 'She done it nice.'

31 OCTOBER
Cash was the first yearling in British racing history to win a race, doing so at Newmarket today in 1791 and beating a three-year-old who was giving away three stone in a match race. Yearling racing was banned in 1860.

1 NOVEMBER
Jockey John Egan was fined 8,000 Aussie dollars – then £3,340 – today in 2008, for calling two vets inspecting his Melbourne Cup mount, Yellowstone, 'a couple of tinpot Hitlers.'

2 NOVEMBER
'It was hysterical. It made front page news,' said jockey Darryll Holland today in 2008, revealing that fellow rider Richard Hughes, who forgot his riding boots, caused a stir in Hong Kong by instead riding out in trainers.

3 NOVEMBER
There was no closed-circuit TV or camera patrol films at Bangor today in 1989 – the camera crew went to Bangor in North Wales instead of Bangor-on-Dee.

4 NOVEMBER
Amateur rider Marco Alliata won a race at San Siro, Milan, today in 1998, boding well for his future. He was 77 years old.

5 NOVEMBER
'I hope she finds the whole thing funny,' declared racing fan John Milton today in 1997 after naming the race he sponsored at Newton Abbot in honour of his ex-wife ... 'The She's Finally Gone Handicap Hurdle.'

6 NOVEMBER
Racing Post stalwart and golf specialist Jeremy Chapman hit the punting heights today in 1993. He and your author attended a live broadcast of the Breeders' Cup at Ascot racecourse – and Jeremy backed the winner of the Classic – Arcangues, which was returned at 133/1.

7 NOVEMBER
Champion jockey Fred Archer won the Liverpool Autumn Cup on Sterling today in 1873. Grateful owner Thomas Roughton gave him a short-barrelled gun as a winning present – the weapon with which Archer would take his own life.

8 NOVEMBER
No starting prices were returned for the 14-runner 1m handicap at Southwell today in 1989. SP reporters explained that only one bookie displayed a full list of odds, so no market was formed. Winner, Admiralty Way, paid £9.80 on the tote.

9 NOVEMBER
Reportedly considering a comeback today, in 2004, Derby-winning jockey Alan Munro explained that he had quit in 2000 to learn karate, in which he became a black belt.

Reality star turned ITV Racing presenter Chris Hughes.

10 NOVEMBER
Azabu Juban, a three-year-old, won at Wolverhampton today in 2008, having been off the track for seven months after 'all her hair fell out, she was completely bald,' according to trainer Jonathan Jay.

11 NOVEMBER
'One guy tweeted me saying, "My daughter would never sit and watch horse racing with me, but now she's seen Chris from Love Island she's sat watching the whole coverage."' Love Island contestant turned ITV Racing presenter, Chris Hughes, today in 2019.

12 NOVEMBER
'We came to think about the fact that condoms – just like Ladbrokes – are all about safe transactions,' declared that company's Swedish boss today in 2008 as the company handed out Ladbrokes-branded condoms to students. Insert your own comments about premature withdrawals.

13 NOVEMBER
Police with whistles were stationed around the racecourse at Derby in very foggy conditions there to direct jockeys and their mounts today in 1899. The cunning plan failed as runners veered off course, and went round a cricket pavilion, where two of them crashed into a set of hoardings.

14 NOVEMBER
Bookies were hammered hard as 11/10 Royal Mark won at Windsor today in 1973, the day Captain Mark Phillips wed Princess Anne.

15 NOVEMBER
'Among the bizarre experiences life has brought, standing outside a toilet at Market Rasen racecourse, unveiling a plaque with my name on it, ranks highly,' wrote the *Racing Post's* David Ashforth today, in 2007, having declared the track the best in the land for its WCs.

16 NOVEMBER
Replacing divots on the track at Kempton today in 1983, course worker Edwyn Barnes, 75, looked up to see the runners heading towards him. Knowing Card bowled him over en route to finishing second. Barnes survived.

17 NOVEMBER
The Sun newspaper launched today in 1969, with the front-page headline story 'Horse Dope Sensation'.

18 NOVEMBER
Roy Davies won on Milliondollarman at Worcester today in 1981, followed by Hywel Davies winning on Rogairio, followed by Granville Davies winning on Santoss.

19 NOVEMBER
A race-rigging plan was scuppered today in 1991 when stewards at Newmarket in South Africa spotted that the turf had been deliberately cut short along the complete length of the outside rail, probably to enhance the chances of the horse drawn out there. They moved the stalls.

20 NOVEMBER
Chaos ensued in the bars at Ballarat in Melbourne in 1991, when winning jockey Gary Murphy won the track's big Cup race – and invited the 13,000-strong crowd to have a drink on him.

A pensive David Ashforth of the Racing Post who awarded Market Rasen the best racecourse toilets in 2007.

21 NOVEMBER
'You don't have to pay for cryotherapy, all you have to do is come to Newcastle and stand naked in a field,' said booted and hatted broadcaster Matt Chapman today in 2019, standing fully clothed and enveloped in a large overcoat, talking to shivering jockey Jason Watson who had just won a race on Big Daddy Kane.

22 NOVEMBER
Trainer Arthur Goodwill died today in 1994, aged 82. Turning up at trainer Harvey Leader's stables to be an apprentice jockey as a boy, he was carrying a violin, and for the rest of his life was universally known as 'Fiddler'.

23 NOVEMBER
Rolling Stone, Ronnie Wood, owner and punter, revealed his most embarrassing racing moment today in 2007, confessing: 'I got thrown out of the Royal Enclosure at Royal Ascot for not having a top hat.'

STRANGE STUFF

24 NOVEMBER
American jockey Julie Krone became the first female ever to win a race in Japan, today in 1990.

25 NOVEMBER
Guy Willoughby rode his first winner under Rules, Inn From The Cold, at Carlisle today in 2004, before returning to his job as an explosives expert. As his winner's trainer Len Lungo noted, 'Guy may not be the best amateur around, but I assure you he is better at riding than I am at bomb disposal.'

26 NOVEMBER
Jamie Osborne claimed today in 2008 that he had named a dozen yearlings after the 12 days of Christmas – Three French Hens, Five Gold Rings, Six Geese A-Laying, etc.

27 NOVEMBER
In the 2004 Mackenzie & Selby Hunter Chasers & Point To Pointers Annual, published today, a horse called Knickers had 'never looked like coming down', while Centurion had 'the speed of a 100-year-old.'

28 NOVEMBER
Asked today in 2008 about an alternative career, jockey Mattie Batchelor was in no doubt – 'A male escort. With my charm and charisma I'd have been a natural.'

29 NOVEMBER
Vets Jack Murphy and Sean Arkins of the University of Limerick announced research today in 2008 which they said showed that 'the hair on a horse's head curls can tell you whether it is right or left-hoofed, which in turn can help determine the direction a horse favours to race.'

30 NOVEMBER
Catherine Unsworth was the only person to stake a 2/- (10p) tote bet on Coole at Haydock today in 1929. The outsider won, and Catherine was paid out at record odds of 3410/1.

1 DECEMBER
Alex Greaves rode her first winner today in 1989, Andrew's First, at Southwell, and on this date in 1993 she rode Sharp Sensation, her future husband 'Dandy' Nicholls's first runner as a trainer, at Southwell, only to receive a £400 fine for allegedly not giving the horse every opportunity to win.

STRANGE YEAR

Jockey Alex Greaves rode her first winner on 1 December 1989.

2 DECEMBER
The 1993 Grand National, which ended up as a no-race, finished second today in 1993 in a contest to award a 'Turkey of the Year' title to 'the most ridiculous person or event of the last 12 months', sponsored by the British Turkey Federation. Winner of the award was England football manager Graham Taylor.

3 DECEMBER
'Lights were erected at each corner of the course to direct the riders,' it was reported by the Irish Racing Calendar of perhaps the first floodlit meeting, run at Baltinglass on this date in 1791.

4 DECEMBER
Born today in 1956, jockey Hywel Davies, who won the 1985 Grand National on Last Suspect, answered 'Sleeping' when asked his favourite recreation.

5 DECEMBER
Hollie Doyle rode her 107th winner of the calendar year, Class Clown, at Southwell today in 2019, setting a new record for the number of winners in a year by a female jockey, held by Josephine Gordon. The day before she'd been beaten into second by boyfriend Tom Marquand – and told interviewer Matt Chapman: 'he won't be coming home tonight'. He tweeted in response: 'Never have I made a bigger mistake when riding a winner.'

6 DECEMBER
Reporting today in 2019 that Cornelius Lysaght, 54, was to leave the role he had held since 2001 as BBC Racing Correspondent, *Times* writer Rick Broadbent noted: '*The Daily Mail* suggested he was a white, middle-aged man sacrificed on the altar of the shouty phone-in, the latest victim of the BBC's lust for a younger audience.'

STRANGE STUFF

Terry Biddlecombe rode a remarkable race on 13 December 1968.

7 DECEMBER
The Times reported in a photo-story that 'fires turn the sky red over Royal Randwick Racecourse, Sydney', today in 2019, explaining that this was an effect of ashes from Australian wildfires.

8 DECEMBER
The 13 runners contesting a chase at Huntingdon today in 2019 had to be alert to avoid an unusual additional obstacle in the race as an empty dustbin rolled across the track.

9 DECEMBER
A two-mile hurdle race at Haydock took longer to finish than the Grand National, run over more than twice the distance, after the runners mistakenly missed out a hurdle today in 1992, only to be warned after completing almost a full circuit that they must return to jump the omitted obstacle or the race would be voided. It took 12 minutes 19.6 seconds to complete the race. The fastest Grand National time is 8 mins 47.8s, by Mr Frisk in 1990.

10 DECEMBER
The House of Commons considered an early-day motion today in 2008; 'That this House regrets proposals being discussed by the BBC to reduce the number of days of British horse racing it intends to cover from the present level of 27 days per year to just 13 days by 2010.'

11 DECEMBER
David Hunter, clerk of the course at Fakenham racecourse floated the suggestion today in 2019 that Holkham Beach, some 12 miles away from the racecourse, would be an ideal location on which to introduce racing on the sand to England, to rival the likes of Laytown.

12 DECEMBER
Lord Oaksey, then known as John Lawrence, jumped clear at Plumpton's second last on Pioneer Spirit in a handicap chase today in 1964, only to fear he had taken the wrong course and double back on himself – only to find French Cottage under Bill Tellwright running towards him and going on to win. Oaksey was fined £25, went home to run a bath to soak his cares away, only to forget he'd done so, until the ceiling collapsed.

13 DECEMBER
'Dark Jet is so far in front he can fall and still win,' declared Sandown's racecourse commentator today in 1968, just as Terry Biddlecombe's mount came down at the last, slithering along the ground on his belly, with Biddlecombe somehow staying put, then galvanising the horse back into action and going on to win by five lengths.

14 DECEMBER
Lord Poulett, who owned chaser The Lamb, had a dream that the horse won the Grand National, ridden by Tommy Pickernell. When he awoke, today in 1870, he set about booking Tommy to partner the horse in the big race, and they duly won the 1871 running.

15 DECEMBER
The tenth annual London Pantomime Horse Race took place in Greenwich today in 2019. The event, raising money for local charities, including 'Harpenden Riding for the Disabled (RDA)' regularly attracts an audience of thousands. The 'runners' follow a course which involves several pubs, obstacle courses and a 'space hopper challenge'.

16 DECEMBER
The bookies took a hammering as all seven favourites won at Plumpton today in 2019, returning

accumulative odds of 541/1. This was Plumpton history – ironically made at the very meeting where a new history of the course was being unveiled!

17 DECEMBER
'Let's stop paying our licence fee,' demanded former trainer Jenny Pitman today in 2008, protesting at the BBC's threat to cut their coverage of racing.

18 DECEMBER
Awaiting the outcome of a three-way photo finish at Lingfield today in 1991, owner of eventual 11/4 winner Super Sally, Leonard Seale collapsed and died of a heart attack without hearing the result.

19 DECEMBER
Actor Edward Underdown, who died today in 1989, aged 81, appeared alongside Humphrey Bogart in 1953 movie *Beat The Devil* – and also dead-heated with John Hislop as 1938's leading Flat amateur rider.

20 DECEMBER
As the area suffered a drenching, Radio 5 Live reported in their sports bulletin today in 2019 that 'There's an inspection taking place right now at Ascot Raincourse.' Racing did finally go ahead.

21 DECEMBER
Violet Cohen's Lucky Yankee finished fourth of 17 in Lingfield's 2.15 race today in 1985, but no punters had backed the errant greyhound, who escaped her owner's clutches to overtake all but three of the field.

22 DECEMBER
Born today in 1964, Derby-winning jockey Willie Ryan (Benny The Dip) was scathingly honest about why he was quitting in 2004: 'I feel I've had my best days as a jockey and the right thing to do is to be honest with myself and the people I ride for.'

23 DECEMBER
The Times carried a photograph today in 2019 of a dozen grey racehorses ridden by a dozen jockeys wearing Christmas jumpers, with an explanatory line: 'The Jockey Club celebrated "the 12 greys of Christmas" by inviting a dozen racehorses to pose at Newmarket.' The horses were: Uncle O; Hi Ho Silver; Winter Snowdrop; Temple Lord; Moveonup; Eclair de Guye; Arabescato; The Third Man; Grey D'Ars; Split Down South; Defoe; Glenn Coco.

24 DECEMBER
Widnes Sixth Form College students were blamed today in 1986 after the stuffed remains of great racehorse Brown Jack, which stood at the Stable Grill restaurant in the town, were found damaged and minus an ear, lying on the ground.

25 DECEMBER
Born today in 1833, jockey John 'Tiny' Wells, winner of eight Classics, once turned up to ride out wearing an Alpine hat with feathers, a suit in Gordon tartan and a pair of red Morocco slippers.

26 DECEMBER
It happened today in 1899 – and is still recalled today – in the Thorneycroft Chase at Wolverhampton, Good Friday fell on Boxing Day.

27 DECEMBER
Potters Corner was the 8/1 winner of the Welsh National at Chepstow today in 2019 – as, according to tweets, 'several course officials had to physically remove an in-running punter who tried to retrieve his drone.'

28 DECEMBER
The highest odds in Irish Tote history – £289.64 for 10p – were paid out on Gene's Rogue at Limerick, today in 1981.

29 DECEMBER
92-year-old owner Lady Anne Bentinck died today in 2008. She gave trainer Sir Mark Prescott an unusual gift – the skin of legendary 19th century racehorse St Simon, Ascot Gold Cup winner and great sire, owned by her grandfather.

30 DECEMBER
Manhattan Boy won at Plumpton today in 1986. Nothing very unusual about that – except that he ran at the course 64 times, winning 14 of them including five Peacehaven Hurdles – an individual record for the track. Manhattan Boy ran 24 times elsewhere, winning none of them.

31 DECEMBER
All 14 riders in Tramore's Newtown Chase finished the race a circuit too early today in 2007. Five realised and set off again with 9/4 favourite Aussie, ridden by Andrew McNamara, winning.

JOCKULAR JAPES

HUGHES SORRY?
Suffering a broken arm when battling to retain his champion jump jockey title from a stern challenge by Brian Hughes in early 2020, 42-year-old Richard Johnson vowed to return as quickly as possible, and was indeed back 37 days later, riding a double at Musselburgh on 27 February 2020, bringing him to within 18 winners of leader Hughes. After his first comeback winner, Johnson declared: 'I'd say I was blowing more than the horse.'

NOW, LOOK – I'M WATCHING!
Lester Piggott and two other jockeys deliberately delayed the start of a race at Ayr in July 1983, when the three apparently wanted to watch the Magnet Cup at York which was being televised, but was running ten minutes late, thus clashing with the Ayr 'off' time.

The Ayr stewards weren't happy and interviewed Piggott, Walter Swinburn and George McGrath, warning them a fine was the likely outcome. Asking Irishman McGrath for an explanation, he denied taking any interest in the York race. 'But you were seen with these jockeys at the television,' the stewards told him. 'Sure, I was watching the television, but I wasn't looking at it,' came the reply.

Impressed by McGrath's logic, the stewards decided they couldn't win and abandoned plans to impose a fine, reported the Irish Field newspaper.

HOUR-LONG RACE
Jockey Eddie Hide and Swaying Tree set off in Ripon's 4.30 Yorkshire Handicap in August 1980, and the horse duly won the race – but over an hour later, and with another rider, Jimmy Bleasdale, in the saddle.

Fourteen runners started the race, but after one furlong of the scheduled six, a red flag was waved, and six of the jockeys stopped their mounts. Eight, though, ran on to complete the course, with Wynbury passing the winning post first.

At 4.35 the race was declared void.

At 4.48 it was announced that there had been a false start.

At 5.04 it was announced the race would be re-run.

Nine of the runners were withdrawn.
Eddie Hide had been kicked and was replaced as Swaying Tree's jockey by Bleasdale.
At 5.30 the race was re-run.
Swaying Tree, one of the six who had been pulled up in the original running, was the winner.

NICO'S NECK

Jockey Nico de Boinville's family tree 'features 19 ancestors who were beheaded during the French Revolution,' revealed *Times* journalist Rick Broadbent in a February 2020 interview in which the race that 30-year-old Nico's mount Altior lost his unbeaten record over fences to Cyrname was mentioned, prompting the response: 'Usain Bolt gets beat in one race and you don't write him off for the championships.' De Boinville added, 'It's one of the odd juxtapositions of our sport – we need to be emotionless, but there is so much of other people's emotions riding on it.'

Pondering on the life of a jockey, Broadbent observed, 'It is a life of serial losing punctuated by fleeting success.'

Jockey Nico de Boinville never written off.

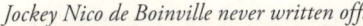

STRANGE STUFF

WELL PISSED OFF

Desperate to lose a pound or two to make the weight before a race at Fontwell, jump jockey Steve Smith Eccles resorted to using an unconventional short-cut known as a 'pee-pill' because of the effect it has.

The rider underestimated how long the pill would take to kick in and was at the start for his first race of the day before 'the urge overtook me. Within seconds I was frantic to relieve myself.'

He took drastic action, he revealed in 1988, forgetting that although the pills create an urge, they can also make it take longer to satisfy that desire – 'I jumped off my horse and sprinted down to the first fence where, with a sigh of satisfaction, I set about losing a few ounces. I stood there with my breeches round my ankles for about five minutes before at long last the action started.'

The race was delayed by three minutes as a result but worse was to emerge when Smith Eccles discovered that TV cameras had caught him unburdening his bladder and his discomfort was 'beamed live into the nation's betting shops'.

YOU'RE A DAD LOSS, SON ...

'I obviously feel let down to some extent,' commented jockey Michael Hills with commendable restraint and understatement in July 1990 as word spread that he had been sacked as stable jockey – by his father, trainer Barry Hills.

A LEG-END

Jump jockey Ian Watkinson, active during the 1970s, earned himself the nickname 'Iron Man' – hardly surprising after he won the 1976 Oxo National at Warwick, on 3/1 shot Jolly's Clump, riding the four-mile chase with a broken leg, which he had known he had pre-race. Yet, revealed colleague Steve Smith Eccles, 'he persuaded a doctor to set the broken bone in a splint and inject him with strong painkillers.'

On another occasion he rode great chaser Tingle Creek to victory despite a dislocated knee, then, not long after, having had a cartilage removed at a time when this would mean three or more weeks out of action, was back within three days, with his stitches still fresh, winning on another of the great jumpers, Night Nurse.

However, another of his many injuries was hardly his fault – riding a dodgy jumper of a 12-year-old hurdler turned chaser, he was rolled on by his mount when it fell during a Sedgefield race. Semi-conscious, he was loaded on to a stretcher, and the bearers decided to run him to the ambulance room, only for one of them to trip and fall, dropping the woozy Watkinson, who crashed face down on to the tarmac – breaking his nose.

PHOTO NEGATIVE TURNED POSITIVE

As they came to the last in the Growise Champion Novice Chase at Punchestown in April 2018, Al Boum Photo seemed to have the race at his mercy, only for jockey Paul Townend to react to the shout he was sure he heard, and swerve his horse violently to the right to bypass the fence, also taking out Finian's Oscar as he did so.

The result was a 21-day ban for the jockey and much abuse from punters. However, trainer Willie Mullins and the horse's owners kept faith in the combination and Townend was again on board as Al Boum Photo ran out 12/1 winner of the Magners Gold Cup at the Cheltenham Festival just under a year later.

SO, HE DID MEAN IT!

He'd said it before – 'I'd love to get off one in Punchestown, pull the saddle off and tell Willie that I won't be out for the next one,' when asked whether and when he might eventually retire. But few there at, or watching, the 2019 Gold Cup at Punchestown realised that Ruby (christened Rupert) Walsh was set to do just that, as he had been telling people he expected to ride at the 2020 Cheltenham Festival.

However, after the Willie Mullins-trained Kemboy passed the post in front and Ruby jumped off, to be told 'Well done' by Mullins, he responded: 'You'd better find a rider for Livelovelaugh later.'

That was it. The end of a glorious riding career – and the start of a new one as a TV pundit, having made his views on such people very clear in the past: 'I hate lazy journalism. I pick reporters up on simple things like form. I hate sloppiness. I hate bullshit.'

Walsh did not appear to be the sentimental type about his mounts – 'People often think jockeys get attached to their horses, but we don't. The jockey just gets on and off.' He also epitomised the 'hard as nails' physicality of jockeys. Having had his spleen removed in 2008 he declared: 'It would have been worse if it was a kidney or my bladder. Take an antibiotic and a few injections and away you go. As long as it's not your brain or your neck, the rest will heal.'

The record-breaking jockey – who was the leading jockey at the Cheltenham Festival 11 times in 2004, 2006, 2008, 2009, 2010, 2011, 2013, 2014, 2015, 2016 and 2017 – has another record to boast about, having been mentioned in a song by singer/songwriter Christy Moore called 'The Ballad of Ruby Walsh', which appears on his album Listen. The song is based on Christy's own experience of watching the jockey at Galway races and includes the lines 'Ruby Walsh, he saved me life below at the Galway Races – Ruby hold her back, give her the craic and up she'll go …'

STRANGE STUFF

Happy days as Al Boum Photo wins the Cheltenham Gold Cup in 2019.

WHAT A GUY!

Racecourse doctor Guy Mitchell, 45 at the time, became the first person with just one eye (his left) to officially take part in a race, which he did in July 2019 at Newbury.

Another Guy was the first amputee jockey to win a race, Captain Guy Disney, doing so in February 2017. He won the Royal Artillery Gold Cup, on his horse Rathlin Rose, at Sandown.

BRYTER THAN AVERAGE!

Bryony Frost has swiftly established herself as a major figure on the jump racing scene. As well as her undoubted ability as a jockey, she also has an unconventional take on many aspects of her life. Recovering from a collarbone fracture during 2019, Bryony spoke to the *Racing Post* about her attitude to her professional life:

'To me, I'm a separate person. I have this really strange way of never looking at myself as me. I struggle to say "I". It's always "we" because it's me and my horse. It's not me. I find it impossible to think of it being about me. This body isn't actually mine. My body is my career and my horses' careers. It's so weird. It's like I'm stood over there looking at me over here.'

Bryony Frost has quickly established herself.

And this connection to her mounts was emphasised after her dramatic victory in the 2019 Cheltenham Festival's Ryanair Chase on Frodon, explaining to the Post's Lee Mottershead: 'Two out we landed a bit tight, but at that moment he leant into my hands and said "Don't you dare let go of this. I want you with me because I cannot do it by myself. Are you with me, or are you not? I need to hear you growl at me." She also said after the race: 'We were so in sync our heartbeats were probably together.'

Bryony's attitude was summed up by her remark that: 'I'm living to make memories, and Frodon made a fairy-tale a reality.'

FRANKIE, I DO GIVE A DAMN

Having failed a drugs test in September 2012, Frankie Dettori lost his job riding for Godolphin. So, whilst serving a suspension, he went into the Celebrity Big Brother House, where he wore a flat cap, dressed up as a tin-pot dictator, stayed in for three weeks and ended up in fifth place, reflecting, 'I don't think I made too much of a fool of myself.' On 16 May 2013, during a Channel 4 interview with Clare Balding, he admitted taking cocaine in 'a moment of weakness'.

STRANGE STUFF

GORMLESS GORMAN?
Rookie jump jockey George Gorman, 17, was cruising to victory at Newbury in March 2012 in only his second race. With one fence to negotiate in a three-mile chase, he and equine partner, second favourite, Merry Vic were several lengths clear – only to mistakenly miss out the fence completely: 'In a few seconds I've gone from the highlight of my life to the worst moment of my life,' sighed the distraught rider.

PITMAN GESTURE
Former top jump jockey Richard Pitman, who rode Crisp into second place in the Grand National of 1973, Red Rum's first victory, and who was once married to trainer Jenny Pitman, made an amazing sacrifice in February 2012, at the age of 69, when he donated a kidney to a complete stranger.

HOLLAND TO CHINA
Darryll Holland became the first British jockey to ride full-time in South Korea during 2013, following that landmark up by becoming the first British professional jockey to ride in Mainland China.

WHAT A DIFFERENCE A DATE MAKES
On 13 October 2011, the *Racing Post* reported, 'Richard Hughes quits in protest at new whip rules.'

After those rules were amended, Hughes decided to carry on riding – and almost exactly one year later, on 15 October 2012, he achieved one of British racing's more extraordinary feats when he rode the winners of seven of the card's eight races at Windsor.

UNIN-TEN-DED TIP?
Observant punters may have noticed that Danny Brock was looking forward to partnering Mazovian in the 4.15 at Southwell in July 2012 – when he turned up in the paddock ready to mount – before the 3.45 race! Sure enough, when he returned half an hour later he and Mazovian duly galloped to a 10/1 victory.

NAP OF THE DAY
Frankel's jockey Tom Queally claimed he had been sleepwalking when accused of drink driving in 2014.

Queally was more than twice the limit when found asleep at the wheel of his BMW, but he claimed he had not been drinking.

30-year-old Queally's lawyer, Nick Freeman, also known as 'Mr Loophole', claimed he was 'morally totally innocent' as he was 'sleep-driving' at the time, that there was a history of sleepwalking in the Queally family, and that he had been doing it since the age of five.

Despite the claims, Judge Bridget Knight disqualified Queally for 22 months, fined him £1,350 and ordered he pay the prosecution costs of £3,500.

CARR CRASH

Looking back over her career as a jockey after becoming a trainer, Ruth Carr recalled a hot day when she was riding at Cartmel – 'I was tailed off, and as I pulled up and hacked back, the drunken crowd started pelting me with beer cans and doing donkey impressions.'

She must have felt such an ass.

USEFUL ADVICE ...

'A smile can take you a long way.' Jockey Cieren Fallon.

MISTAKEN IDENTITY

'Aren't you Wilson Pickett?' Lester Piggott revealed in 1986 that he was 'pretty speechless' to be asked by a young girl if he was the renowned soul singer whilst buying ice cream in London's Finchley Road – 'my resemblance to him is tenuous to say the least.'

COMPLICATED COMPLIMENT?

'The biggest compliment I can pay her is that we don't regard her as a lady rider, we simply regard her as a rider, and right now she's as good as anyone, male or female' … Eddie O'Leary, racing manager for the Gigginstown operation, with his take on Rachael Blackmore, who rode 12 winners in five and a half years, before suddenly driving home 90 during 2018-19, finishing second only to Paul Townend in the Irish jump riders' championship.

Some may suggest that his compliment is perhaps a little back-handed, and not quite the type of approval Rachael and other female jockeys would entirely approve of, even if they are too well mannered to complain that surely every jockey, male or female, is entitled to be called 'a rider'.

Rachael is a perfectionist, even to the point where she criticised herself for her 'half-hearted attempt at punching the air' after winning on 50/1 Minella Indo in the Albert Bartlett Novices' Hurdle at the Cheltenham Festival – 'It didn't really turn out the way I wanted. I'll need to work on that … it was poor, very poor.'

STRANGE STUFF

DOUBLY SYLY?

Sylvester Carmouche III, a jockey with a poor race record in recent years, was arrested in March 2015, reported the *Daily Racing Form*. West Virginia police charged him with attempted murder, arson, and cruelty to animals after he allegedly set fire to his girlfriend's house when she and her children were inside.

Fortunately, no one was injured in the late-night incident. According to the reports, the woman said Carmouche allegedly started the fire after an argument at the house. Carmouche was arrested on a Tuesday night not far from the home in Mercury Village.

Carmouche had had two mounts this year, both at Mountaineer Racetrack, and had only 26 mounts in the previous year, without a win. However, during a five-year period from 2006 to 2010, his mounts won more than $1 million each year.

Many racing followers who heard of this story thought they recalled the name. They were right. Carmouche is the son of Sylvester Carmouche Jr, who received a ten-year ban for an infamous incident in 1990 during which he hid his horse in a fog bank shortly after the start

Eddie O'Leary, racing manager of the Gigginstown operation.

Venetia 'Lady Whiplash' Williams.

of a one-mile race at Delta Downs in Louisiana. He restarted the horse as the other horses in the race approached the stretch, and won by 24 lengths.

VENETIA WHIPPIAMS?

Riding 200/1 outsider Marcolo in the 1988 Grand National, Venetia Williams suffered whiplash after taking a tumble at Becher's Brook.

But, recalling that experience in a 2014 BBC Radio 4 interview, she remembered the reaction to her subsequent arrival in hospital: 'I fastened my whip with an elastic band to my middle finger so that I wouldn't drop it. When I fell at Becher's I was carted off unconscious in the ambulance and I arrived at the hospital with my whip still attached to my finger – I think they thought Lady Whiplash had arrived.'

A fortnight later Venetia was back in the saddle but in another fall broke her 'hangman's bone' in her neck, resulting in three months in traction, which, unsurprisingly, ended her career.

But she had unfinished business with the Grand National and, now a trainer, won the race in 2009 with 100/1 shot Mon Mome.

STRICTLY FOR THE BIRDS

According to his Wikipedia page, retired jockey Michael Hills 'has a series of hobbies, such as darts and snooker, he also breeds Canaries and Finches'. Oddly, though, there is no mention of the incident that marked what was supposed to be his final day in the saddle, when, in November 2012, aged 49, he arrived at Newmarket to take his five booked rides prior to retirement. However, he then failed two breath tests and was suspended from riding.

Nonetheless, he remained on course to receive a presentation and a rousing send-off from fellow jockeys, including twin brother Richard, who just happens to be the same age.

WHAT ELSE COULD GO WRONG?

Chris Meehan was unshipped during a hurdles race at Italian course Merano in July 2016. As he fell, he was kicked in the face, not only knocking him out but breaking his nose and leaving a 27-stitch gash in his jaw. The Irishman was helped by the starter, who had come over to him. 'He put me in the recovery position, with my right leg out straight.'

They waited for the arrival of the course ambulance – which, recalled Meehan – 'came up alongside us and reversed on to my leg. They stopped it on top of my leg, so I started screaming; it broke straight away.'

Once he was safely in hospital and recovering, Meehan reflected: 'What makes it worse is my father, brother, auntie – they're all ambulance people – my father teaches people how to drive the ambulance. You couldn't make it up.'

GETTING THE ELBOW

US jockey Randy Romero was successful, but accident-prone. In 1983 a freak fire in the jockeys' room at Oaklawn Park saw him suffer burns over 65 per cent of his body. He broke eight ribs and a collarbone during the 1990 Breeders' Cup, returned in 1991 and promptly broke his left elbow at Gulfstream Park. Screws were inserted and three months later he came back at Belmont Park, but the elbow had not set properly, and broke again. It had become infected. A cast was put on until January 1992. He rode again in April 1992, but was still troubled by the elbow, so doctors in California grafted three inches from his hip, to his elbow, securing it with screws. After a four-month rehabilitation Romero returned to the track.

A movie, *Casey's Shadow*, is based on Romero's life. The downside of his career was the number of racing-related injuries he suffered, requiring more than 20 operations. It seemed to run in the family – his father Lloyd J Romero was a Louisiana state trooper who trained quarter

JOCKULAR JAPES

Paddy Brennan, a strong advocate for gumshields.

horses. A drunk driver crashed into his police car and permanently disabled him. Randy retired in July 1999 having ridden 4,285 winners.

BITING COMMENT

'There's no reason a young rider can't wear one and they should be. If they get used to wearing one when they're coming through, then in five or ten years everyone would be. I feel so strongly about it because it can save lives. I'll keep talking about it until it's compulsory.' Leading rider Paddy Brennan called on the BHA to make it compulsory for jump jockeys to wear gumshields when riding in Britain. (February 2020)

REFROCKED LESTER

On 6 June 1988 the Central Chancery of the Orders of Knighthood announced that 'The Queen has directed that the appointment, dated 1st January, 1975 of Lester Keith Piggott to be an officer of the Civil Division of the Most Exclusive Order of the British Empire shall be cancelled and annulled and that his name shall be erased from the Register of the said Order.'

Thus one of the finest British jockeys of all time was disgraced by losing the honour bestowed on him over 13 years earlier. However, a scheme driven by racing journalist Neil Morrice resulted in nine life-size bronzes of Lester being created by sculptor William Newton, and in June 2019 The Queen herself unveiled one of them at Epsom prior to the running of the Derby and was smiling broadly alongside Lester himself as she did so, signalling that he had been forgiven for his sins, which had resulted in a year's jail term for tax evasion during the 1980s.

The other statues were placed at racecourses and other significant racing-related venues.

TWITTERATI

TURNER'S TWITTER

On 31 December 2019, Hayley Turner posted a tweet summing up her decade:
'My decade …
3 Group 1 winners
2 broken ankles
3 Crushed vertebrae
Broken pelvis
Retired
OBE
Unretired
Victoria Cup win
Shergar Cup Silver Saddle
Royal Ascot win
Shergar Silver Saddle again
Crushed another vertebrae
I hope the next decade is as eventful.'

ALL OF A TWITTER, BUT FUKUTO

On Twitter, in 2020, David Stevens, aka @PompeyDave, observed: 'Just looking at tomorrow's @NewburyRacing card, how did Fukuto get past the @BHAPressOffice name police?!'

However, surprise, surprise, along came a BHA comment from an earlier date, declaring: 'Technically we have the power to refuse to accept entries if a name has a "vulgar, obscene or insulting meaning" but having reviewed the horse's start in France, it was pronounced Fu-K-oo-To in commentary, which we had no concerns with.'

Thought another twitter user – 'It was named in France and apparently is in usage in Swahili …'

STRANGE STUFF

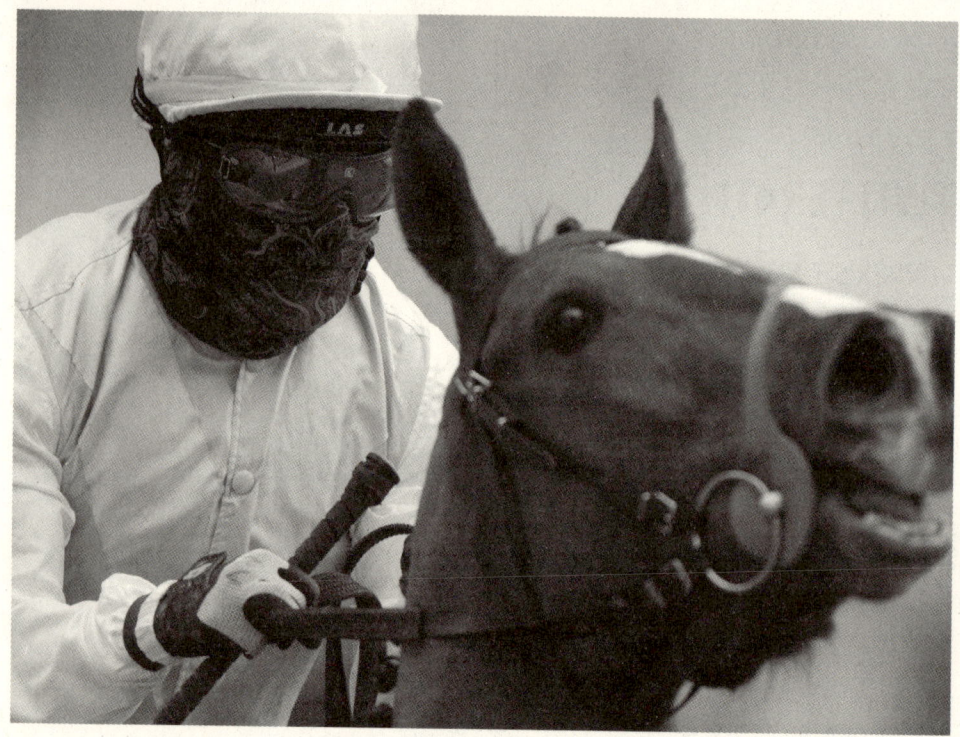

A masked Adrian Nicholls, racing in 2014 at Southwell, became the first jockey to be fined for a tweet.

Which encouraged one Rhys Williams, @Rhys_N_Williams, to note: 'Good thing for commentators that no one considered Tossoff or Wanka Tanka to be worth buying from France in recent years.'

SWEET

Jockey Patrick Harty tweeted on 10 February 2020: 'I've got my first ride on a racecourse in eight years coming up on Thursday at Clonmel. Should be good fun. I'm prepping by eating an entire box of Maltesers.'

TWEET T**T?

Adrian Nicholls became the first jockey fined for a tweet when, during August 2013, his somewhat ungrammatical outburst after being given a two-day ban for misuse of the whip at Thirsk, where he had won on Rocket Ronnie, saw him tell the world, or at least his 5000+ followers: 'F**k the 2 days I got great 2 bang 1 in!!'

He was fined £100 to rub salt into his wound.

Jockey Robbie Dunne was full of excitement and anticipation for the outcome of the World Heavyweight title showdown between Deontay Wilder and Tyson Fury in February 2020, which was staged following their previous encounter which ended in a draw. Paying his £25 fee to watch, Robbie was ready at 4am to watch the big fight – only to be frustrated as he was unable to persuade his television to show the action: 'I've paid for it and can't get it on.'

He then threatened to throw his remote through the screen in a tweet to his friend and fellow jockey, resulting in Tom Scudamore tweeting: 'Whilst everyone is rightly praising the incredible performance of @Tyson_Fury please spare a thought for those that paid their fees, got up at 4am and couldn't get their telly to work @robertdunne15.'

RUDDY YOUNG

On the night in early November 2019 that the ruddy-cheeked 26-year-old Joseph O'Brien, earlier interviewed alongside his father Aidan on TV looking barely old enough to vote, added the title of youngest ever trainer of a Breeders' Cup winner (Iridessa) to the one he already held for being the youngest jockey to ride a winner at the event, James A Knight tweeted: 'Think I have the unique distinction of having been an owner in his yard and being blocked by him on twitter!'

MAFIA MATT?

Stuart Akister (@StuartAkister), tweeted on 24 February 2020 – 'I think Matt Chapman has just suggested he's worried the BHA will order a mafia style hit on him ...' after the controversial pundit, aka @MCYeeehaaa, had written in his *Sun* newspaper column: 'The control it wants to have over people in the sport really is very scary indeed. More than ever I lock my doors and windows at night.' He had earlier mentioned that the BHA had been 'complaining about me as they always do.'

HAVE TO PLUMP FOR ELSEWHERE

A Coral betting shop customer tweeted that he was a little perplexed to read a notice scrawled over a newspaper's Plumpton card in his local branch that the meeting had been: 'ABONDEAD'.

BACK TO THE FUTURE

The first official emoji to mark a British horse racing festival was launched for the 2020 Cheltenham Festival. The Gold Cup emoji, developed by The Jockey Club and Twitter, was designed as a replica of the original Gold Cup, dating back to 1924.

WHAT THE DICKENS?

A LOSING WINNER?

Author Charles Dickens was ripped off by a Scrooge of a welshing bookie in 1852. He revealed what happened in an obscure 'Weekly Journal' publication, dated 26 June 1852, which he 'conducted' in the mid-19th century, explaining that he placed a bet in one of the newly introduced betting shops of the day – yes, they were legal for a few years.

He wrote, 'Our neighbourhood yields an abundant crop of Betting-shops and we have not far to go to know something about them. Passing through a dirty thoroughfare near Drury Lane Theatre we found a new Betting-shop had suddenly been added under the auspices of "Mr Cheerful."' Dickens added that he had his suspicions about Mr Cheerful's integrity so 'resolved to lay a bet and see what became of it.'

Stepping into the 'small establishment so very like that of the apothecary in Romeo and Juliet … we expressed our desire to back Tophana for the Western Handicap, to the spirited amount of half a crown.' The bet was duly accepted, booked and Mr Cheerful 'handed us over his railed desk the dirty scrap of pasteboard in right of which we were to claim seven and sixpence sterling if Tophana won,' suggesting rather short odds of 2/1 were offered.

Dickens waited until, to his delight, Tophana duly won the race. 'We returned with our document to Mr Cheerful's establishment and found it in great confusion, filled by a crowd, mostly greasy, dirty and dissipated, all clamouring for Mr Cheerful.'

But Mr Cheerful was nowhere to be seen. Instead, there was a 'miraculous boy, all alone, and unsupported, but not at all disconcerted,' who explained, 'Mr Cheerful had gone out on 'tickler bizniz' and wouldn't be back till late.' Would Cheerful return tomorrow, wondered Dickens? No, explained the boy, 'Coz it's Sunday and he always goes to church a' Sunday.' Monday, perhaps? 'No. He's going to a sale a' Monday.'

Mr Cheerful's book of bets was discovered in the shop – 'Mr Cheerful had received about £17, and even if he had paid his losses, would have made a profit of between £11 and £12,' discovered Dickens, who observed ruefully: 'It is scarcely necessary to add that Mr Cheerful has been so long detained at the sale, that he has never come back.'

DICKENS OF A TIPSTER

Not only was he ripped off by a dodgy bookie, but Charles Dickens also made the acquaintance of a dodgy tipster, which he was happy to use as the basis for an article:

'In one sporting newspaper for Sunday, June the fourteenth, there are nine and twenty advertisements from Prophets, who have wonderful information to give – for a consideration ranging from one pound one, to two and sixpence – concerning every "event" that is to come off, upon the Turf.

'Each of these prophets has an unrivalled and unchallengeable "Tip", founded on amazing intelligence communicated to him by illustrious unknowns in all the racing stables.

'Each is perfectly clear that his enlightened patrons and correspondents MUST win; and each begs to guard a too-confiding word against relying on the other.

'They are all philanthropists. One Sage announces "that when he casts his practised eye on the broad surface of struggling society and witnesses the slow and enduring perseverance of some, and the infatuous rush of the many who are grappling with a cloud, he is led with more intense desire to hold up the lamp of light to all."

'He is also much afflicted, because "not a day passes, without his witnessing the public squandering away their money on worthless rubbish."

'Another heralds his reappearance among the lesser stars of the firmament with the announcement "Again the Conquering Prophet comes!"

'All the prophets write in a rapid manner, as receiving their inspiration on horseback, and noting it down, hot and hot, in the saddle, for the enlightenment and the restoration of the golden age.

'This flourishing trade is a melancholy index to the round numbers of human donkeys, who are everywhere browsing about. And it is worthy of remark that the great mass of disciples were, at first, undoubtedly to be found among those fast young gentlemen who are so excruciatingly knowing that they are not by any means to be taken in by Shakespeare, or any sentimental gammon of that sort.

'To us, the idea of this would-be keen race being preyed upon by the whole Betting-Book of Prophets, is one of the most ludicrous pictures the mind can imagine; while there is a just and pleasant retribution in it which would awaken in us anything but animosity towards the Prophets.'

BOOKIE AND BETTING BANTER

FIRST MILLION POUND PUNT?

Terry Ramsden was one of the biggest punters ever to tread British racecourses – I'll always remember him calling me the day before the 1986 Grand National, 'I've already backed him big but I fancy another small bet on my horse Mr Snugfit.' 'Certainly, Mr Ramsden, how much?' 'Fifty grand, please.'

One of his trainers, the flamboyant Rod Simpson, recalled Ramsden having 'the first million-pound bet ever taken on a single horse.' This was on Simpson's Mausolee in a 15-runner National Hunt 'bumper' race on the Flat at Edinburgh – since renamed Musselburgh – which was a 3/1 chance, but 'if Terry had tried to get his money on in the ring the price would have disappeared faster than a snowflake at a crematorium.' The horse was being ridden by seven-pound claimer, Dean Gallagher, who was told by Simpson 'Just go and win.'

Mausolee was on the heels of the two leaders going into the final half furlong, and Dean 'had to ride like a demon to get up on the line to win by a short head.' The horse returned 3/1, and Simpson wrote that Ramsden 'got stitched up over the price.' Obviously, at 3/1 he would in theory have won £3million, but a bet of anything like that amount staked at a racecourse would see the odds slashed in moments. 'I think he did get it all on,' wrote Rod. 'But he complained he was stitched up over the price, he told me he couldn't even get on at evens.'

'It was the first £1 million bet taken on a single horse. But it wouldn't be his last.' And that twenty-five grand each-way on Mr Snugfit, along with the other hefty wagers he'd already placed on his horse? With three to jump in the National, jockey Phil Tuck had to persuade Mr Snugfit to put his best foot forward and the pair made up countless lengths to run through beaten horses to make it home in fourth, thus landing his each-way wagers. It made him a relatively modest profit on the hefty, mega-dosh outlay.

PHIL YOUR BOOTS ...

PHILLIP TILSON was, of course, delighted. He had just picked out the first, second and third home in the 1993 Derby ... and he'd done it in the correct order – not easy – 15/2 Commander In Chief won, with 150/1 chance Blue Judge second and another 150/1 shot, Blues Traveller, third.

BOOKIE AND BETTING BANTER

Rod Simpson trained for one of the biggest punters, Terry Ramsden.

STRANGE STUFF

Phillip was reckoning on a five-figure payout for his Tricast wager, requiring the first three in the right order to win, when he took his betting slip up to the counter at the Ladbrokes' shop where his bet had been placed.

They refused to pay him, and offered him his stake money back – claiming that the Tricast was not a bet they offered customers, and his had been accepted in error. Phillip was not best pleased and complained to the *Sporting Life* newspaper's arbitration service between bookies and punters. *The Life* appealed to the bookie's better nature and persuaded them to pay Phillip £30,000. Mr Tilson had, though, now learned that punters placing the same wager with bookies who were offering the bet were winning far more than £30,000.

Phillip's case was amazingly taken up in an Early Day Motion, tabled in the House of Commons on 9 June 1993, when it was supported by no fewer than 41 MPs, declaring:

'That this House is appalled by the actions of the bookmaking firm Ladbrokes who have refused to pay in full Mr Phillip Tilson a punter from Mansfield over £100,000 for a winning tricast bet which he laid with them on the outcome of the English horserace, the Derby, a bet that successfully predicted the first, second and third horses in the correct order in that race; believes the company should fully honour this customer's winnings and not persist in seeking a settlement of this bet on any negotiated lower amount.'

Ladbrokes were unmoved. So Mr Tilson took his case to another arbitrator, Tattersalls, who also found in his favour – but to the tune of just £700. Having cost himself some £29,300 by appealing, Mr Tilson was about to receive yet another hard knock, as it emerged that he was just 17 years old, under the 18-year-old threshold for betting with a bookie.

Ladbrokes gave him his stake money back.

UNLUCKILEE BACKING A LOSER

75-year-old Newcastle man Jack Lee watched all six of his selections in his accumulative £2 Scoop 6 bet romp home in October 2004. But Jack was soon deprived of £857,714 of winnings as Babodana was disqualified by stewards and placed second.

Jack was left with a very small consolation of £90 for his place-only accumulator. However, having won £4,000 – 'my biggest win' from another bet he placed on the same day, Jack was philosophical about his luck – 'That's gambling for you,' he told a *Racing Post* reporter, 'I feel very sorry for the trainer and owner.'

The next week the now still-waiting-to-be-won Scoop 6 fell to Mancunian Stuart Bolland, to the tune of £1,132,657. He magnanimously declared that he would be making a £15,000 gesture of goodwill to Jack, without whose disappointment his winnings would have been far smaller. A ceremony was set for the hand-over on 18 November. On the eve of the presentation, Jack Lee died.

RUGGED UP

The Times' 'Feedback' column debated the original derivation of the term 'carpeted', meaning 'told off', in February 2020, and reported that Brian Needham had written in to declare it 'a horse racing term – when jockeys were summoned to the stewards' room following a misdemeanour they stood on a mat in front of the stewards' panel. If found guilty they were admonished while "on the carpet."'

Interestingly, two books devoted to the meaning of racing terms both fail to endorse this definition. Leigh Woodhouse's 2005 Racing Lexicon does not mention the term at all, but Gerald Hammond's 1992 *Horse racing: A Book of Words* gives a definition of an alternative race-related use of the word 'carpet' – 'Racecourse slang for 3/1. Double carpet is 33/1. The origin is rhyming slang – "carpet bag" equals "drag", a 19th-century form for a prison sentence of three months' hard labour.'

INTERNATIONAL RACING

AMERICAN ANTICS
PEA PATCH
Ellis Park racecourse in Kentucky is known as 'the Pea Patch' after a soybean crop which flourishes in the track's infield during the summer. In November 2005 the track was shut down by tornado damage, but later reopened.

DUEL DOWNED
Opening in 1990, turf track Dueling Grounds, named in honour of its history of 19th-century duels being fought on the site, was renamed Kentucky Downs in 1996.

WIRED UP
Pimlico racecourse in Baltimore is believed to be the source of the racing-related use of the word 'wire', dating from 1870 when a cord was tied across the course, with prize money for the day's events securely held inside a bag which was wired to the cord. Reportedly, winning jockeys would retrieve the cash from the wire after passing the finish line in front.

MOUTAINEERING
Waterford Park racecourse, on the banks of the Ohio River in West Virginia, launched on 19 May 1951, with the horses competing on a track of golden sand while planes landed on the infield, disgorging owners and punters. The track name changed to Mountaineer Park, the planes stopped flying in after an accident, and the racing surface was no longer sand, but a kind of gravel, against which horses were protected by blinker hoods with wire mesh over both eyes to protect them from flying stones.

THANKS A MILLION
A terrible fire virtually destroyed Arlington Park racecourse and its buildings housing its records in 1985, just 25 days before it was due to host its famous signature race, the Arlington Million. However, thanks to an incredible effort by those associated with the course saw it was prepared

in time to host what became known as the 'Miracle Million', which was won by British-trained horse, gelding Teleprompter, trained by Bill Watts. In 2021 plans were announced to sell 'all 326 acres of Arlington Park property for redevelopment'.

TALL TALE

Hoosier Park racecourse, near Indianapolis airport, staged an event dubbed 'World's Tallest Jockey' on 18 October 2003, when reportedly 7ft 7in tall basketball player Manute Bol briefly became a jockey in a charity event – despite having arthritic knees.

PUNCH DRUNK

As the eight runners contesting the 1999 Maryland Breeders' Cup Handicap at Pimlico, USA, charged towards the winning line, they were confronted by 22-year-old Lee Chang Ferrell, who had scaled an infield fence and was now standing in front of the runners – as they passed, somehow managing to avoid him, Ferrell threw a punch at the favourite, Artax, missing the horse but hitting jockey Jorge Chavez.

The horse lost all chance of winning and Pimlico later refunded the $1.4m wagered on him. Ferrell later claimed he had been attempting to commit suicide. Artax was not harmed and went on to win the Breeders' Cup Sprint, earning $1.6m.

TOASTING BOB

Bob Baffert-trained Bayern was a photo-finish winner of the $5m Breeders' Cup Classic in 2014 at Santa Anita, touching off the Jamie Osborne-trained, Jamie Spencer-ridden, Toast Of New York. A relieved Baffert had reportedly been 'spooked' by a visiting trainer who, it was said, had decorated his own quarters with voodoo-type dolls of his rival handlers, including Mr B.

THE DONALD'S DERBY DISPUTE

EVEN former US President Donald Trump became embroiled in the row over the outcome of the 2019 Kentucky Derby after the 145th running of the great race, watched by 157,729 racegoers, saw Maximum Security, partnered by Luis Saez, crossing the finish line a length and three quarters ahead of Country House – whose connections promptly lodged an objection.

Stewards duly investigated, focusing their attention on an incident on the home turn when Maximum Security seemed to drift off his rail-hugging position, easing three other horses out with him and allowing Code of Honor to nip through on his inside to lead. Maximum Security battled back to pass the post ahead.

Twenty minutes after the race had finished the stewards announced that Maximum Security had been disqualified and 65/1 shot Country House confirmed as the winner, the second promoted winner of the historic event, after Dancer's Image's disqualification after failing a drug test in 1968.

Country House's trainer Bill Mott called it a 'bittersweet victory', while Maximum Security's owner, Gary West, suggested this was 'the most egregious disqualification in the history of horse racing.'

Donald Trump rowed in with an unprecedented racing tweet: 'The Kentuky [sic] Derby decision was not a good one. It was a rough and tumble race on a wet and sloppy track, actually, a beautiful thing to watch. Only in these days of political correctness could such an overturn occur. The best horse did NOT win the Kentucky Derby – not even close!'

The West team filed an unsuccessful lawsuit in the US District Court demanding reinstatement for Maximum Security, whose next race saw him beaten at 1/20, before winning at 4/5 next time out only to have to survive another stewards' enquiry for victory.

RUFFIAN TO THE RESCUE

Nineteenth-century casino gambler Charley Harrison found himself in Salt Lake City, USA, in 1859, where a friend of his, Tom Hunt, also a gambler, had got himself into serious trouble and was 'the star attraction at a lynching party'.

Harrison hatched a plan to save his friend. He had illegally acquired a stolen racehorse called Border Ruffian, on which he rode to the scene of the lynching, bringing Hunt's horse along too. Harrison held up the would-be lynchers with his six-guns, freed Hunt, whereupon the pair of them fled. Leaving their pursuers behind, the pair rode into an outlaw gang, who shot Hunt's horse, so Harrison had to swing him up on to Border Ruffian's back and 'double-mounted on the powerful Border Ruffian they managed their escape' wrote historian/writer Robert K DeArment in his book Knights of the Green Cloth.

But this wasn't Border Ruffian's only unusual involvement with illegal activity. A couple of years later, in May 1861, Harrison was now living in Denver, and ownership of Border Ruffian had been passed to another gambler, Colonel A B Miller, who had put his equine pride and joy up against another famous racehorse of the region, Rocky Mountain Chief, owned by one Bill Greer.

There was a gold nugget valued at some $95,000 up for grabs for the winner of the race, contributed by donations from spectators. The race was held over three heats of one mile, with two wins needed to claim the nugget.

Harrison had no loyalty to his former equine saviour and bet big against the Ruffian, but the Chief's trainer, Tom Hunt, was betting against his charge and to ensure he lost held on to the horse's head before releasing him at the start.

Ruffian took heat one but Hunt was run out of town by aggrieved local punters. Harrison backed Chief to win the next two heats – and to ensure that he levelled the scores he rode alongside the runners as they approached the finish, pulled out his gun and demanded that Chief's jockey should whip the Chief, which, to save his life, he did, prevailing by a narrow margin.

With the score at 1-1, Colonel Miller announced he was withdrawing Border Ruffian from the contest, handing the $95,000 nugget to Greer, while Harrison was paid out from his bets. Greer and Harrison sat down at the card table that night – and the latter duly won the nugget from him. Harrison died during a raid by native Americans in 1863.

WINNER BY A LONG NECK

Kempton Park in the UK has organised reindeer, pig and camel races for its racegoers to enjoy – but Fair Grounds in the USA responded in January 2013 by staging ostrich and zebra races on their seven hour 'Going Wild' card.

Canterbury Park in Minnesota also staged ostrich and camel racing in 2012, when another feature of the day was a race commentary by a caller inhaling helium.

MAR-VELLOUS

'Some of my favourite performers are horses!' Old Blue Eyes himself, Frank Sinatra, no stranger to a racecourse, quoted by William Murray in his 1976 book *Horse Fever*, in which he records how Sinatra's fellow crooner Bing Crosby was to a large extent responsible for the opening of Del Mar racecourse on 3 July 1937. He also records that Bing's High Strike won the very first race, and that Crosby also broadcast a half-hour radio show from the track every Saturday, as well as making his song 'Where The Turf Meets The Surf' synonymous with the course – it became famous for being played there before the first and after the last race.

CAUGHT ON THE HOP

A sudden surge of positive tests for an illegal painkiller in American racing during 2012 was blamed on the substance dermorphin – which occurs naturally in the skin of a South American frog – hence it soon acquired the nickname of Frog Juice.

FRENCH FROLICS
BATTLE BETS

During a World War Two attack on Caen, which coincided with the 1944 Derby and was named Operation Epsom, historian Catrine Clay revealed in her book '*Trautmann's Journey*' that officers embraced the spirit of this theme – 'They put up boards in the midst of battle, listing the runners and riders and took bets, then listened to the result on the wireless.'

STRANGE STUFF

UNDER ORDERS AT 8.45PM
Mont-de-Marsan racecourse, south of Bordeaux – in the town where successful Arc-winning trainer Patrick Biancone was born in 1952, laid claim to the title of earliest rising racecourse when, in July 1993, their first race took place at 8.45am.

ARRETEZ-VOUS, ARRETEZ-VOUS, ARRETEZ-VOUS, ARRETEZ-VOUS, ARRETEZ-VOUS, ARRETEZ-VOUS
One of the jockeys fell from his horse as a January 2011 race at Cagnes-sur-Mer racecourse got underway. The racecourse commentator called for the field to stop racing on six separate occasions but the remaining runners continued for the whole seven and a half furlongs, despite spectators booing and jeering. An enquiry was held but stewards bizarrely permitted the result to stand.

BOG STANDARD CAR
Assistant trainer to Andre Fabre in France at the time, John Hammond took stable runners to race at Deauville in August 1985. Next morning he emerged from his hotel only to find his car completely wrapped in lavatory paper.

OUI, MA CHERE
France's first official races for women riders took place 'at a fashionable Riviera Sunday meeting' in March 1961, with one of the rules of qualification, according to the Irish Field newspaper, being 'married women must have the consent of their husbands before taking part in any race.'

CASH CONSCIOUS
Jockey Alfred Gibert was run away with during an August 1989 race at Clairefontaine racecourse (which claims to be the world's most floral track, as 'there are 60,000 flowers scattered around the course') only for fellow rider Cash Asmussen to forfeit his winning chance by riding after Gibert and bringing his horse under control – later winning an award for 'the year's most sporting gesture'.

HUNGARY FOR WINNERS
BULLET-PROOF
Hungarian jockey Pál Kállai rode what proved to be his last of over 3,000 winners on 24 September 2006 – at the age of 72. He died on 13 October, ten days after his 73rd birthday, less than a week after collapsing at Kincsem Park racecourse in Budapest, where he was due to ride the favourite for the local St Leger.

During his career Kállai was indicted on two counts of conspiracy, race-fixing, and/or attempting to fix races. He was cleared of one count but convicted of attempting to fix a race at Garden State on 21 December 1974. The jury was told that he asked another jockey to hit his horse, Way To Reason, over the face with his whip because he had to stop it, and he couldn't hold it. Some fix, anyway – Way To Reason won the race.

Between the 'fix' and the trial, Kállai had also become a target for the Mafia, probably because he wouldn't play dirty like some of the other jockeys. In 1976 the Mob moved beyond veiled threats, beyond beating him up in an elevator at Atlantic City, and into open warfare. Marta Kállai remembers the incredible stories her husband told her in an interview with Steve Dennis published in the *Racing Post* in 2019:

'He was married to Marlyn, his second wife, at that time,' she says. 'One night their dog was killed, castrated and hanged on the gatepost, with the obvious implication that he would be next. He was sent letters saying they knew where his daughters went to school. They were after him.

'There was a race in which they wanted him to finish fourth. He wouldn't listen, he wouldn't do it. They told him they were going to shoot him. He said, "Go ahead, I am on a fast horse, too fast for you." So he was behind the starting gate, waiting for the race, and someone put a gun over the fence and shot him. The bullet went through his silks but he was wearing a thick undershirt and luckily the bullet hit the zip. He rode the race anyway – this is Pál, remember – and finished third, with the bullet still stuck in the zipper.'

KINCSEM'S CAT
Hungarian-bred Kincsem won all 54 of her career starts, contesting races in five countries against top opposition, including the 1878 Goodwood Cup, her only visit to Britain. The mare refused to travel without her favourite cat.

IRISH INCIDENTS
RACING INTO DANGER
Police had to read the riot act on three separate occasions during a race meeting at Irish course Banogue on 3 May 1859, including an incident during which a carriage containing two gentlemen, Colonel Dickson and Sir Richard De Burgho, who were entertaining family members, was destroyed by a mob, who also assaulted those present.

IN TOO DEEP?
Back in the saddle after recovering from a broken leg in late 2012, Irish jockey Andrew Lynch, best known for partnering top chaser Sizing Europe, had been taking regular dips and paddles in the sea to help with the ultimate healing process.

A happy Danny Mullins; a less happy time was his driving an ambulance in 2013 which resulted in a ten-day ban.

Returning from racing at Down Royal, Lynch, then 28, decided to take a paddle on the way back, at Gormanstown beach. The tide was out and it was dusk, so 'I had to drive out nearly a mile to get to the water. I was on the phone and had waded in just up to my knee when I saw a helicopter with a light in the distance. It started circling me. Next thing the spotlight's on me, then it's on the car and then the helicopter comes down real low next to me, nearly blowing me over, and a lad comes down on a rope.'

It transpired that coastguards watching Lynch had been apprehensive about his actions – 'I went over to him and he said it looked very bad with the car coming out so far and me getting out and walking straight into the sea. He thought I was going to commit suicide and was so worried he'd called the Garda too.'

Lynch was able to convince them of his motives and the incident clearly did him little harm as on his next ride he partnered Our Vinnie to win at Cork.

FIGHTING FINISH

Local race fans were determined to fix the outcome of a race organised over open fields at Limerick in 1833. They planned to hurl stones at English rider George Smith, or even to pull him from his mount, to stop him winning at all costs.

Forewarned, Smith, riding Fidler, had come up with a cunning plan. Heading off in his jockey kit and colours, he took a clear lead before stopping to don an overcoat and hat before spurring his horse into a clear lead. As he approached the fences where stone-carrying spectators were gathered, Smith shouted at them to move as the favourite, who was winning, was approaching.

Assuming Smith to be just an interested party out following the race, they did just that, permitting Smith to avoid personal damage and romp to victory.

This type of attempted race-rigging was not only an Irish phenomenon. Australia's *Ararat Advertiser* reported on an 1860 meeting at Victoria's Great Western Race Club: 'Supporters of the favourite Black Boy, surged onto the track to prevent the second horse, Punch, from winning. This caused supporters of Punch to set up a great barney around the judge, and it was as much as the one sober policeman could do to stop the fighting. Just as the last race was about to start, fighting broke out again and the day's racing terminated in a general free fight.'

DRIVEN DANNY

Having pulled up his mount Private Treasure in a novice hurdle race at Bellewstown on 5 July 2013, jockey Danny Mullins, 21, was so impatient to return to weigh out for the next race that he annexed a nearby ambulance.

Mullins later explained to the stewards he felt assistance was slow in coming forward, so 'in the heat of the moment' he jumped into the Order of Malta ambulance and drove himself back, so that he had time to weigh out for the following race. As a result, Mullins was banned for 14 days, reduced on appeal to ten days – with the remaining four days suspended for one year.

PROUD OF PRIDE

Pride Of Ballyara, owned by Dr Joe Mullarkey in the mid-19th century, won a great many races in England and Ireland. With the proceeds of their wagers on the horse, during the Irish Famine the Mullarkey family used the winnings to buy food for local residents in and around Tubbercurry.

The horse was retired from racing in 1845 and then used to pull food carts laden with grain around the neighbourhood. When the horse died it was given the ultimate compliment and was buried in the Mullarkey family plot in Ballyara Old Cemetery, under

STRANGE STUFF

Yutaka Take was deeply affected by the death of Japan's Deep Impact in 2019.

a headstone declaring: 'Tread softly oer this spot. If blood can give nobility a noble steed was he. This slab is in remembrance of a famous thoroughbred that netted a fortune for the Mullarkey family.'

DRAMATIC DOUBLE
The local clergyman, Reverend Cleary, rode a winner at county Limerick track, Fedamore, in 1845. But that wasn't the end of his dramatic day and he was called on later to give the last rites to a spectator, Pat Grady, who was hit head-on by a horse and died of a fractured skull.

JAPANESE JOTTINGS
DEEPLY MISSED
'I put my hands together [in prayer] in front of an empty stall without its owner,' he said. 'He was truly a special horse to me. Only I know how he ran like he was flying in the sky. I told him, "thank you" … he was the precious treasure.' Bereft leading Japanese jockey Yutaka Take following the death of one of the country's greatest racehorses and stallions, Deep Impact, in July 2019.

HOW OTHERS DO THINGS
'In Japan riders are required to be in jockey quarters the night before racing and forfeit their mobile phones, only recovering them after the action Peter Scargill. (*Racing Post*, 9 January 2020).

KIWI KAPERS
DELAYED RETURN
Kiwi jockey Johnny Wairoa had a bad fall over fences in 1929 – and rode his next winner at Gisborne on Merry Crooner during the 1950/51 season after a 22-year gap.

MONKEY BUSINESS
Racing began at Gate Pa from 1874. In 1880 a grandstand was constructed, and during that year it was reported that 'punters paid out 2/6d, and a canary or monkey would pick a number out of a hat to give them a tip for the next race.'

SHADY FINISH
Partnering In The Shade in the 1931 Taranaki Cup, jockey R S Bagby was thrown out of his saddle, only to land on his feet, but on top of the running rail. The quick-thinking rider somehow managed to jump back into the saddle, and ride on.

STRANGE STUFF

SIXCESSFUL
After an amazing day winning all six races at Beaumont in 1931, jockey J W Dooley finished second in all six races the very next day.

BOOKIE BLOW
In 1886 Christchurch became the first New Zealand town to prosecute a bookmaker, fining him $50.

LADY ALL AT SEA
New Zealand racehorse Ladybird swam ashore in 1886 after arriving via boat at Manukua Harbour, then walked to Ellerslie where she won a race, then returned by ship to Dunedin before winning there again.

SHEEPISH RESULT
Sheep disrupted racing at Omakau in 1909, resulting in the runners having 'to gallop off the course to avoid straying muttons.'

TIMESLY TIPS
The Manawutu Times was prosecuted in 1923 for printing racing tips.

WHIPPER WALSH
A ban on the practice was imposed after jockey David Walsh rode Colman to win at Trentham in July 1948 whilst carrying two whips to keep his mount on the straight and narrow.

FALLING INTO CONFUSION
During the 1930 Lawford Chase at Riccarton in 1930, all five runners fell. Four were remounted. Jockey A E Ellis had parted company with Pekrette, but spectating jockey F Langford jumped up on the horse – only to fall at the last. Langford then chased and caught the horse, remounted, and, despite being minus a bridle, finished, albeit fourth and last.

WALK-TALK-GALLOP
Fifteen runners contested an 1895 race at Manaia, Taranaki, in which they had to walk one circuit of the course, then trot one circuit, then gallop the final circuit. The winner completed the course in 16 minutes, 51 seconds, paying just over 15/1.

INTERNATIONAL RACING

DON-OLD
17-year-old Donald won at Hawke's Bay in June 1907 – partnered by a jockey four years younger than himself.

Carbine, one of the top horses of his day, so disliked racing in the rain and getting his head wet that his trainer would, if necessary, walk down to the start holding a large umbrella over his head.

RACEGOER LEGS IT
At Trentham in 1911, jockey A Watson rode Clem in a 6f sprint, only to break his leg when he hit a spectator leaning over the inside rail in the straight. The spectator ran away after the incident.

STEELY RIDER
The New Zealand Enforcer Referee of February 1922 reported that 'F McCabe, the NZ horseman now riding in England, wears a steel cap. It will be interesting to see if any of the English riders use one in the future.'

ONLY RUNNER LOSES
At the off-time for the 1899 Jockey Club Handicap at Reefton, New Zealand, the starter dropped his flag to start the event ... however, the only horse declared for the race, Speculate, had for some reason not made it to the start line.

Reported the *Otago Witness* newspaper: 'The Starter dropped his flag and sent an imaginary field galloping down the course. The consequence was the Club saved the stakes, owing to the jockey after the manner of his kind, not coming up to time.'

HAVE HELMET, CAN RIDE
Glenorchy Race Day is a unique card of races in New Zealand's south island, which has taken place annually for over 40 years on the first Saturday of the year, organised by the Glenorchy Rugby Club, and attracts large crowds. Races include: Walk Trot Gallop; Trotting Cup; Relay Race; Stockmans Race; Saddling Race; Double Banking; Ladies Gallop; Open Gallop; Locals Gallop; Quarter Mile Sprint. Although anyone with a horse can register (only rule is that a helmet must be worn), the meeting describes itself as 'not riding for the faint hearted or inexperienced.'

LUCKY ROD
Rod Stewart was the owner of the appropriately named Blooming Lucky which won on the Otago Racing Club's Gold Cup day, run at Wingatui racecourse in 1997. Mr Stewart and his good lady, Rachel Hunter, were present to see the race and pose for photographs with the horse appropriately clad in a tartan sheet.

STRANGE STUFF

NOT SO MAGNIFICENT SEVEN
Wingatui staged a remarkable seven-runner Flat race in April 1914. They all lined up at the barrier start, only for four of the runners to be left at the start, taking no part. Of the remaining three runners, the jockeys of the runner-up and third failed to weigh in and were disqualified, leaving Afton Loch as the winner and only official finisher.

OZ ACTION
HAIRY PETE'S CUT
Aussie jockey Peter Morgan was booked for a few rides at Victoria Park near Adelaide in 1972. When he arrived at the course the South Australian Jockey Club representative took one look at him – and stood him down immediately, because his hair was too long.

GUN WHIPPED OUT
Racing was interrupted at Flemington in Australia on 19 February 1966, when Walter Hoystead held up the runners and riders at gunpoint for 16 minutes to publicise his campaign to ban whips.

OBJECTIONABLE RACE
In a race run at Warialda in New South Wales in 1994 the runner-up objected to the winner; the third objected to the winner – and to the runner-up; the fourth objected to the winner – and the runner-up and the third; the fifth objected to the runner-up and the third. The stewards went into a huddle before deciding to uphold only the objection by the runner-up to the winner and struck out the rest.

RUNNING TO THE LINE
Experienced rider Sid Curran rode Pyramid Park at Gold Coast Turf Club in June 1972, but during the 14-runner race he was dislodged from the saddle as his mount stumbled.

But, recalled Curran, 'I landed on my feet, ran alongside for a couple of strides, and vaulted back into the saddle. I rode to the line, finishing eighth.'

FREAK DEATH
1991 Prix de l'Arc de Triomphe winner Suave Dancer was sent on secondment from the National Stud to stand in Australia – only to die from a lightning strike in 1998 in Melbourne.

ROUGH RESULT
Trainer Bob Hoysted was literally pissed off, at Moonee Valley in 1984, because stewards had refused to allow his horse, River Rough, to urinate in his pre-race 'swabbing stall'. Claiming

the horse would be, er, inconvenienced by running with a full bladder, Hoysted withdrew him from the race.

MICK'S DEADLY DEED
Racing magazine *Racetrack* reported in 1995 that during the 1920s when jockey Mick Hayes was the go-to rider for fancied runners in big races, he had been expected to partner a serious contender in a Randwick, Sydney, event. However, when a jockey change was announced that J Nugent would now take the ride, the odds drifted rapidly.

However, just before the off, the horse's odds were slashed by bookies as money poured on, and the combination duly won. When the jockey returned to the winner's enclosure he was recognised as Mick Hayes and despite many complaints by punters and bookies that they had been misled, Hayes was able to supply proof that he had changed his name by deed poll to Nugent.

FATAL FROG
President of Australia's Nerang Jockey Club, the Hon J C Appel, died in 1929 after drinking water from a tank which, it transpired, had been polluted by the presence of a dead frog.

HUNG UP BY THE ROOS
Few racecourses can boast as mystical and atmospheric a backdrop as the volcanic Mount Diogenes, also known as Hanging Rock, immortalised in the haunting 1967 book by Joan Lindsay and the 1975 movie *Picnic At Hanging Rock*.

But the 500 racing fans who arrived at the track in January 2011 were disappointed when the only sport they got to see was the fruitless efforts of course officials to keep the course clear of kangaroos, after a troupe of the animals invaded the track before racing could start.

The seven-race card was abandoned and the only action spectators saw was when, to raucous cheers from the crowd, one 'roo ran a finish down the home straight'.

OIL GIVE YOU A WINNER
I attended a 2010 race meeting at Gold Coast Turf Club, spotting the message: 'On Track Thoroughbred supply the "Good Oil" free of charge to patrons.' I was baffled and had to ask for an explanation, eventually discovering Good Oil to be a tipping service.

23 RACES ON THE CARD
Cranbourne Racing Complex in Victoria claims to offer a unique racing experience, according to Vanessa Yates of the Turf Club there – 'Cranbourne has three tracks. Turf, harness and a

greyhound track in the middle. On one day of the year we race all three codes on the same day. This equates to a total of 23 races – eight thoroughbred, seven harness and eight greyhound.'

RANDYWICK RACECOURSE

Asked to name the strangest thing he had ever seen on a racecourse, Aussie rider James McDonald told the *Racing Post* in June 2015, 'A couple having sex in the bush at a twilight meeting at Randwick. They weren't that bothered about being seen – they were right next to where the horses trotted in and out.'

HORSE THAT NEVER WAS

This case did not involve a thoroughbred racehorse, but it should give any existing or potential owners food for thought.

On 25 June 2015, Harness Racing New South Wales (HRNSW) concluded an inquiry that commenced on 11 February 2015 in relation to licensed trainer Mr Michael Day (Snr) fraudulently obtaining payments from an owner for the training of a standardbred horse that never existed.

Explained the HRNSW, 'The particulars of this charge were that Mr Day (Snr) between 2009 and 5 May 2015, by way of dishonesty and deception, received money for training fees and other expenses for a horse referred to as "MIRIYAN", a horse that did not and does not exist. These actions, involving dishonesty and deceit, are detrimental to the Harness Racing industry.'

WHIP ROUND

Shane Scriven was ultimately banned from riding for five months for stealing an apprentice's whip during an April 2011 race at Ipswich in Australia. The stewards took a dim view of 45-year-old jockey Scriven stealing apprentice Ben Looker's whip over the last 100m of the race.

Earlier in the race, he had his whip accidentally knocked from his hand. After the winning post, he handed Looker's whip back. Scriven's mount Requested was beaten a nose by Seeyou with Toronto Dancer, ridden by Looker, a half-head away third.

Requested was disqualified and Looker's mount promoted to second. The incident was not reported on the day by either jockey, and was only noticed a few days later when stewards were looking at the film for another matter.

At the eventual hearing, stewards said they regarded the matter very seriously given that:
Scriven's conduct put his and Looker's safety at great risk.

His actions were designed to improperly improve his prospects in the race while disadvantaging another rider's chances.

Actions such as this might tarnish the image of racing, so any penalty must serve as a deterrent.

Throughout his 30-year career, Scriven had had battles with weight and he told the inquiry he might not be able to come back after a lengthy suspension. But stewards determined the bizarre incident warranted the penalty.

Scriven appealed and was allowed to ride pending the final decision – winning the prestigious Doomben Cup as the case dragged on.

The ban was subsequently reduced to three months on appeal. Scriven duly made a comeback, but announced his permanent retirement in September 2012.

FOOD FOR THOUGHT

When Australian trainer Bryce Stanaway was refused a sandwich by a course official at Pakenham in Victoria during a July 2015 meeting, he was so upset that he promptly scratched all three of his runners from the two races remaining – Trinidadian, Entirely Perfect and Traveling Wilbury. He realised he should have just swallowed it when his actions earned him a $2,000 fine.

BRINGING UP THE REAR

Riding Miss Royale at Canterbury racecourse, near Sydney, in April 2018, jockey Blake Shinn, 27, was the only rider who couldn't see the end in sight during the race – as the jockey's breeches slipped down during the race, leaving his nether regions fully exposed to spectators.

Shinn finished second and explained, 'I tried to give my fellow jocks a bum steer.'

GOING SWIMMINGLY

Aussie trainer Brad Smith took his five-year-old colt, Rebel Rover, for a piece of work on Sandgate beach in Brisbane – only for the horse to spook, shed his rider and charge into the sea, where he started swimming – and kept on swimming – and kept on swimming.

Eventually, after Brisbane Water Police were called in, Rebel Rover was finally rescued with a lasso, having swum some 11km out into 4m deep water. Closer to the shore the jockey jumped back on and Rebel Rover was returned safely to dry land.

The horse had some previous – having recently served a ban for playing up in the stalls.

KICKING OFF

A female Australian jockey, 27-year-old Nikita McLean, who punched her sister, also a jockey, at a Hamilton meeting during April 2013 because the sister had slept with her husband, vowed to make peace with 18-year-old sister Jackie Beriman after she had her five-and-a-half-month suspension for the sibling assault halved by an appeals board.

'He [McLean's husband] had it off with her younger sister,' the judge noted.

'I'm committed to try and restore my relationship with Jackie and will work hard to achieve that,' McLean said.

The feuding sisters were being told by others to smoke the peace pipe to end a private war that had captivated public interest.

The chief executive of the Victorian Jockeys' Association, Des O'Keefe, said he expected a 'satisfactory resolution' to the feud that had caused concern in the jockey's room as well as damage to racing's image.

FAR KENELLE?

A horse called Kenelle was a regular runner in races contested at provincial tracks in Victoria, Australia, during the 2002–08 seasons.

RELATIVELY UNUSUAL

Brisbane jockey Colin O'Neill rode Summer Park to win at Rockhampton, Australia, on 1 October 1973. The next race on the card was won by Rocky Way, ridden by Pam O'Neill, Colin's wife.

66/1 St Adam dead-heated with 9/2 favourite Sazerac over hurdles at Bendigo in Australia on 29 January 1994, ridden respectively by Rodney Durden – and his son, Craig.

Sisters Carlene, Ramona and Leonie Wehr filled the first three places in the Stuart Handicap at Alice Springs on 24 July 1982. Three brothers, WD, RJ, and FH Skelton did likewise in the New Zealand Winter Cup at Riccarton in August 1961.

Five members of the Payne family – Therese, Maree, Bernadette, Patrick and Andrew – rode in one of the races on the Ballarat card of 17 November 1994, with Patrick, Therese and Maree occupying the first three places.

ON YER BIKE, ALF

Alf Gard, legendary Aussie racing commentator and a colourful, controversial character, died aged 90 in 2013.

Gard was a pilot with the RAAF during World War Two, then began with the ABC in 1950 as an all-round sport commentator, covering football, cricket and tennis, but in 1958, Gard replaced Jack Havey as the ABC's race commentator.

He held the position for 28 years until the corporation terminated his employment after an outburst on the live TV program *Today's Racing*.

Alf was the regular racecourse commentator at Victoria Park in Adelaide and on one celebrated occasion he was calling a race, during which he noticed a runner moving through the field and quickly challenging the leaders.

Spotting the fast finisher's black cap and red silks, Gard told spectators, 'It's an incredible run. I've never seen anything like it – he's absolutely storming past the field on the outside, absolutely mowing them down …'

Desperately checking his racecard to discover the name of the horse and jockey in the red and black, Gard was devastated when his assistant hissed at him, 'That's not a horse and jockey, it's a bloke in a red jumper with a black helmet riding a motorbike on the road outside the course.'

GOOD AS GOLD

Avoca Shire Turf Club in Victoria, Australia, has a history dating back to 1857. It is in an area known as Victoria's Pyrenees and boasts an unusual incentive for visitors to seek it out. As well as a number of nearby winemakers, the Club notes that: 'The Pyrenees also holds its place in the history of Australia's Gold Rush with many prospectors still striking it lucky in areas of the Pyrenees today.'

Black Caviar wins the Diamond Jubilee Stakes at Royal Ascot in 2012.

STRANGE STUFF

WINX WIZARD OF AUS

Australian 'super-mare' Winx triumphed in her last-ever start in the Queen Elizabeth Stakes on 13 April 2019, at Royal Randwick (inevitably renamed Rand-Winx by the media) in front of a crowd of 43,844, starting in the outside barrier and scoring a third successive victory in the race, and her 33rd victory – of a total 37 – in a row, 24 of those in Group 1 races.

The two longest winning streaks are by Camarero (56 successive wins in restricted company in Puerto Rico from 1953-55, amongst 73 in total) and Hungarian mare Kincsem (54 wins while undefeated from 1876-79).

The win increased Winx's earnings to over AUS$26 million (£14,564,743), a world record by converting international earnings during a given year to British pounds using the currency exchange rate at the beginning of that year.

Paying tribute to the eight-year-old, foaled on 14 September 2011, the *Racing Post's* Lee Mottershead declared: 'Racing is showbiz on hooves. Winx seemed to know that ... possibly more than any other horse ever has, she made people feel better. Not a bad way to go out.'

Winx's exploits almost over-shadowed those of another Aussie super-mare, Black Caviar, foaled in August 2006, who was retired on 17 April 2013, undefeated in 25 races, including 15 Group 1 victories. The closest she came to losing was when she raced for the first time overseas in England at Royal Ascot in June 2012.

On the 30-hour flight she was clad in a specially designed 'compression suit' which helped blood circulation. The race on 23 June attracted a crowd of 80,000 and was broadcast live in Australia, where crowds watched the event on a big screen in Melbourne's Federation Square. Racing over a straight six furlongs on rain-softened turf, Black Caviar won the Diamond Jubilee Stakes by a head from French-trained filly Moonlight Cloud.

Jockey Luke Nolen sent the mare past Soul inside the last quarter mile, but after establishing a clear lead, he began to ease Black Caviar. Moonlight Cloud moved up on the stands side to draw almost level before Nolen began driving Black Caviar again in the final strides as racegoers, TV viewers and Aussies watching in Melbourne began to gasp and fear defeat.

Nolen said that his over-confidence had been a factor in the closeness of the finish: 'It was an error that every apprentice is taught not to do, and I got away with it today.'

It was reported that following after-race X-rays Black Caviar had sustained an 8cm muscle tear somewhere in the race. However, an examination by vet Peter Angus and chiropractor Michael Bryant later revealed that Black Caviar sustained a grade-four tear of the quadriceps and a grade-two tear of the sacroiliac during the race.

Shortly after her retirement, a life-sized bronze statue by sculptor Mitch Mitchell of the champion mare was unveiled in the township of Nagambie, where she was foaled at Gilgai Farm.

HORSING ABOUT

RECKLESSLY LOOKING FOR PIZZA THE ACTION?
As the tapes went up for a two-and-a-half-mile chase at Uttoxeter in March 2019, Reckless Behaviour lived up to his name by whipping round and unseating jockey Sean Bowen.

He then crashed through the rails, dashed out of the track and headed for the streets of Uttoxeter, finally being spotted and caught by a lady emerging from a pub, thinking she was sober, until she realised there was a racehorse just about to enter the Domino's pizza outlet. She managed to grab his reins and hold on to him until assistance arrived.

Reckless Behaviour may have missed out on the pizza joint, but just a couple of months later in May, six-year-old horse Charlie Brune found himself in a local pub, along with his trainer, Tom Shanahan, celebrating the fact that they had just won twice in 26 hours – a Wexford hurdles race, backed from 33/1 to 10/1, and another at Tipperary the very next day.

His trainer had never saddled a winner in the previous 30 years, so was keen to enjoy the wins and the 'few quid' he won betting on them: 'I was on my way home and I told Maggie Ryan in the Horse and Hound pub in Dualla that I was coming in for a few pints. I told her the horse was coming in with me. It was tricky getting him through the doors. We had some craic. It was mighty.'

CHARMING
The winner of the 'best turned out' award for Aintree's App At Virgin Bet Chase on 9 November 2019, the day before Remembrance Sunday, was James Ewart-trained Charmant, who had a poppy in his tail.

PULLED UP SOCKS?
Chicago Socks made his racecourse debut at the age of nine, in a novice stakes race over 1m 3.5f at Windsor in September 2019 – making quite an impression in the process. Trained by William de Best-Turner, the horse not only finished last – by an estimated 223 lengths or more, which was too far for the judge to measure by conventional means – but he was given a *Racing Post* Rating of zero – 'and he only got that because we don't give negative numbers,' said *Post* handicapper Sam Walker.

The trainer promptly closed down this possibly unique racing career by retiring Chicago Socks, remarking: 'I was hoping the other horses would carry him along. That didn't happen. He's not a racehorse. He's going to go and be a dressage horse.'

The horse suffered more embarrassment – he was shown on the racecard as a colt when he is a gelding, and his trainer, who from his last 350 runners had enjoyed three winners, admitted: 'It wasn't a very good day.'

The *Racing Post's* Jonathan Neesom's in-running comment was: 'Reluctant to enter stalls, reluctant to race, pottered around in his own time, beaten nearly half a mile (100/1, tchd 80/1).'

WEIRDO

'The horse is a weirdo, I've never known one like him. He lives outside, won't go in the stable no matter how much it has rained, the only time he goes in is to eat.' Trainer Gary Moore on Plumpton scorer Age Of Wisdom. (15 February 2020, *Racing Post*)

A GRIM FATE

Partnered by a rider whose name would come to be associated with a certain fence at the Grand National, Captain Becher, the winner of the 1836 St Albans Steeplechase, run at the Hertfordshire course, Grimaldi, came home in front, but sadly collapsed and expired shortly after passing the winning post.

In recognition of this brave winner, the Honourable Frederica Beauclerk composed the following tribute:

'Woe worth the chase, woe worth the day
That cost thy life, my gallant gray.
The racers pass the eager throng,
They shout, Grimaldi's won a head!
But in this world what joy lasts long?
Ah, woe is me – Grimaldi's dead!'

MANE CHANCE

Groom Dawn Henry came up with a seasonal ploy to boost the chances of her charge, Jo Foster-trained Sigurd at Wetherby on 26 December 2019 – Dawn plaited tinsel into the mane of the horse – who was inspired to a 15/2 victory.

HARDEST PART IS WINNING

Having worked for 15 years with the Arena Racing Company, Jim Allen decided to take up training – in America. The hard work paid off when he won a race with a horse who had had to come through all sorts of adversity before getting his head in front at Presque Isle Downs, including: 'a very close encounter with an Eastern Diamondback rattlesnake, a million black and brown widow spiders and Hurricanes Hermine and Matthew – all of which tried but failed in killing Hardest Part.'

After the win, Allen announced in November 2019 that he would be returning to the UK, telling the *Racing Post* from the States: 'I picked Hardest Part up from Ascot Sales before I came out here. He'd broken a leg in his first breeze with Godolphin but they operated and saved him, inserting three screws, which he still has, and when he was well enough they sent him to the sales. I got him for £3,000 unraced, and he's now won over $40,000. I didn't do anything with him for a year and a half as I was busy developing a 147-acre training centre in Florida that had fallen into disrepair. I left the horse out for the entire time in a huge field hoping his leg would hold up and strengthen as he grew.'

HOW CORKY POPPED 50/1 QUESTION

Nicky Henderson's long-serving head lad retired from the role after 41 years in 2019. When Corky Browne was working for Fred Winter before joining the Henderson stable, he took a gamble on his future by promising his then girlfriend Diane that he would marry her if the horse he was looking after at the 1966 Grand National won the race.

Anglo was a 50/1 chance to do so, which suggests Corky was expecting to remain single – but did indeed win the big race – and Corky was as good as his word: 'If it hadn't been for her I probably wouldn't have got through it all. She has put up with a lot.'

BETTING BLIND

By the time he was 12 years of age, Laghat (the name reportedly means 'Kick') had run 119 times, winning 26 races. The horse, born in Italy in 2003, was blind. He wasn't born blind but caught a virus as a yearling.

Breeder Giuseppe Rosati Colarieti did not want the horse to be left to his fate, so asked trainer Emilio Borromeo, whose charges had won several Group races including the Italian Derby, if he would try to school the colt to race.

The horse was restless overnight in his box, so amateur rider Federico De Paola experimented by putting a 20-year-old former show jumper in with Laghat. They got on well. In January 2006 Laghat contested a selling stakes race at San Rossore in Pisa, partnered by apprentice Giuseppe Virdis. They won. And did so again a fortnight later.

STRANGE STUFF

Corky Browne, head lad to Nicky Henderson, pictured with his plaque to mark his retirement.

Federico De Paoloa bought the horse, riding him in some of his races over the next few seasons – 'He has a sixth sense which tells him where to put his legs; when we approach the finish it's him who gives me the signal and that extra burst of speed.'

Added the jockey: 'He has won 19 races and some of them have been important ones – in one race he won the 25,000-euro top prize. We have never had a crash with any of the other horses in any of the races we have been in and sometimes there can be as many as 16 in a field.'

Author Enrico Querci even wrote a novel based on the horse's life 'Laghat, Un cavallo speciale'.

COFFEE FOR THE LADY?

Having finished seventh of 14 at Warwick in July 2014, two-year-old Tantric Lady was so full of running that she bolted without her rider, eventually pulling herself up outside the Costa Coffee branch in Warwick town centre. A surprised local shopper held on to the reins until racecourse staff arrived to return her to connections.

BLOODY HELL – WILL SHE DYE ?

A horse wearing a noseband dyed red was withdrawn from her 7f race at Wolverhampton in March 2013 when the dye was mistaken for blood after she was thought to have banged her head whilst entering the stalls.

As a result Sixties Queen was withdrawn, much to the annoyance of trainer Alan Bailey – 'It was absolutely ridiculous – I put a handkerchief up her nostrils and the red mark was clearly dye.' The dyed noseband was to support the Comic Relief charity appeal, with Arena Racing Company donating £250 for each runner wearing a red noseband.

Clerk of the Course Fergus Cameron said, 'The vets were called as they thought the horse may have cut herself, but they believed what they found was dye. However, they were called back after the starter and jockey expressed further concerns.'

Bailey claimed the two owners were left out of pocket by £600, taking into account entry fee, transport and jockey's expenses. The day raised £10,500 in total for Comic Relief.

GRISLY END

The magazine which prides itself on chronicling matters bizarre and inexplicable, *Fortean Times*, told readers in its issue 280 of a four-year-old, bay thoroughbred horse with a white star on its head, which had met a truly grisly end, as reported by the *Australian Queensland Times* in May 2011: The horse 'had its head skinned after being shot through the heart in its paddock near Esk, Queensland, sometime between 8 May and May 12.'

STRANGE STUFF

However, there was no sign of the skin at the scene, and a police spokesman commented: 'It was someone who was quite skilled, who knew what they were doing.'

In July 2016 a retired racehorse died after being shot in the head with 'a handgun' in an apparently random attack as he grazed near his south-east London stables in Chislehurst. Shocked staff at the yard had checked on the horses as normal at around 3pm and found 'Woolfie' slumped on the ground with a bullet wound to his head. Stables manager Justine Bowdery said, 'The police said the gun used is highly dangerous. It wasn't an air rifle. This was a proper handgun. The yard's been here for 30 years and nothing like this has ever happened.'

The 11-year-old grey thoroughbred was originally trained by Gary Moore and raced under the name Woolfall Treasure, being ridden by jockeys including A P McCoy and Richard Hughes. After retiring in 2013 after 42 Flat and 15 jump races, Woolfie had been owned and cared for by Myra McKenna, 58, and lived at the stables.

A distraught Ms McKenna said, 'He'd had a leg injury in April and he'd been kept in for all that time until Thursday when I took the decision to let him go out again. I'd spent two years nursing him back to health, feeding him up and he was just up to health again.'

Greats together; Frankel and Sir Henry Cecil after winning the Champion Stakes at Ascot in 2012.

FRANKEL FACTS
Many people's idea of the greatest racehorse to run on the Flat, Henry Cecil-trained Frankel, raced 14 times, winning 14 times, collecting £2,998,302 in prize money – but exerting himself by racing for a total of a mere 23 minutes and 24 seconds.

He weighed 123 lbs when he was born on 11 February 2008, eventually bulking up to about half a ton, and standing 163.8cm. His diet consisted of Canadian oats (on average 23lbs per day), American and English hay, as well as alfalfa, bran, calcium, carrots, chaff and corn.

If you had bet £1 on Frankel to win each time he ran you would have made a profit of £5.97, mainly because he started as odds-on favourite in all but one of his races. His top speed was 43.19mph during a race at Goodwood – twice as fast as Usain Bolt's peak pace.

BROOMING LUNATIC?
One of the worst examples of a horse turning on its jockey occurred at the 1866 Chesterfield Cup, run at Goodwood. Already aware that his mount Broomielaw was not the best tempered of animals, jockey Harry Custance, one of the leading riders of the day, had received permission for the colt to be led, rather than cantered, to the post, while he followed on foot.

When Custance removed his coat to mount, Broomielaw suddenly charged at him 'open-mouthed, roaring like a bull'. While a stable lad used Custance's coat as a blindfold to cover the horse's head, Custance bravely – some said foolishly – jumped into the saddle, only for the 'savage animal' to endeavour to dislodge him 'by bucking, kicking, plunging and rearing', eventually going down on his knees 'to tear out the turf with his teeth'.

This display delayed the start by half an hour, and it took a 'long tom' whip being cracked beneath his hocks to get him to jump off – only to win by three quarters of a length.

The horse never ran again.

Custance survived this experience to win the Derby in 1874 (he'd already won it on Thormanby in 1860 and Lord Lyon in 1866) on another 'vile-tempered horse' called George Frederick – and then became the first – and only – man to both ride a Derby winner and then become the official starter of the great race – which he did in 1885 when Melton won.

TRUCULENT TRAINERS

GOSDEN GOSSIP

He is unlikely ever to send out a horse to win the Grand National, but one of John Gosden's owners did win the great race – albeit on the silver screen. Actress Elizabeth Taylor played 12-year-old Velvet Brown, who dressed up as a boy to win the National, only to be disqualified, in the 1944 movie *National Velvet*.

Champion trainer John Gosden has eclectic interests.

As an owner, said Gosden, after her death in 2011, 'if she could have run a petting zoo for horses, that would have been perfect for her.'

Another of Gosden's celebrity owners is artist and Rolling Stone Ronnie Wood, who described him as 'Mr Rock 'n' Roll – he knows all the words to Dylan songs, he knows all the Stones' songs.' The latter is some claim – I'm far from convinced even Messrs Jagger and Richards, who wrote most of them, could claim that!

Wood chose his racing colours of white with a red sash to match those of his favourite beer, Red Stripe.

Gosden, who admits to being a huge Neil Young fan, studied economics at Cambridge University, where he was a successful sportsman and won 'blues' for both discus and javelin.

Gosden is also a keen fan of art and opera: 'Some people get on that narrow-gauge railway and have nothing except racing to talk about, but it would drive me mad. I guess I'd be happiest if they built a racecourse in Hyde Park … but from here [his training centre] I can dart into London, 60 miles, go to the opera, the ballet, see a band.'

DOPE

'Because the horses involved were not racing at the time, I did not realise that what I was doing was in breach of the rules of racing,' was Mahmood Al Zarooni's 'explanation' after it emerged in April 2013 that 11 horses he trained for Godolphin had failed dope tests. He was banned for eight years.

TON-UP TRAINER

New Zealand trainer Barbara Blackie had her stable star, Diplomat, coming under orders at Ashburton racecourse on 23 July 2019 – three days after her 100th birthday. The horse did not win and Barbara sadly passed away several weeks later, still almost certainly owner of the title of 'world's oldest racehorse trainer'.

ARMLESS ENOUGH

Trainer Sylvester Kirk decided to try riding a different kind of conveyance from his more usual equine one in June 2004. However, getting into a supermarket trolley for a ride around his local branch of Tesco proved an unwise move – and resulted in two fractured arms, reported his local paper, the *Swindon Advertiser*.

The paper quoted a supermarket spokesman as saying, 'Mr Kirk was apparently riding one of our shallow trolleys down the aisle – we don't wish to elaborate any more.' Said onlooking shopper Mrs Sandy Holmes: 'He was just like a bloody kid thinking he was on a bloody roller-coaster.'

STRANGE STUFF

TAKING THE P***?

A £1,000 fine sounds a little pricey for a wee mistake – but that's the punishment Newmarket stewards levied (lavied?) on former Desert Orchid trainer David Elsworth for relieving himself in the equine sampling unit at the racecourse in July 2014.

And it happened on the day Elsworth's Arabian Queen won the Group 2 Duchess of Cambridge Stakes. The trainer was reported by the BHA Equine Welfare and Integrity office and the head groundsman, who alleged that he had 'acted in an improper manner on licensed premises, in that he had entered the equine sampling unit and contaminated the bedding which, in turn, had to be cleaned in preparation for the following day's racing.'

I'm a wee bit surprised Elsworth didn't tell them to 'p*ss off'!

BAD MANNERS

As a rookie trainer, champion all-weather handler Mick Appleby remembered that on his first day working for John Manners, proof arrived quickly of the latter's renowned eccentricity: 'After midnight I heard a loud noise. I looked out of the window, and saw Johnny mowing the grass, in his long-johns, with a torch tied to the lawnmower. He was as mad as a hatter.'

MAKING A MARK

Mark Johnston (born 10 October 1959) is a Scottish trainer based in Middleham, North Yorkshire, and a qualified vet. On 23 August 2018 Mark Johnston became the most successful British Flat trainer of all time when Frankie Dettori rode Poet's Society to win the 3.00 at York at odds of 20/1 to give Mark his 4,194th winner. Trainer Mark Johnston's dad was a TV aerial wholesaler ... but he shouldn't be confused with EITHER MARK JOHNSON, 1990 USA Champion Apprentice, born 15 November 1970, OR TV and racecourse commentator MARK JOHNSON, also 2019-20 President of the Jersey Race Club and who, in 2009, became the first British commentator to give the Churchill Downs racecourse call for the Kentucky Derby.

EARLY DAYS OF RACING

FIRST RACING
It can never be proved just when and where the first organised horse racing took place, but amongst the contenders are the 776BC Olympic Games, and in England, races staged by Emperor Septimius Severus (145AD-211AD) (not to be confused with the four-year-old Pennsylvania-bred colt of the same name racing in the States during 2019) at York – or Eboracum as it was then known.

Another source suggests: 'The first races to be recorded in England took place under King Athelstan's reign in the 9th century.'

NOTT FIRST FEMALE JOCKEY?
In June 1798, the *Sporting Magazine* carried an intriguing story, revealing that: 'A person who had been in the Nottingham work-house for upwards of 16 years as a man, with all the habits of one, dying last week, was discovered to be a woman. This woman had been a groom under the late Sir Henry Harpur, went under the name of Jockey Jack, had many times rode Sir Harry's horses in a race over Nottingham course and was esteemed a good rider.'

STONE ME, RACING RULES!
It was revealed in mid-2016 that a 2,000-year-old inscribed tablet of stone, known as 'Horse Rock', discovered in Turkish province Konya, was found to be outlining horse racing rules, including:

'A horse cannot compete in another horse-race if it finishes first in any given race.'

'An owner cannot have another horse compete in one race if he or she owns a previous winner.'

Commented Professor Hasan Bahar of a local university: 'This is a sign of gentlemanly conduct in the races. It offers a chance for others to win as well, unlike modern races.'

DEADICATED ARTIST
Great equine artist George Stubbs, born in 1724, studied the anatomy of racehorses, often using dissected corpses to do so. Indeed, Ralph Nevill, in his 1908 published *Old Sporting*

Prints wrote of the artist, who, he said, 'became the fashionable horse painter of his day' that he 'never ceased to study ... even carrying a dead horse on his back up to his dissecting room.'

THE WAY WE WERE ...

'Shall we one day see "American style" starting stalls? Or a dirt track so that racing can take place daily for three weeks or so? This, many would argue, is not prophecy but nightmare!' stated racing writer Les Scott, reviewing the 1960 season in 1961 *Ruff's Guide to the Turf*.

'In recent years go-ahead bookmakers have introduced many new types of betting on many new races. I visualise that the time is not far off when these firms will be competing with their overseas counterpart and betting on events such as the Kentucky Derby, Durban July Handicap and the Melbourne Cup.' Stated Gerry B Warner, editor of *Racing Review Annual 1952*.

A 1952 advertisement for the *Racing Review* magazine explained why JOCKEYS like the publication – 'They focus their main attention on race-finish pictures'; BOOKMAKERS 'gain plenty of pointers for ante-post prices.' BLOODSTOCK AGENTS 'enjoy studying detailed reports about the progress of horses they have sold abroad.' And women? WOMEN 'rush to read about the latest racing fashions, or over cocktails discuss some exotic hat that appeared in one of our pictures'!

WHAT A RELIEF ...

Racecourse facilities for spectators have improved gradually over the years, but an idea borrowed from the former Lewes racecourse might still prove popular if reintroduced. A 1994 history of the course, written from oral memories, *Lewes Remembers Racing & Race Days* included one local's memory of how 'the older men and ladies used to erect what one could only call 'privacy screens' and, if you'll pardon the expression, they used to stand and shout at the top of their voice: 'Piddle and poop a penny.'

But it was the only place one could go, except for the bushes.'

In September 2014 Lewes marked the Golden Anniversary of the closure of the course with a parade to the site of the track – but there was no sign of a 'Piddle & Poop' site ...

PLUS CA CHANGE?

Violence amongst racegoers at some racecourses has become a recent problem. However, I am unaware of anything to match the activities at the summer meeting of 1835 at Swansea's track.

Some 8,000 turned up to the meeting when the entire population of Swansea was an estimated 13,265.

Not all had come for the racing, believes historian of the course Robin Campbell, who wrote – 'alcohol, gambling and sex were what they had come for – and a tidy bit of violence on the side …'

Quoting a source from 1902, Campbell explained in his book All Bets Are Off how one local described what he witnessed when a conflict broke out between the 'boyos' of Neath, and the military stationed in Swansea: 'We saw flashes of metal flying about in the sunshine, bludgeons descending on the heads of combatants, and a general melee … blood was everywhere, and the combatants, more particularly the Neath men, presented a ghastly spectacle. The disturbance, which practically became an absolute riot, lasted a long time.'

CAR VERSUS HORSE

Online footage of a 'unique encounter between four wheels and legs' staged and filmed in 1927 at La Chappelle racecourse in France, prior to the running of the prestigious Grand Steeple-Chase de Paris, shows a horse and jockey racing against a car (probably a Peugeot) and driver in a race in which both combinations had to jump a number of hurdles.

Further details have proved elusive, but watch for yourself online.

OF COURSE THEY DID

COVID CRISIS

French track Compiegne became the first European racecourse to stage a meeting with no access for the public because of the Coronavirus crisis with its card on Monday, 2 March 2020. Chantilly followed on the next day.

The Japan Racing Association had already begun refusing admission to their racecourses from Saturday, 29 February 2020 for the same reason, while in Hong Kong 101 off-track betting offices had been closed and admission to Sha Tin and Happy Valley reduced, from early February.

CAUSE FOR CONE-CERN

A racegoer and his 75-year-old mother, who had spent £200 enjoying themselves in Salisbury's racecourse restaurant during the summer of 2009 and decided to enjoy a stroll on the members' lawn whilst licking ice-creams were threatened with ejection from the course by the track's general manager, Jeremy Martin.

To the astonishment of other racegoers, Martin declared, 'We can't have people wandering around eating food.' There was more … 'People pay extra for exclusivity in members. They don't expect to bump into someone carrying an ice cream.'

There was an icy backlash to this episode, to the extent that, in a desperate attempt to regain the PR initiative, at their next meeting Salisbury offered their first 99 racegoers … free ice cream, and a gentleman identified as Mr Jeremy Martin – surely no relation to the Jeremy Martin who had complained about the earlier ice cream scandal – commented, 'We are a listening racecourse, and will be allowing ice creams in members from now on … we won't be coning off special areas.'

NO ONE HAD THE FOGGIEST

The seven runners set off for the last race on the card, the 3.40, 6f apprentice handicap, at Lingfield on 16 January 2013, but 40 minutes after the race had finished punters only knew that Baby Dottie had won, in the process giving rider Sophie Ralston her first career victory.

The race had been run in foggy conditions, with visibility deemed acceptable at the start. However, 'swirling fog' apparently blanketed the final straight and judge Dave Smith was only able to determine the identity of the first past the post.

The in-coming jockeys were interviewed by the stewards as they weighed in, in an effort to determine the full result, after which it was decided that only the winner, and Spartic, identified by being the only runner wearing cheekpieces, deemed the runner-up, could be officially placed.

Not best pleased was trainer Dominic Ffrench Davis, who was adamant that his Brandywell Boy had finished third and believed he had, er, missed out on £302 prize money. 'We looked at all available views from the integrity camera coverage, but were unable to identify the other horses. We were advised we could not take into consideration any other views,' explained stipendiary steward Terence Brennan.

Spread betting company Sporting Index settled bets by regarding the final five runners as finishing joint third.

PREGNANT PAUSE

A racegoer telephoned Edward Gillespie, when he was running Cheltenham, 'to ask me to check which day the Gold Cup was run on many years ago, because she'd met a bloke here, gone back to his hotel and got pregnant, but never revealed to her husband her suspicion that the baby was not his. The husband died and she was looking up her cycle from the year. The answer proved the father of her son might be still around and he was 'really lovely'.

DROP THAT

Jockey Ronan Whelan was suspended for three days for excessive use of the whip at the Curragh on 22 May 2010. The stewards later 'reviewed' their decision on the basis that the jockey had dropped his whip on leaving the stalls.

WHAT A FEET

US magazine *Time* reported in 1923 that after jockey Steve Donoghue had won that year's Derby, at Epsom, on Papyrus, his third consecutive victory in the race, 'tales are told of subjects literally kissing his feet when he entered a café shortly after winning the Derby.'

BUCK OFF

A contemporary report of racing at York in 1718 noted that 'Crutches started a very hot favourite for the Plate, but Thomas Buck, finding his horse winning in spite of all his efforts to stop him, with courage worthy of a better cause, threw himself off when leading at the distance post.'

STRANGE STUFF

Edward Gillespie had a strange request for help when at Cheltenham.

TAUNTONED?
Taunton Stewards accepted the reason put forward by connections of Mrs J Woodman's runner on 27 February 1930 for the horse's non-participation in the race it was entered for – that the horse 'couldn't be found'.

Now, where has that nag gone, I know I left it around here somewhere ... excuse me, have you seen ...?

The same course staged a selling race in September 1988, after which the winner attracted a bid of 1,100 guineas – followed by one of 2,800 guineas, then increased to £1million – by a man who was promptly removed by the local constabulary, protesting that he was a member of the SAS. The horse eventually sold for 1,880 guineas.

In February 2011 jockey Conor O'Farrell on Arrayan had jumped the last at Taunton and gone eight lengths clear with a few yards to run, only to become unbalanced on the run-in, slithering off the horse to the ground.

LOSING STREAK
'Weakening when hit streaker, pulled up.' The formbook entry for eight-year-old Boxing Match, after his run at Fontwell in May 1995 was disrupted when 29-year-old spectator Stephen Brighton disrobed by the side of the course and ran straight into the path of the horse and his jockey, Rodney Farrant.

WHEN 12 BECAME ONE
Twelve runners were set to contest a novice hurdle race at Worcester in July 2012 – only for 11 of them to be withdrawn as trainers organised a protest against what they considered the poor level of prize money on offer – a mere £3,000.

Only one horse was left in, Nigel Twiston-Davies-trained Moulin De La Croix, which duly ambled round to win and collect the £3,000 – which was then distributed amongst the trainers of the other 11 withdrawn horses to pay the mandatory fines imposed on them by the BHA.

COARSE COURSE COMMENTS ...
'This place is brilliant – as long as you don't want to eat, drink, have a bet or go to the toilet,' according to a racegoer at the newly refurbished Longchamp track in Paris for the 2018 Prix de l'Arc de Triomphe meeting, reported by former editor Bruce Millington in the *Racing Post*.

FURIOUS END TO RACING
They had been racing at Robert-Town in West Yorkshire for some 30-plus years and were aware that part of the course in certain races involved crossing a local main highway. In June

1857 a meeting took place at the course in which three jockeys, William Middleton, William Lomax and James Beaumont, were battling flat out for victory during a race, after which they found themselves in trouble with the law – and were charged with 'riding furiously over the public highway'.

They were found guilty and that was the end of racing at the course.

LET'S HAVE A BUTCHERS AT THIS MEATING ...

They raced at Longhorsley in Northumberland for the best part of a 40-year period after the inaugural meeting took place in August 1832, at which, with no alternative available, the local butcher's scales were borrowed in order to weigh the jockeys.

DIFFERENCE OF OPINION

A race meeting at Wigan on 6 July 1761 featured a race when two horses owned by different owners but with somewhat similar names – or, perhaps opinions – lined up against each other in the 'Give And Take' race.

In the event, Mr Greathead's Sweetest When Clothed won the race, with Mr Cowling's Sweetest When Naked finishing third.

LONGEST DAY?

Racegoers had to be sharp to catch the beginning of the meeting at Presteigne, Wales, held on Tuesday, 3 June 1849, which boasted 'an early morning session', during which Hector won the Presteigne Stakes, and Mountain Maid the Broadheath Stakes.

At this point the meeting took a break while patrons enjoyed an unhurried, possibly quite liquid, lunch, before resuming activities at the 'evening session' in which the Scurry Stakes brought the entertainment to a close, the race being won by Mr Partridge's Clockwork.

A meeting at Welshpool in October 1845 must have seemed to last all day for the gallant Glaucus, owned by Mr Shepherd. Having lost to Deception in the Tradesmen's Plate and then finishing behind Linnea, he must have thought he'd done enough for one day, only to contest the Tally Ho Stakes, finishing runner-up to Kilgram.

Even that wasn't enough to satisfy Mr Shepherd, and a probably knackered Glaucus somehow found reserves of energy to win the closing Selling Stakes – and possibly then being sold at auction for his efforts ...

Another 19th century meeting in Wales, at Raglan on 27 January 1866, was a little sparse of competition with only two match races as entertainment, in one of which the runner-up, True Blue, was then disposed of by its frustrated owner by means of a raffle, won by a gentleman from Crickhowell.

THREE TIMES A LOSER
They raced intermittently at Maldon in Essex from 1738 until 1784. In the January 1738 inaugural meeting all three horses entered for a £10 Plate were losers. One ran around the wrong side of a marker post, another did complete the course but was disqualified for carrying the wrong weight, and the other fell, and was fatally injured.

LIFE WAS NEARLY A BEACH
Set to contest a 6f race at Yarmouth in October 2019, Richard Spencer-trained Jean Valjean had other ideas, so persuaded his jockey, Sean Kirrane, to bail out, crashed his way through a running rail, found his way on to the adjacent golf course and headed for the beach.

Kirrane blamed the first-time visor for spooking the three-year-old gelding, who was caught and walked back to connections.

LEICESTER LUNATIC
With one of seven furlongs still to run, the jockeys and horses contesting a race at Leicester in June 2014 were joined by a two-legged interloper as a male racegoer, dressed in shirt, trousers and shoes, ducked under the rails and joined in. As the horses went past him he ducked under the rails and returned to the grandstand enclosure only to be swiftly thrown out of the course.

Although his name had not been ascertained, a photograph of the man, apparently in his 20s, and described as 'idiotic and a lunatic' by clerk of the course Jimmy Stevenson, was circulated to other tracks by the Racecourse Association in an effort to ensure he was not allowed into any other course.

Another incident of this kind had happened at Ascot the month before but concerns that it may become a widespread craze were thankfully not realised.

KISS OFF
Racegoers were shocked when 50/1 outsider Millie's Kiss won at Yarmouth in July 2017 – particularly as the horse had not even been entered for the race. Stable mate Mandarin Princess had been due to contest the event, only for Charlie McBride the trainer of both horses to saddle the wrong one of the two.

When the mix-up was revealed annoyed bookies paid out on the runner-up, the favourite Fyre Cay, as well as on the 'official' result. 'Another fine mess,' declared Coral spokesman Dave Stevens, calculating it would cost the company £50,000 – although quite how is difficult to fathom as few would have backed the 'winner', and had the 'real' runner contested the race it probably would not have won anyway.

The mix-up was discovered by the integrity officer, 'who scanned the horse and found it to be the wrong horse' according to stipendiary steward Tony McGlone, crediting the introduction of a microchipping identification for revealing the error.

NOT BRIGHTON EARLY

I was at Brighton races on Thursday, 17 October 2019 with a group of friends to see the final day's racing there for that year. All started well. We chose horses so that we could have a group entry to the Placepot bet – in which entrants are required to find a placed horse in each of the first six races to win a dividend declared after the races have been run, reflecting the difficulty involved.

After the first two races, we still had two Placepot lines running for us and were optimistic about our chances of collecting a dividend once all six races were over, until an announcement was made, explaining that the next four races were being abandoned due to 'a patch of false ground' on the course.

This meant that the Placepot dividend would now be settled purely on the races already run – and that we had lost virtually half our stake money, despite still having had every chance of winning the whole thing.

If that wasn't bad enough, there had been seven races scheduled on the day and the false ground did not affect the course used for the seventh race. So they brought that race forward to the time scheduled for the third race to ensure people wouldn't be forced to hang around for almost three hours until the seventh, due at 4.40, was run.

Well, that should have been the sensible thing to do, but no, Brighton instead decided that the last race would be run at the scheduled 4.40 time. To be fair to them, I believe they were bound by the rules to do so. This meant we would be staying, as one of my favourite horses, King Crimson, who had won at up to 25/1 for me in the past, was involved.

Many others were not so patient. Probably over half the crowd left, and most of the bookies followed them, leaving only three or four still there. King Crimson duly took part, albeit not much of a part, in the race, was again freely offered at 25/1, and duly finished well down the field, thus rounding off a memorable day at the races.

On social media, allegations were made that the final race was only retained to avoid the track having to refund everyone's admission charge if only two races were run and to encourage people to remain where they were and to carry on spending money – betting on races from elsewhere, which were screened on the closed-circuit system, and on more food and drink. But I am given to understand that once two races are run, no refunds have to be made.

NEWBURY NIGHTMARE SAGA CONCLUDED

Four years after racing had to be abandoned at Newbury on Saturday, 12 February 2011, after two horses collapsed and died under unique, freak circumstances in the paddock prior to the opening race, the sorry saga was concluded.

Fenix Two, owned by J P McManus, and Marching Song, whose connections included triple Gold Cup-winning owner Jim Lewis and Grand National-winning jockey Graham Thorner, were about to be mounted when they both fell to the ground. They had both been electrocuted. A third horse, Kid Cassidy, also collapsed, but recovered, while The Merry Giant was also reported to be 'badly traumatised'.

In February 2015 the *Racing Post* reported that Newbury chief executive Julian Thick had been 'praised for his role in bringing the saga surrounding two horses electrocuted at the track to a conclusion'.

J P McManus had already been compensated by the course's insurer, while connections of Marching Song had considered legal action.

Jim Lewis told the *Post*, 'It's taken a long time and was stress we could have done without. When Julian Thick took over at Newbury he was very keen to see the whole thing put in its place and I think it was through his efforts that we got a settlement.'

TOSS THIS IN

'The rider of Pancake Day reported that the colt ran flat,' was the deadpan comment put forward by connections to officials at Southwell in February 2015 to explain a disappointing performance.

RACE-IST COURSE?

Stratford racecourse launched a promotion offering free admission to Irish racegoers, only to scrap it after being advised that it could be construed as racist. Course officials had been hoping to swell attendance at their meeting on 15 March 2010 on the eve of the Cheltenham Festival by inviting Irish racegoers heading there free entry upon proof of nationality.

But course managing director Stephen Lambert revealed – 'I was told that we could have been done under the Race Relations Act 1976 by not allowing other citizens, including those from England, into the races for free ... we really do live in crazy times.'

WEATHER OR NOT TO RACE

During the hot summer of 2019, Southwell racecourse brought its 25 July jump card forward to start at 11.25am in a bid to combat the heatwave – but temperatures rose quickly, to as high as 35C, and the final two races had to be abandoned.

STRANGE STUFF

In April 2018 on a day of freakishly high temperatures reaching 79F/26C, and when many horses would still have their winter coats, Cheltenham abandoned a steeplechase.

BEV REV

All four races at an 1800 race meeting at Beverley racecourse were won by the Reverend M R Goodricke of Sutton on the Forest. He was no novice rider though, as, riding under the name G Crompton, in 1797 he won the St Leger on his own horse Lounger, and in 1801 he won the same race again, this time on another of his own horses, Quiz.

FANCY THAT

A hooker in England's 2019 Rugby Union World Cup squad at the age of 28, Jamie George, is a keen fan of fancy dress – and as such turned up at that year's Cheltenham Festival dressed as a most unlikely, very overweight jockey – he's 6ft tall and weighs around 17 stone 11lbs, and was wearing J P McManus colours of green and yellow hoops.

TOO LONG

'Seven or eight-race cards, with this needless, interminable 35 minutes between races, is really turning people off. Some of these meetings going on for nearly four hours sees racegoers heading for exits long before the end of the card,' says Glyn Linder of Norwich in a letter to the *Racing Post* on 1 February 2020.

FAMILY GAMBLE

Julian and Christine Gamble from West Sussex are such fans of racing and racecourses that they named all six of their children after different tracks. Despite being regulars at Fontwell, the couple chose the names: Alden Ascot; Sophia Tralee; Isobelle Ayr; Cicely Naas, Juliette Chantilly and Eleanor Cheltenham for the half-dozen offspring.

'We enjoy a day at the races so much that we decided to make the sport a more permanent fixture in our household by naming the children after racecourses,' explained Christine.

LET'S GO ROUND AGAIN

Many races have been lost when jockeys have ridden a finish lap of a race too soon, but in a 1991 hunter chase at Thorpe, Portonia passed the post ahead in a the two-mile contest, giving rider Kathy Ross her first winner – only for the combination to set off to go round again. 'The rider had over-estimated the number of circuits and did a lap of honour to turn her own private race into a 4m2f affair,' reported hunter chasing's annual *Mackenzie & Selby*.

FOUR HEAVEN'S SAKE
Having ridden his fourth winner of the day at Worcester in September 2014, all-conquering champion jump jockey A P McCoy was probably looking forward to celebrating with a libation of some kind – only to be greeted by a hail of foul-mouthed abuse from an irked racegoer, who had presumably not backed McCoy's winners, who compounded the offence by also hurling a beer can at the rider.

Arena Racing Company responded quickly by banning the man and two of his companions from all of their courses.

JUMP TO IT
Tom Scudamore lined up alongside ten fellow jockeys at the start of a hurdle race at Cartmel in July 2014 – only somehow to set off on the wrong track and jump the first fence on the chase course.

Scudamore admitted he'd been 'very unprofessional' in response to the 12-day ban he received.

ALL IN THE BEST POSSIBLE TASTE
'14 hot girls' in the relevant 'swim' wear, contested the inaugural Bikini Mile over, according to different reports, a quarter of a mile or half a furlong, at Hollywood Park racecourse on 14 July 2006. They (were) paraded pre-race to a trumpet fanfare and installed in the starting stalls before sprinting for a $500 prize.

Conditions of entry included – 'Girls of all ages and races may apply. Must look great in a bikini. Must also have a great personality, fun spirit, and be able to run a bit.'

The annual event continued for a number of years, even spreading across to Australia where the Gold Coast Turf Club instigated a similar event. Reported *The Guardian* in 2010: 'The Turf Club chief executive, Grant Sheather, acknowledged some may see the event as degrading, but said it would be done in "good taste". "When people say 'Gold Coast' you think of beach, you think of girls and you think of bikinis," he said, before remembering the script. "It's a marketing ploy to build racing," he added.'

In December 2009 the website eBaum's World said of the Bikini Mile in what one imagines was a sarcastic criticism: 'what better way to kick off a horse race than to race man's other pieces of property, women.'

BREEDING HELL
When their stallion Rabelais, standing at stud in Maisons-Laffitte in France, began to find his fertility waning at the age of 28, his owners put him in the care of a Professor Voronoff, whose

STRANGE STUFF

revolutionary technique involved acquiring another horse and grafting 'parts of this animal's reproductive glands on to Rabelais.'

Although the operation was pronounced successful, Rabelais died several days later – as had Belgian stallion Ayala and a German one, Ard Patrick.

When the Thoroughbred Breeders' Association became aware at their 1928 AGM of these experiments by the professor, they moved to ban them from taking place in Great Britain, passing unanimously the motion that 'this Association strongly disapproves of the practice of gland grafting'.

LONG SHOTS

KNIGHTMARE?
Political correctness gone mad? Interviewed on *Sky Sports Racing* in December 2019, former trainer Henrietta Knight was telling viewers some fascinating inside stories of her career, at one point using the phrase 'pissing with rain', at which point the presenter apologised for her use of 'language'.

NOT FOR THE SQUEAMISH
'He gave it a local injection in its balls. Then he pulled out a dreadful instrument that looked like a pair of outsize garden secateurs. Snip, snip, and the horse's balls fell into the straw. Then a little terrier rushed in and started eating them,' said racing writer Jeffrey Bernard (1932–97) on watching a horse being gelded.

BIG ASS FANS BREED CONTROVERSY
The 2019 Breeders' Cup courted controversy by allowing sponsorship of one of the races under the title 'Big Ass Fans Breeders' Cup Dirt Mile' – which was only enhanced when the media presenters on the night seemed to do their best not to name the full title of the race, prompting one tweet demanding to know: 'Why is NBCSN graphics & presenters not giving the Dirt Mile its full sponsored name? Big Ass Fans Breeders' Cup Dirt Mile. Is ASS such a terrible word?'

At The Races explained: 'Race six on Breeders' Cup Saturday is the wonderfully named Big Ass Fans Dirt Mile, of which this will be the thirteenth renewal.'

The Kentucky-based company involved explains on its website: 'In 1999, the Big Ass Fan Company was born. Kind of. Then called the HVLS Fan Co. [that's High Volume, Low Speed – catchy, right?], we first made our mark selling massive ceiling fans that spun slowly but moved astounding amounts of air. The fans kept large spaces that lacked air conditioning, such as factories and dairy barns, feeling cool and comfortable – and soon enough, plenty of other customers wanted in. Things moved fast after that (and kept moving). Only a few years later, we officially changed our name after customers kept calling and asking if we made "those big-ass fans". When churches wanted to install fans to keep congregations comfortable, we developed the first silent fan motor to meet their needs.'

STRANGE STUFF

The sponsorship was launched earlier in the year: 'We are delighted to welcome another dynamically innovative global company in Big Ass Fans as a Breeders' Cup corporate partner and official race sponsor of the Dirt Mile,' said Chris McNamara, Breeders' Cup senior vice president of corporate partnerships. 'The reputation for quality, dependability, and ingenuity of Big Ass Fans' exceptionally engineered products is a perfect complement to the character and international prestige of the World Championships. Big Ass Fans has proudly served the equine industry since our company's inception, so partnering with the Breeders' Cup is a natural fit,' said Big Ass Fans CEO Lennie Rhoades.

One wonders what odds would be available from the bookies about any race in the UK being able to decorate a race with such a title?

NOT JUST HORSE TURDS, THESE ARE KENTUCKY DERBY WINNER TURDS

Resin-coated droppings from 1997 Kentucky Derby winner Silver Charm were offered for $200 per turd by artist Coleman Larkin in 2019.

To be fair to him, he was selling them to give 'a portion of' the proceeds to Old Friends Farm, Georgetown, a thoroughbred retirement facility, and home to Silver Charm. This is what was on offer:

'16-ounce mason jar with Silver Charm horse dropping preserved and suspended in clear epoxy resin. Equal parts art and novelty, these gorgeous nuggets of digested Kentucky bluegrass and whatever else horses eat were daringly harvested by the artist himself, fresh from the haunches of legendary 1997 Kentucky Derby winner Silver Charm.'

And purchasers received a unique guarantee with their product from Larkin: 'I personally guarantee they'll last longer than you do. Even if I have to kill you myself.'

But is Larkin really a horsey person? A tweet of his suggested not: 'Horses aren't that great. They have one giant toenail on the end of each leg that never stops growing and they really like mints. That's insane. Possums are better.'

SEMENGLY SHAKEN – AND STIRRED

A senior NHS general manager at Hammersmith Hospital utilised £200,000 of the £57m budget she was responsible for to import thoroughbreds and horse semen from top European stud farms which she used to inseminate four of her own mares at the stud farm with which she was involved, it was reported by *The Times* in January 2011.

During the same year, but apparently unconnected to the fraud, racehorse semen milkshakes were a bizarre attraction on the drinks menu at the annual Wildfoods Festival in New Zealand. Racehorse owner Lindsay Kerslake, who charged 10 Kiwi dollars a time, explained: 'We get the semen in the same way breeders do, using an artificial vagina, and storing it. You often hear from a female perspective that semen has an alkaline taste, so I thought we'd better make it more user-friendly. Think of it like a milkshake.'

BETTING STORIES

A word, or several with which to introduce this chapter: Betting/gambling can and should be fun, fascinating, affordable and enjoyable. But, like some of life's other attractions – drinking, eating, taking drugs, smoking and so on, it needs to be handled with care. We begin the chapter with a cautionary few words, which deserve your concentration, tweeted in late February 2020 by popular British boxer David Allen to his 109,000+ followers:

'I love horse racing, and, being totally honest, I ****ing loved gambling, but if you have a problem with it, face it, stand up to it and get help, or it will ruin your life – trust me, been there. x'

AVENGING PUNTER

Actor Patrick Macnee, son of Lambourn racing trainer 'Shrimp' Macnee, shot to fame playing the urbane, unflappable John Steed in the wildly popular 1960s TV series *The Avengers*. Born in 1922, always impeccably turned out, he also was fond of a bet. He opened an account with 'a new bookie named William Hill,' he wrote in his 1988 autobiography *Blind In One Ear*, but the arrangement did not work out well.

'Having backed a stream of winners, I was collecting my winnings when a skeletal gentleman with broken nose and cauliflower ears sidled up: "You," he rasped, "Git out the back. The guv wants yer."'

William Hill was a gentleman. With great courtesy, he explained that given my father's reputation, my patronage was no longer acceptable.

'I do so enjoy doing business with you, Mr Hill.'

'Yes, son, but I can't afford you.'

ARGY BARGY

Victor Rosales wasn't messing about. He was going racing in Buenos Aires, Argentina, in 1990 determined to land a huge win from his massive bet, the equivalent of £10,000 on 12/1 shot Broncaro.

Rosales watched nervously as the three-year-old left the stalls; watched apprehensively as the horse failed to match strides with his opponents; watched disbelievingly as the horse finished last; watched, distressed, as the horse came back in from the course.

Devastated Rosales pulled out a revolver and shot … the horse.

STRANGE STUFF

FRANKIE IN TEARS AS REALITY KICKS IN

Master Of Reality, partnered by Frankie Dettori for Joseph O'Brien, was second past the post behind winner Vow And Declare – the third time in that position for Frankie in the great race – in the 2019 Melbourne Cup.

But he'd bumped the Aidan O'Brien-trained Il Paradiso, who finished fourth after his late surge through the field was impacted by the interference.

As a result, placings were altered, with Prince Of Arran and Il Paradiso, who had finished third and fourth, being moved ahead of Frankie and Master Of Reality.

'I want to cry,' was Dettori's only reaction after the two-mile contest.

However, an Australian punter was left crying tears of relief and joy as a result – because it meant a payout of almost A$800,000 (£425,000/€494,000) from a A$10 stake on the Lexus Melbourne Cup finishing positions, after an anxious 20-minute wait for the result of the stewards' inquiry.

The Sportsbet client had placed A$10 (£6.13/€5.27) on a first-four prediction.

Being demoted cost Master Of Reality's connections a whopping A$750,000, but won the fortunate bettor A$793,842.

Dettori, who described the interference as 'very minimal' to the stewards, was hit with a nine-meeting suspension.

'Safe to say our punter would have been incredibly happy with Frankie Dettori's aggressive ride,' Sportsbet's Rich Hummerston said. 'This is the modern day rags-to-riches story.'

ABOVE AND BEYOND?

Working for, or as, a bookmaker obviously involves working at racecourses – usually taking and looking after bets. But duties can often take a different turn, as the on-course clerk to the late William Hill, Ron Pollard, discovered in the late 1950s.

'William had brought his mistress to the races with him. But suddenly, and unexpectedly, his wife, Ivy, turned up at the races, too,' recalled Ron. 'Bill did not turn a hair. He said to me quietly, "Your job this afternoon is now to keep Mrs L [the mistress] in the bar. No matter what she says, she is not to come down here." Ron duly performed this tricky task effectively, but wryly remembered, 'Mrs L and I got rather tipsy!'

Another of Ron's off-beat duties was to hide the evidence should authorities come to the office looking for any sign that cash bets (then illegal of course) were being accepted at the head office.

'Usually,' said Ron, 'a police insider might tip the bookie off, for a "consideration."'

One day, though, a late tip-off that the constabulary were on their way resulted in Ron having to improvise and act quickly.

'When the police did arrive, the thousands of pounds normally lying about in the office were nowhere to be seen – they were locked in a small cupboard with me for protection, with just a small amount left on the table for the police to see.'

FISHING FOR BUSINESS

He claimed to have been 'the world's oldest bookmaker,' but when 99-year-old Morry Peter died in 2009 fellow bookies recalled how he had once nailed a large plastic fish to his odds board at the races, with a large slogan declaring 'Plaice Bets Only'.

Morry may have been channelling a memory of 19th-century bookie Big Bill Fisher who, on Derby day 1882, lived up to his surname by placing in front of his pitch an aquarium – with rods and tackle leaning against it – with live fish in it.

This attracted a big crowd of clients, many of whom lumped on 11/2 winner Shotover. However, when they returned to collect their winnings, Fisher turned out to have been the one that got away – he'd fled the course, never to be reeled in and caught.

THE £360,000 FALL

Clear over the last fence at Taunton in January 2009, Topless, ridden by James Davies, was five lengths ahead of the rest on the run-in, and set to clinch the final leg of a Tote Super 7 bet worth a third of a million pounds for punter partners Dave Nevison and Mark Smith, who had already seen their £84 combination bet include the first six winners.

As the couple mentally counted their winnings, the horse took a drift to the left. Jockey Davies used a slap of his whip to keep her running straight, whereupon she jinked right, and the rider parted company with her some 20 yards from the winning line.

Watching at home on TV, 53-year-old Nevison 'was just totally shell-shocked. Ten minutes after the race I went on the longest run I've ever been on. I usually go about two-miles and I think I must have run ten, and didn't feel a thing.'

Nevison did not bear a grudge and even went to Chepstow the next day to commiserate personally with the jockey. 'It put me off betting for quite a long time and made me question what I was doing,' added Nevison.

BOOKIE'S UNFAIR BET ON TRAFFIC HOLD UP

Bookie Betfair was accused of deliberately causing a traffic snarl-up in central London when a trailer lorry carrying a giant model of an octopus apparently broke down on a pedestrian crossing at Oxford Circus during the morning rush hour.

Commuters and delayed drivers took photographs of the surreal sight until the truck was finally moved to ease congestion, leaving the bookie's spokesman Barry Orr claiming the model was part of an advertising shoot and issuing an apology to inconvenienced commuters and drivers.

BY GEORGE ...

He placed his first Grand National bet in the 1940s and kept on doing so every time it took place, until 2015. But George Atkinson, from Swaffham, Norfolk, who died aged 104, having been dubbed Britain's oldest punter, was NEVER able to back the winner.

To mark George's passing, his bookie, William Hill, gave his family a £104 each-way free bet on the winner of the 2016 running of the race – which turned out to be 33/1 Rule The World – to end the long-running Atkinson jinx. The winnings went to charity.

DESERVED PUNISHMENT

No attempt to rob a betting shop can ever be regarded as anything other than criminal behaviour which deserves significant punishment. Rory Seager attempted to rob a betting shop in Ilford, Essex, threatening staff with a 'bomb'. When the staff members retreated to a secure area of the premises, Seager hurled his 'bomb' across the shop floor and left – before being apprehended and arrested later in the day.

The 'bomb', it transpired, was a 99p tin of John West pilchards, purchased from a local corner shop.

In May 2015 Seager was given a two-year suspended sentence, along with two years' supervision by the probation service and was ordered to undergo mental health treatment.

YES, WASN'T THAT LUCKY?

Fertiliser salesman Fred Craggs, from Thirsk, North Yorkshire, realised he had hit the jackpot with his 50p bet on his 60th birthday in February 2008, but sat through a family meal without telling anyone

When Isn't That Lucky romped home in front to start off his eight-horse accumulator, Fred Craggs had still regarded his bet as a 'throwaway punt' to celebrate his 60th birthday. By the time A Dream Come True also won, to make it eight out of eight and beat odds of 2,000,000/1, he was a million pounds better off.

I was spokesman for William Hill at the time, and it was one of our shops in which he'd placed his bet. I told the *Daily Mirror* through gritted teeth (seeing my annual bonus disappearing over the horizon!): 'We are delighted that the wait to discover the identity of our fortunate client is now over, and that he has been in touch and arranged to receive his winning cheque – we can now put him forward for inclusion in the *Guinness Book of World Records*.'

BOOKMAKING ON A BICYCLE ...

... was the headline in the *Lincolnshire Echo* of Thursday, 3 October 1895, which reported that: 'A man named Cole was fined 40s at the Police Court for street betting. He had a novel way of conducting his business. Mounted on a racing bicycle he defied the police, and having collected his betting papers at certain points, he went away at express speed. When captured he denied bookmaking. His assistant, a man named Crisp, was fined 10s.'

BOOKIE LOST HIS SHIRTS

Bookmaker Jack Walsh literally lost his shirt – and another one, too, reported the *Sporting Life* in 1965. Staines, Middlesex layer Walsh's housekeeper had washed the shirts and hung them out to dry – but when she came to take them off the line, they'd vanished.

'It must be that one of my punters, having lost his shirt on the horses, decided to get a little of his own back,' said Walsh, adding, 'He's a better judge of shirts than horses – he took two made-to-measure shirts that cost eight guineas each.'

NABBED

A man wearing black-and-white pyjamas and wearing a mask attempted to rob a betting shop in Saracen Street, Glasgow, walking up to the counter, indicating that he was carrying a weapon and demanding that staff fill up plastic bags he placed on the counter 'or I pull this out.'

However, 41-year-old Duncan Haldane had failed to notice that there were police officers in the shop wearing hi-visibility yellow vests and carrying out a licensed premises check. They promptly came out from behind the counter, grabbed the would-be robber and handcuffed him.

He was given a five-year sentence in early 2016.

DEAR DIARY – I'M NICKED

Reported *The Week* magazine in December 2011, 'A robber who denied taking part in a raid on a bookmaker's was charged with the crime after police found his diary.'

Jonathan Ochola, 21, was convicted of being the getaway driver while an accomplice stole £500 from the Hampshire shop, and had insisted he was home, watching TV when the robbery happened, but his diary entry for the day read: 'Go Porsmouth [sic], Robbery happens.'

Detective Constable Mel Sinclair, of Hampshire Constabulary, said, 'You do not normally get a good piece of evidence like that. He was foolish enough to put it in his diary and admitted in interview it was stupid.'

STRANGE STUFF

CELEBRITY PUNTERS

US movie star Mickey Rooney died aged 93 in 2014. A keen racegoer and punter, he once explained, 'I lost a $2 bet 65 years ago and have spent about $3million trying to get it back.'

Robbie Williams bet £20 each-way on Rule The World, the 2016 Grand National winner, winning some £700 – because that was also the name of a hit by his group Take That. He tweeted after the race: '20 quid each way "rule the world" grand national. GET IN!!!!!!!!!!!!'

Long-running presenter of BBC TV's *Antiques Road Show* the late Hugh Scully enjoyed a bet, telling the *Express* newspaper in August 2000: 'I was very bad with money in my twenties and enjoyed reading the *Sporting Life* and backing horses. I vividly remember receiving a letter from my bank manager saying the bank would not cash any more cheques to a Mr William Hill.'

ONE GOOD TIP DESERVES ...

Broadcaster and racing fan John Inverdale caught a cab from Dublin airport to the Aviva Stadium where he was presenting the BBC TV coverage of the 2014 Ireland versus Italy Six Nations rugby union match.

Arriving at his destination, John paid the driver, giving him a decent tip, whereupon the driver handed him a small piece of paper, on which was written the name of a horse he told John would win at the imminent Cheltenham Festival.

Refusing to reveal that name until after the race, John was quids-in as More Of That stormed to a 15/2 victory in the Ladbrokes World Hurdle.

I was with John, a keen racing enthusiast, at Ascot for a 2018 Flat meeting during which he tipped the assembled guests a 16/1 winner in the shape of Getchagetchagetcha. We were there to celebrate the victory in the 2017 William Hill Sports Book of the Year by author Andy McGrath with his Bird on the Wire about cyclist Tom Simpson. John and I were both judges for the award and remembered a similar occasion when another of the judges, the late Hugh McIlvanney, had been in attendance and brought with him on his arrival the news that he had spoken to trainer Mick Channon on the way in, who had recommended that he should have a punt on one of his runners later in the afternoon.

Having told all of the guests in our box to back the horse, Hugh was in deep conversation with a fellow Scot as the runners set off in the relevant race. As the occupants of the box cheered the horse on, Hugh suddenly realised he hadn't got round to putting on his own bet.

Naturally the horse romped home, a 6/1 winner. All of the guests – bar one inconsolable Scotsman – were in celebratory mood for the remainder of the afternoon. Hugh accepted their thanks for his tip with a gritted teeth grimace, rather than his usual grin!

Mr Inverdale understood just how Hugh was feeling. John had been a co-owner of a horse

Broadcaster John Inverdale is a keen racing fan.

called Make A Stand, but decided to sell off his interest. A season or two later Make A Stand was the 7/1 winner of the 1997 Champion Hurdle.

ANY MOORE?

Having been told by friend, fellow Arsenal supporter Frankie Dettori, that Ryan Moore would have a good day at the races on Friday, 23 June 2019, Piers Morgan 'piled on Moore in the first race. He lost.'

Deciding he should have stuck with Dettori's mounts, he did so in the second race. 'Moore won.'

Now he had to stick with Moore in the third. 'Frankie won.'

'Ripping my hair out,' wrote Morgan, 'I piled back on Moore in the fourth. He lost.'

He backed Moore again in the fifth. Again he lost. 'Disgusted, I piled what was left of my cash on to Frankie in the final race. Moore won.'

Once calmed down, Morgan reflected that 'acclaimed theologian Dean Inge said "Gambling is a disease of barbarians superficially supervised."'

STRANGE STUFF

SENDING OUT THE RIGHT SIGNALS
Jockeys' agent, Dave 'Shippy' Ellis, who said it was the funniest thing he ever saw on a racecourse, couldn't quite believe the lengths that his jockey Greville Starkey was going to win a bet with a fellow rider during a high-profile race.

Ellis revealed during a 2015 *Racing Post* interview that he 'was watching Greville winning his bet struck in our local pub with Frankie Durr, that he would give clear hand signals to fellow jockeys when leading the field in the long-distance race on TV at Goodwood. It was amazing what Greville would do for a fiver in those days.'

The best winning bet Ellis himself ever had was on 50/1 shot Fort Fox, trained by Mick Ryan and ridden by Graham McCourt, at Huntingdon – 'the horse was later brought right into the bar at the Newmarket Moat House, and rewarded with carrots from the chef.'

MAJOR UPSET
83-year-old Pauline Nye, a retired army major from West Sussex, quite fancied the chances of Lights of Broadway at Taunton on 9 January 2012, so staked a tenner each-way on the horse with Hills as much because she was a fan of jockey Mark Grant.

Not long after placing the bet, Pauline was £2,400 better off as Lights of Broadway romped home at 200/1. 'I watched on television and they could have heard me in the next town when I cheered her home,' said Pauline.

WINDOW CLEANER PANES BOOKIES – AT THE DOUBLE
Terry Burrows was awarded the title of the world's fastest window cleaner by the *Guinness Book of Records* in 1995 – but the Romford man inflicted pane on bookies William Hill and Betfred – cleaning up with £41,439 from a £1 each-way Lucky 15 in January 2010 with the former, then repeating the performance via Betfred for £39,998 in September 2012.

He told the *Racing Post*: 'I've cleaned up.'

FIRST OF MANY
Former Manchester United boss Sir Alex Ferguson, a committed racehorse owner over the years, confessed that his first-ever bet was 'sixpence each way, or something' on 1961 Grand National winner, the grey Nicolaus Silver. The next grey to win was Neptune Collonges in 2012.

BETTER LATE THAN NEVER
Pensioner Bob Holmes, 76, had the morbid task of clearing out the paperwork left behind when his father-in-law Joe Robertson died in 1978.

BETTING STORIES

Jockeys' Agent 'Shippy' Ellis recalled many amusing betting incidents.

However, Bob, from Renfrewshire, did not get round to the task for some while – 39 years, in fact. Going through the letters, receipts, tickets and bills, he came across a betting slip showing £1 at 11/1 for Red Rum to win the 1974 Grand National – and initially thought it must be a receipt for his winnings.

Closer examination showed it was the actual bet, and for some reason Joe had never claimed his winnings.

More in hope than expectation, Bob contacted William Hill, in whose shop the bet had been placed. Once they confirmed that the slip was genuine, Hills declared it a record 'lost' slip and paid out £130 to happy Joe – the extra cash allowing for inflation

MILLION QUID FIVER

Conor Murphy, then 28-year-old second head groom to trainer Nicky Henderson, thought he'd give himself a little 2011 Christmas present to enjoy for a few months by betting that five of the boss's horses would win at the forthcoming Cheltenham Festival.

He staked a £50 accumulator on Sprinter Sacre, 6/1; Simonsig, 12/1; Bobs Worth, 6/1; Riverside Theatre, 10/1 and Finian's Rainbow, 8/1.

They all won.

Although the accumulative odds made the full payout exceed £3 million, Bet 365's rules limited him to a maximum payout of £1 million.

Conor went on to become a trainer.

ARC AT THIS BET

Shortly before the 50th Prix de l'Arc de Triomphe took place in 1971, one gambler was so convinced the horse would win that he strolled into a William Hill betting shop, slapped a large pile of banknotes on the counter, and told the counter clerk to place the whole bundle on Mill Reef at 4/6 to beat the best horses in the world.

The notes came to £14,000 – the equivalent, according to an online UK inflation calculator, to £196,248.86 today.

Partnered by Geoff Lewis, Mill Reef duly romped home.

BANKS OF SCOTLAND

When flamboyant and successful Scottish bookmaker John Banks (father of current day flamboyant and successful bookmaker Geoff Banks) was asked for his 'business interests outside racing' for the 1970 *Directory of the Turf*, he answered: '40 money factories, in other words, betting shops and credit department.' He added: 'My favourite hobby is my work.'

HAMMER TO CRACK NUT?

'Course bookmakers help tracks by providing colour and atmosphere and being part of the occasion of going racing, and the tracks could help out the layers here. An exclusion zone around the betting ring for under-18s might be difficult to enforce but a badge or wristband for those not old enough to gamble could help, although it is not exactly foolproof.' Bill Barber in the *Racing Post* after seven on-course bookies were deemed to have taken £5 bets from a 16-year-old at Royal Ascot 2019 and faced hefty fines as a result.

ANIMAL ANTICS

HAMMING IT UP
Jockey Martin Dwyer, 2006 Derby winner on Sir Percy, acquired the usual tally of injuries during his career – broken hand, fractured ankle, damaged elbow and so on, but perhaps uniquely also claimed 'a blemish on my chest – from a hamster bite.'

FAIR ENOUGH
A 1902 ad in the St Louis Post-Dispatch for the annual agricultural fair held at the Fair Grounds promised 'racing all week on a one-mile track' and such attractions as 'performing seals and sea lions, a daring balloonist, a wonderful high wire act and a one-legged trick cyclist'.

LUCK OF TUCK DUCK
Jockeys had to divert their mounts around a fence near the grandstand at Sedgefield in May 2013, after a nesting mallard and her six eggs were discovered in the innards of the jump. It is illegal to disturb the nest of a wild bird during the breeding season so clerk of the course Phil Tuck had no option but to miss out the fence during races.

DON'T BEE SILLY
Racing at Chantilly was delayed for half an hour in July 2013, to allow experts (firefighters in beekeeping suits) to move a swarm of bees from their position close to the winning post.

FISHY WINNER
Preparing for an imminent day's fishing in May 2019, Craig Brazier had only two pounds – the cost of a jar of maggots to be used as bait – left in his pocket.

But instead of buying the bait something told him to use the £2 to pay for a Scoop6 bet in the Betfred shop over the road – as a result of which the Nottinghamshire man was soon £1,342,599 better off as all of his selections duly obliged to make him an instant millionaire.

NOT SO HANDY
In July 1903, Nat Moore, a young bookmaker who worked at Delmar racecourse in the USA, was attacked by a small alligator that was on exhibition at a nearby amusement park. He reached his hand out, assuming the animal was stuffed, but found otherwise when the 'critter' crushed his right forearm. The track, no relation to Del Mar, which had opened in 1901, closed in 1905.

HARE RAISING
After Patavium won at Doncaster in July 2010, trainer Edwin Tuer revealed he'd fancied his horse to go well following a recent gallop when 'a hare was sprinting along in front of him, but he caught it up, stepped on it and killed it, and flicked it up in the air – I've never seen anything like it.'

DOGGED GAMBLER
When renowned gambler Simon Cawkwell's daughter was attacked by a neighbour's dog and bitten on the lip in the mid-eighties, it resulted in legal action, with the neighbour paying £1,200 in compensation.

Cawkwell told gambling magazine *Inside Edge* that he then, in 1985, placed the compensation payment 'on Shadeed to win the 2,000 Guineas', which the horse duly did at odds of 4/5.

'This established a very nice fund,' added Cawkwell, which he ended up investing and 'transforming into a useful six-figure sum.'

The money was used 'to fund my daughter's entire schooling. And it was all thanks to that dog.'

THE HOOVER CLEANS UP – BUT EMUS BEWARE
The controversial voiding of the London National Chase run at Sandown on 7 December 2019 upset the seven jockeys who were banned for ignoring the yellow flag which signalled 'void race' after one of the runners suffered a fatal injury – but it also upset bookies and punters, as confirmation that it had become a no-race took many minutes to come through – even course commentator Simon Holt hadn't realised what was being signalled – so some punters had already been paid out on the 'winner'.

Many who bet on the race, though, and believed their selections had been beaten, just discarded their tickets. But, once the race was officially voided, those tickets could be cashed back in for the original stake money as every runner was regarded officially as a non-runner.

And as a result, 'The Hoover' cleaned up, a Tote worker revealed to the *Racing Post*, telling them that the man earned that sobriquet for his modus operandi of collecting up as many discarded betting tickets as he possibly could in the hope that some which have been thrown away are actually worth money.

He was able to cash in on the void race and despite being aware of what was happening there was no choice but to pay him out as the tickets he handed in for payment were legitimate. However, he may well not have got away with it in Australia, where, rather than 'Hoover', they call such people 'Emus'. As the racecard for Royal Randwick in Sydney, pointed out (twice) when I was there in November 2006, 'Racecourse emus – people systematically picking up betting tickets – will not be tolerated on the Australian Jockey Club's racecourses. Anybody found so operating will be deemed to be an undesirable and will be banned from the racecourse and dealt with according to law.'

Interesting – presumably any such tickets picked up by emus would otherwise just end up being thrown away as litter – therefore saving the betting operators on the track having to pay out any money, thus contributing to their profits. Or am I merely being cynical …?

NOT JUST A ROO-MOUR

Writing in the 1952 *Racing Review Annual*, *News of the World* racing writer Kenneth Bryceson recalled visiting four-time champion jockey Frank Wootton, an Australian who rode 187 winners in the 1911 season, only to discover that 'his method of keeping fit was to spar a few rounds every morning with a boxing kangaroo he kept in the grounds of his house at Epsom.'

Bryceson noted: 'The kangaroo had a punch like the kick of a mule – Frank seemed to think it was great fun!'

WINGING IT

The runner-up in the 7.10 race at Brighton on 8 July 2014 was, uniquely, a seagull, which crossed the line between winner Jewelled, ridden by Richard Hughes, and third-placed Sagesse, partnered by Luke Morris.

When the photo-finish print was unveiled there, splitting the two was a seagull unleashing a flying finish.

Principal of the judging team Nick Bostock declared that the only similar example he could recall of something obscuring the official photo was at Cheltenham when a punter 'obviously in his enthusiasm at backing the winner threw his *Racing Post* in the air – and the paper obscured most of the horse as it crossed the line, but the nose could be seen.'

Whether the offending Brighton bird was related to the ones that spooked winner Celestial Girl during a race at the same course almost exactly four years earlier, giving her rider Chris Catlin the successful excuse that she swerved to avoid them as she hung right on the run in, was unclear.

Other interactions between racehorses and birds include the stray swan hit by Dark Energy at Kempton in May 2014 as the horse shied, and soon after unseated his jockey, while at Wolverhampton in August 2007 the leader Liz Long reacted to loose geese on the track and faded out of contention.

Probably the worst incident of this type occurred in Melbourne, two needing hospital treatment in 2005 when a whole flock of seagulls flew into the 11 runners at Sandown. Five jockeys were unseated, only five horses completed the course and the race was declared void.

FOUR OF A KIND: MONOLULU, BERNARD, McCRIRICK, CHAPMAN ...

Monolulu, to Bernard, on to McCririck, then to Chapman ...

PRINCE AMONG MEN

Baggy trousers, flamboyant waistcoat, lion's claw mascot round his neck, spectacular plumage on his head. Not John McCririck, but Peter McKay, of Scottish descent born in the Danish West Indies in 1881, but who changed his name to the exotic Prince Monolulu from Ethiopia, and in 1920 started visiting racecourses, posing as a tipster.

His appearance rapidly gained him an audience and a tip for 100/6 Derby winner Spion Kop in that same year, not only enriched his finances by £8,000, but boosted his racecourse reputation no end. 'The crowd mobbed me, they thrust pound notes into my hand, they pushed ten bob notes, half crowns, shillings and even tanners into my pocket.'

His catchphrase, 'I gotta horse!' drew the crowds, as did his whole schtick and engagement with racegoers. He became a national institution, using his slogan, 'God made the bees, the bees made the honey; you have a bet and the bookies take your money!' He was reportedly the first black person to appear on British TV on 2 November 1936. He appeared in a string of films from the 30s to the 60s and even had a record released, featuring his race-track spiel.

Here's an eye witness account of Monolulu by respected racing writer Michael Church, who saw him in action at the 1953 Derby, 'standing on a box ... bedecked in a plumed headdress and sundry rabbits' feet ... he assured us that if Sir Gordon [Richards] won the Derby, the Queen would make him Lord Gordon.'

Sir Gordon did win, on Pinza, but did not become a Lord!

Like so many before and since, Monolulu gambled his money away over the years and his profile began to decline. In February 1965 he was very elderly and ill in Middlesex Hospital in London when Dennis Hackett, editor of Queen magazine, dispatched writer Jeffrey Bernard to interview him.

Bernard's biographer Graham Lord explained: 'Bernard took along a box of chocolates and when Monolulu proved too weak to help himself to one, Bernard pushed a strawberry cream into Monolulu's feeble mouth. The "Prince" tried to swallow it, coughed and started choking.

A nurse sent Bernard out of the ward and drew a screen around the bed, but it was too late. Monolulu had choked to death.'

Bernard himself would go on to become a considerable personality on the racing front and others as a journalist – eventually, Keith Waterhouse's 'Jeffrey Bernard Is Unwell' – the phrase which *The Spectator* magazine used to explain his frequent inability to contribute his regular column, almost invariably due to an excess of alcohol – became a successful West End show with stars like Peter O'Toole, Tom Conti, Dennis Waterman, James Bolam queuing up to play Bernard.

Bernard, according to journalistic legend, threw up in front of – some say on – the Queen Mother. On another occasion he was said to have been at a dinner where he stood on the top table and urinated into his soup plate.

He wrote two wildly entertaining columns per week for the *Sporting Life*, racing's leading newspaper – until October 1971 when, aged 39, he arrived legless at an awards dinner for National Hunt racing at which he was guest of honour. 'Two waiters had to carry me upstairs,' he recalled. Next morning he awoke in time to make his flight to the races at Longchamp, quite possibly to see the Prix de l'Arc de Triomphe.

The first person he spoke to there, Henry Cecil, greeted him: 'What a pity you've been sacked.'

His 'Colonel Mad' column in *Private Eye* began in 1977, scurrilously scathing about the great and good of racing under a cloak of anonymity, which once resulted in my then managing director demanding that I tell him who wrote the column, which was also fond of taking a pop at bookies. When I refused he said, 'Can't you at least get him to stop libelling me!?'

Other publications featuring Bernard's jottings included the *Sunday Mirror* – sacked for going on holiday without leaving a column – the *New Statesman,* and the *Spectator*, where he wrote a column called 'Low Life', described by writer Jonathan Meades as 'a suicide note in weekly instalments'.

Jeffrey's local pub in Soho, the Coach and Horses, often figured in his writings and he was found guilty of illegally taking bets there.

Perhaps aware of the inevitable, Bernard allowed Channel 4 to film him for a 'still living' obituary programme. John McCririck, a friend who supported him in court and in the obituary programme, was perhaps Bernard's natural successor as racing's bete noir when Bernard died in September 1977.

WAS McCRIRICK A REINCARNATION?

Larger-than-life racing personality and eccentric John McCririck was noted for his extravagant personal style, which helped him stand out amongst more soberly clad members of the racing media and racecourse scene.

STRANGE STUFF

John McCririck in familiar racecourse pose.

With his in-depth experience and understanding of bookmaking – he'd had a short, financially disastrous experience of being a bookie – Big Mac's deliberately eye-catching, flamboyant style of dress soon made him a ubiquitous figure whenever TV needed a recognisable presence – not just on the racing coverage.

His betting expertise and indifference to criticism of his looks soon won him universal recognition as a media personality, in which he gloried.

But had Big Mac been here before, and was this time merely copying his mode of dress from his earlier existence as a 19th-century Englishman, born in Devon, with an Italian-sounding name – Francis Cavaliero, who became a big cheese in Austro-Hungarian racing, importing horses there from England and becoming secretary of the Austrian Jockey Club for 48 years before he died in 1882?

A photograph of Cavaliero reproduced in John Pinfold's 'The Velka Pardubicka and the Grand National', shows him to be a dead-ringer for McCririck … right down to the mutton-chop whiskers, ostentatious head-wear and flamboyant clothes.

Eventually he fell out of favour, despite blaming ageism, and drifted out of the public consciousness. His media replacement would soon take the limelight in his place …

CHAPMAN TAKES OVER

John McCririck died in July 2019, leaving Matt Chapman to continue the line of entertaining racing eccentrics and dividing opinion over whether they are positives or negatives for the sport. I'm in the 'positive' corner.

In 2018 Chapman, from Guildford, attempted to make the crossover from racing to general public awareness when he seemed to have broken out of the racing straitjacket when he won the role of fronting ITV's ten-week, high-profile show *Dancing On Ice*, featuring a dozen celebrities and, ahem, 'stars' from soaps and 'reality' shows.

Chappers was reportedly 'excited' by the role and put in the work to be up to speed on the lives of those he'd be introducing. But following his debut in the opening show, he faced criticism for his presenting style and was unceremoniously sacked from the show.

Wrote Stuart Riley in the *Racing Post*: 'There was significant criticism on social media … and ITV leaders took the decision to replace Chapman, who drew complaints from some viewers for his boisterous commentary style.'

Or was this quite the case? *The Sun* had an alternative explanation: 'A *Dancing On Ice* source told *The Sun's* Bizarre column: "Matt decided he couldn't make his diary quite work as he thought. He's a big character and a talented sports commentator but he had some mixed reviews in the first show, and he told ITV that perhaps it wasn't for him after all."'

So it was back to his high-profile racing life, as the betting expert and provocative wind-up merchant on *ITV Racing*, the appointment he won in September 2016, and other dedicated racing TV stations.

Website *horse racing.uk.net* described Matt as: 'Without doubt the most outspoken member of the *At The Races* presenting team and his style is certainly one that divides opinion, he is never shy in giving his opinion on the latest issues and is no stranger to getting himself into hot water because of it.

'Chapman is clearly the most colourful presenter in the sport at the moment and as a result he has built up a good following with his forthright opinions and excitable comments making him a compelling watch.

'Indeed the popularity of Matt Chapman was confirmed in 2010 when he picked up the Broadcaster of the Year Award at the HWPA Derby Awards Lunch.

'Chapman is a presenter that will not be popular with every racing fan, his ranting and raving can become somewhat tedious but you can be sure that he will not sit on the fence when asked for a view. He is the perfect presenter to field questions from punters while not being afraid to put the tough questions to trainers and jockeys.

STRANGE STUFF

Matt Chapman presenting for ITV Racing.

'A presenter like Matt is clearly a marmite presenter but that in itself is good for the sport as he gets people talking about racing with his forthright style and controversial opinions. Chapman seems to be growing in popularity, his brand of presenting horse racing is unique and that sets him apart from many other racing personalities who can often be viewed as somewhat bland.'

Matt first became interested in horse racing at a young age, weighing up the pros and cons of the various runners in a race and trying to come up with the winner. The speed and danger of racing was also a fascination, one that he still feels today.

His first job began the day after he left university, when he joined the International Racing Bureau (IRB) which promotes international horse races globally, providing services for trainers, breeders and owners.

He joined the editorial department as the junior member and gained a deep knowledge of international racing. While at university he had worked part time at the *Independent* newspaper on the news desk where he worked with mentors such as John Cobb, Greg Wood, Paul Hayward and Richard Edmondson.

After leaving the IRB, Matt worked for eight years on the news desk of the *Racing Post*. Keen to enter the presentation business, he managed to persuade George Irvine, who ran the Racing Channel, to give him a screen test.

Matt felt particularly proud of being able to describe Sir Henry Cecil as a friend, as well as being voted the Horserace Writers and Photographers Association (HWPA) 2010 Broadcaster of the Year along with winning the 2010 *Racing Post* Broadcasters' World Cup. But he downplays his role as a presenter: 'People who are interested in the sport will watch whoever it is who is presenting.'

Always keen to create a talking point, Matt did it once by NOT talking, after he taped his much-utilised mouth firmly shut in 2017 and underwent a sponsored silence at Newcastle racecourse in 2017 to raise funds for the charitable Voice Of Racing Project.

He always likes to make his presence felt even if that means being controversial.

Matt thinks that racecourses should be improved substantially as often they are the worst place to watch horse racing. And, he has said, the food served at racecourses is usually of poor quality and overpriced. The loos could be better too. He is an advocate of social media as it gives ordinary people the opportunity to communicate with jockeys and trainers, something that previously would have been impossible. The best place for news on racing, he says, is Twitter.

A prime example of the appeal and abuse which can be associated with Chapman was seen in full flow on Saturday, 16 November 2019, when he and ace jump jockey Ruby Walsh jousted and joshed their way through the early ITV Racing morning show, with the retired rider showing occasional signs of a desire to, at the very least, administer a cautionary cuff, as Matt appeared determined to goad and wind up Walsh.

Chapman continued the tirade when the afternoon live coverage of racing began, telling viewers that a horse which had been backed was clearly attracting such support as the horse would have improved since Walsh used to ride him.

When Robbie Power won the opening televised race on West Approach, Chapman was quick to remind viewers that Power had achieved what Walsh had been unable to achieve by winning on the horse at Cheltenham.

So, just like his predecessors Monolulu, Bernard and McCririck – Chapman divides opinions – love or loathe all of them you couldn't, and can't, ignore them …

WHAT'S IN A NAME?

NO FOOLING
Only Orsenfoolsies was foaled in April 2009 and duly given what was felt to be an appropriately amusing name. He was sold for £500 and raced until retirement in January 2020, by which time the 11-year-old had nine wins from 67 races and prize money a fraction under £100,000 to his not-so-foolish name!

NAME GAME
Both horses fighting out the finish of a chase at Keele Park racecourse today in 1896 were named Lambton. Lambton won. Neither was ridden by jockey Mr W. Lambton, who would score a double at the track in February 1898.

BALLY ODD
Irish racecourse Ballymoney staged racing from 1762 until 1880, whilst Irish racecourse Ballymooney did likewise from 1842 until 1846, thus offering potential confusion during the five years the two were both active. Neither should be confused with Irish racecourse Ballymena, which staged racing from 1853 to 1866.

FALLON … the surname of former champion jockey Kieren, a controversial figure for various reasons, who, when his son was born, chose a very similar name to his own – Cieren.

LOBLOLLY STABLES, USA … named not after the expense of owning racehorses, but after a species of pine tree.

SEXYFISH … an also-ran in the inaugural 2020 Saudi Cup, with some £15 million on offer in prize money, the world's richest race. During the meeting in Riyadh, Kiwi jockey Lisa Allpress, who had just become New Zealand champion jockey at the age of 44, made more history by becoming the first woman to win a race in the country where women were not allowed to drive before 2018.

CHARLES WHITTINGHAM … Legendary US trainer Charles Whittingham became known as 'Bald Eagle' for obvious reasons. When applying for credentials in New York, the non-hirsute handler listed his hair colour as 'Brown' – explaining, 'That's the way I remember it.'

WHAT'S IN A NAME?

Father and son, Kieren and Cieren Fallon.

STRANGE STUFF

Rich Ricci, able to laugh at himself.

HITLER … the name of a horse racing at Namibia's Otjakomaue racecourse during 2012. Reported the *allAfrica* website: 'Hitler moved like greased lightning, striking everywhere to rewrite the history books by becoming the first horse in the short history of local horse racing to clinch all available silverware on offer at the Otjakomaue Horse racing Track.'

GEORGE BAKER … the four-year-old horse, owned by George Baker the man, trained by another George Baker, was ridden by still another George Baker, the jockey at Leicester in August 2011 – and won for the fourth time in five starts.

BLACKMAN … was the name under which a two-year-old filly was running in 2002. She had reportedly been named after Australian artist Charles Blackman, famed for his series of Alice In Wonderland paintings. However, reported the *Daily Mail*, following a complaint to racing

WHAT'S IN A NAME?

officials that the name was offensive to Indigenous Australians, Aussie trainer David Hayes was ordered to change it, which he did, to Lady Blackman – accepted by Racing Information Services Australia.

XILOBS GOD ... no backward horse, this one, which contested a Down Royal bumper race in May 2012.

CUT THE LUGSREILLY ... When this horse made its debut in a 2009 Worcester bumper, the owner explained: 'When I grew up in Glasgow there was a legend that a chap called Reilly was angry when a dog used to bark all the time in a pub. Reilly said if the dog did not stop barking he would cut its ears off – and he did.'

The owner? Reportedly, apparently, Sir Alex Ferguson.

BANGOR-ON-DEE's 4.40 race on 9 March 2005 may have had the longest name ever attached to a race ... the 3m LLANFAIRPWLLGWYNGYLLGOGERYCHWYRNDROBWLLLLANTYSILIOGOGOGOCH Handicap Hurdle.

YOU'RE JOKING!

A cunning plan by jockey Paddy Brennan to change his name by deed poll to Joe Coral in February 2012 was foiled when the BHA refused to give permission.

Brennan's name change would have been at the behest of bookies Coral, who were going to place a £200 bet on each of his mounts at the Cheltenham Festival, with profits set to be donated to the Racing Welfare Charity. After the Festival Brennan would have reverted to his 'proper' name.

Coral PR Simon Clare said: 'The BHA took the view that Paddy changing his name would breach the code of conduct between bookies and jockeys.'

BOOKIES MARMALISED

Despite never having had a bet in her life before, someone suggested to Joanna Morgan as she ran her marmalade stall at Goodwood racecourse in 2016 that it may be a good time to break her betting duck as a horse named Marmalady was about to contest a 5f sprint.

Joanna also just happened to be world champion marmalade-maker (for her Radnor Preserves Smokey Campfire Marmalade). The horse was an outsider – but, and why else would I be telling you this? – duly obliged at 16/1. Joanna was then invited to present the race prizes. She didn't reveal how much she staked.

A little earlier in the horse's career she had figured as part of an unusual tribute to Steve Callow, after the 61-year-old publican who loved racing passed away. He was a regular visitor

STRANGE STUFF

to Gary Moore's stable and Marmalady had become a particular favourite, as were Moore's top jumper Sire De Grugy and Ryan Moore's 2010 Derby winner Workforce, who he had backed.

Steve's widow, Janette, 56, came up with the idea of decorating his coffin with images of his three favourite horses, which was enabled by the undertaker, and the cortege was allowed to drive round the Moore stable prior to the funeral.

FAT'S THE WAY TO DO IT

City investment banker Rich Ricci was able to laugh at himself when he named one of his horses Fat Cat In The Hat.

TRUMP THIS

American racehorse Royal Trump had an official name-change in June 2021, after his owner Steven McCanne decided that it had become too controversial to race a horse whose name could be associated with ex-president of the USA Donald Trump.

The Californian entrepreneur said having a horse who might provoke boos from the crowd 'was the last thing the sport (and the horse) need'.

The six-year-old gelding had run as Royal Trump 27 times, winning six, but became, instead, Peaceful Transfer.

OWNERS' ODDITIES

DOME SWEET DOME
Theresa May was in a 1990s racing syndicate that owned a horse called Dome Patrol, which managed to win a race or two, trained by William Muir.

WHEELY DRUNK
Long-term racehorse owner Graham Wylie recalled, in 2016, a memorable day at York racecourse when 'a mature lady who was very drunk passed out, fell backwards, and landed in a wheelbarrow in the Pimm's bar.'

Wylie called paramedics who, when they arrived, 'just wheeled her out of the bar – still holding on to the bottle of champagne she was drinking from.'

TRYING TIMES
Wales and British Lions' rugby centre Jonathan Davies owned a third of Potters Corner, when the horse won the Midlands National at Uttoxeter during the 2018/19 jump season. At the time he was part of the Wales side that beat Ireland in the Six Nations tournament to clinch the title. Trainer Christian Williams told the *Mail on Sunday*: 'The camera went on to Jonathan, and the boys were jumping up and down after the match. They said on the TV they were celebrating their win, but it was nothing to do with the rugby. One of the subs had told him that Potters Corner had won. He is racing mad.'

WEIGHT A MINUTE ...
On 20 April 1903, Aussie racehorse owner Jim 'the Grafter' Kingsley's Gentleman Jim was set to carry 10st 9lbs in the Pace Welter race at Broadmeadow, Newcastle, near Sydney. Despite decent form, the weight saw the horse's odds on the drift.

And despite this, Kingsley was spotted staking substantial amounts on the horse, which duly won – only to cause a sensation when, at the weigh-in, the jockey was accused of being two stone lighter than required. Kingsley stormed that the scales were wrong, stamping his foot and demanding that the jockey should be re-weighed. When he was, the weight was correct and officials ruled bets could be settled.

Later that afternoon, one or two suspicious-minded officials staged an impromptu investigation in the weighing area – and discovered a mysterious wire that disappeared into a hole bored into the wooden floor.

They then found a disguised trapdoor by nearby bushes, leading down to an area where they found evidence of a two-stone lead weight attached to a wire, clearly used to ensure that the jockey's weight could be made to tally with what he'd been allotted.

When checks were made at a nearby course where Kingsley runners had also run and won, similar equipment was uncovered. Kingsley was arrested, charged and convicted of defrauding the Newcastle Jockey Club – he and his jockey were disqualified for life.

A PALL-ING SITUATION

'The use of legal and illegal performance-enhancing drugs. Rampant use of these medications and designer drugs have cast a pall over the landscape and in great part have driven me to abandon racing in America in favour of racing abroad, especially in Great Britain and Europe.' Barry Taylor, whose 32+-year-old Team Valor International claims to be the 'most successful racehorse ownership syndicate in the world', writing in the *Thoroughbred Racing Commentary* in December 2019.

THE ONE IN 25

'My wife thinks I'm one of the 25. She'd go crazy if she knew I owned all of him.' Rodney Masters of the *Racing Post* reported in December 2014 on the victory of a gambled-on two-year-old earlier in the year, owned, said its trainer, by a syndicate of 25, only one of whose members was present to see the race. That one shamefacedly put the record straight in return for retaining his anonymity.

A KIND OF HUSH

Asked by family members what he'd like for Christmas in 2009, a friend of the author, racehorse owner Mike Hush, let it be known that he fancied reading the recently published Freud on Course by fellow owner and one-time *Racing Post* columnist Sir Clement Freud.

Sure enough, on Christmas morning he spotted a book-shaped present from his mother-in-law, placed under the Christmas tree. He ripped off the gift-wrapping in anticipation, and 'I was somewhat speechless when I unwrapped a book on *Dream Psychology – psychoanalysis for beginners* by Sigmund Freud!'

BOTTOMED OUT

Horatio Bottomley was a flamboyant and controversial politician and businessman who was elected to parliament at the General Election of January 1906, when he was the Liberal candidate for Hackney South. After a vigorous campaign he defeated his Conservative opponent by more than 3,000 votes—the largest Liberal majority in London, he boasted.

He was a keen gambler and owned several racehorses, trained privately for him by J Batho, achieving prestigious victories – Cesarewitch, at Newmarket with Wargrave, 5/1, in 1904 (who also won the Ebor two years earlier) and Stewards' Cup at Goodwood five years earlier with 20/1 shot Northern Farmer – winning a reported £50,000 for each of these big wins but he often also lost large sums through unwise bets.

In his biography of the man for whom he had worked, Henry J Houston wrote: 'HB used his racehorses to win popularity in a novel and striking way by introducing them into politics. In nearly every election he fought between 1900 and 1910 he had his 'string' [of horses] paraded through the division, their flanks adorned with appeals for votes.

His racing colours were red, white and black – the colours of the German Emperor. He used these colours on his jockeys during elections, and on several occasions during the war he was told that he should change them.

'There is no need to do that,' he would say, 'for the German Emperor, like my horses, will never win!' His most famous comment came during a lawsuit, during which counsel said to him, 'You keep racehorses Mr Bottomley?' To which he replied: 'No, they keep me.'

However, his career came to a sudden end when, in 1922, he was convicted of fraud and sentenced to seven years' imprisonment. He died in 1933, apparently virtually a pauper.

DEADLY PREMONITION

Owner Mrs W P Cullen had a dream in which the jockey Willie Beasley, hired to ride for her at the April 1892 Punchestown meeting, was killed during the race.

She duly withdrew her horse from the race. But Beasley then got himself a different horse to ride in the race, and fell at the 'Herbs Garden' Bank obstacle. Never recovering consciousness, he died a couple of weeks later.

The name of the horse from which he fell, was All Is Well.

BETTER LATE THAN NEVER, ANY DAY OF THE WEEK ...

Don't Do Mondays won a two-mile novice hurdle at Warwick in March 2013 – the first ever winner for owner Keith Griffin, who had owned 15 horses over 41 years without ever previously troubling the judge.

WINNING OWNER – AFTER TWO HOURS

Two hours after Chris Shirran's impulsive decision to splash out £180 to become a member of the Hoofbeats Racing Club in August 2013, whilst visiting Yarmouth racecourse, she became a winning owner as the club's Honeymoon Express won a 5f handicap on the card.

STRANGE STUFF

LESTER IN DEEP

Bobby McAlpine, eminent racehorse owner/breeder and racecourse chairman at Chester, Bangor on Dee, as well as being on the board at Aintree, was once on holiday with Lester Piggott and his then wife Susan, in Nassau. In his 2012 autobiography, *One Shot At Life*, Bobby recalled that although their host indulged Piggott 'with every conceivable luxury', when Susan asked Lester 'for $10 to go water-skiing' the multiple champion's reply was, 'Go half a mile up the beach and it's only $5.'

In 2011 bookie Victor Chandler, a friend of racing enthusiast artist Lucian Freud, commented that 'Lucian was desperate to paint Lester Piggott, but Lester wanted either money or the finished work in return.'

SIR ALEX A CHAMP AGAIN

Sir Alex Ferguson's horse, If I Had Him, trained by George Baker, became a Champion Hurdler in 2013 – winning that event at a meeting run at Les Landes in the Channel Island of Jersey.

TRAGIC ANNIVERSARY

On the very day that Leicester City supporters marked the first anniversary of the death of the club's late chairman, Vichai Srivaddhanaprabha, the first racehorse he bought, Donjuan Triumphant, ran out the 33/1 winner at Ascot of the British Champions Sprint Stakes, in October 2019.

DEAD LOSSES

A British jockey has both died AND survived to ride again.

Brian Toomey was riding Solway Dandy at Perth, Scotland, on 4 July 2013 in a hurdles race. Three hurdles from home, Brian, 19, was unseated in a heavy fall. He lost consciousness on the ground but was resuscitated by paramedics, who later told him he had 'died for six seconds'.

At this point his injuries were so severe that his chance of survival was slim.

Toomey was placed in an induced coma awaiting life-saving surgery, during which part of his skull was cut away and replaced with a titanium plate.

A very slow recovery ensued: 'I was in hospital for 157 nights.' The eventual recovery took all of two years. He had to learn to walk again and re-take his driving test.

He did manage to return to the saddle in 2015 for a short-lived comeback, from which he retired the following year.

After a brief stint as an assistant trainer in England to Grand National-winning trainer Dr Richard Newland, he eventually returned to Ireland to be with his family as he was feeling very 'down'.

Slowly but surely Toomey came back to the racing world, most recently, now aged 30, riding out for Flat trainer Clive Cox every day absorbing what it takes to be a trainer – his ultimate goal.

Great American horse Man O'War, who won 20 of his 21 races, died in 1947 and became the first racehorse to be embalmed – which took 23 gallon bottles of embalming, compared with an average two for a human.

There was a tragic end to a race at Homebush in Australia in 1847 when jockey George Marsden died after falling from his mount. Another jockey in the race, John Gilligan, was accused of crossing in front of Marsden's mount, causing him to fall. Gilligan faced a charge of manslaughter, was acquitted, and immediately retired.

Although racegoers had seen favourite Simonic pass the post in front at Ascot, Brisbane, in 1940, they didn't get paid out as the judge was unable to confirm the result to enable it to become official – he had collapsed and died during the race.

ROCKING HORSES

ROCK AND RACING

A key member of supergroup Crosby, Stills and Nash, Stephen Stills was living on a ranch owned by friend Mickey Hart during 1969, and as a thank you bought him a racehorse. Then in 1978 Stills released a solo record, entitled 'Thoroughfare Gap', the back and front cover of which showed him in jockey garb – actually riding a racehorse on the front.

To mark the 25th anniversary of the death of founder Rolling Stone Brian Jones, in July 1994 a 12-hour rock festival, featuring many musicians associated with him, was held at Cheltenham racecourse – Jones was born in Cheltenham in 1942.

It may be slightly pushing the definition to call Abba a rock group, but group member Benny Andersson is certainly a keen racing fan, and in October 2019, when she was training his useful filly Lavender's Blue, Amanda Perrett said of him: 'He's very knowledgeable on breeding and racing. He's patient, gives his horses the time they need. He likes to be involved in every aspect of the training and racing of his horses.'

BEATLING ALONG

Paul McCartney featured a track called 'I Can Bet' on his 2015 LP New. Although not generally thought of as a racing man, the Beatle did once splash out to buy a racehorse. He spent £1,200 on Drake's Drum, which he then gave his father as a 62nd birthday present. Whether he disguised it in gift-wrap is not recorded.

The horse raced on Grand National day 1966 – not in the big race, but as a 20/1 outsider, ridden by Norman McIntosh in the Hylton Handicap Plate – and both 'Macs' cheered the horse on at the track, as it romped home at 20/1.

The horse was later retired to Paul's High Park Farm in Scotland.

SUPERNATURAL RACING AND BETTING MATTERS

DURING my lengthy employment by bookmakers William Hill I was frequently asked whether the perfect system for backing winners existed, and sceptically warned anyone claiming that such a thing was possible if they believed that was the case and started placing bets as a result, they would rapidly become very much the poorer.

However, I did notice that there was one rather drastic, possibly supernatural, system which did indeed seem to produce far more than its fair share of winning bets – dead certs you might call them – albeit they were of little use to the people who were causing them to be placed.

The first example of this system I came across was in November 1988, when mourners gathered in Southend to bury keen punter Bill Brown, only to be staggered when the presiding Reverend Bob White told them that the deceased wanted them to place bets on Grey General, a horse running in the 2.30 race at Wolverhampton.

Reverend Bob organised a whip-round, the contents of which were duly placed on the horse – which promptly romped home at odds of 4/1, leaving Bill's brother Jack to explain – 'Bill placed a bet every day – he just wanted to make all his friends happy for the last time.'

Two years later, and some distance away, Roman Catholic priest Father Ed Droxler was presiding over a wake in the USA. He noticed a copy of the *Daily Racing Form* in the deceased's pocket.

Recalling an earlier conversation that day in which Millersville, the name of a Laurel racecourse runner, had come up, Father Ed organised a collection of $60 from the assembled mourners, and dispatched the grieving grandson off to the track to back the horse, which promptly obliged at odds of 6/1.

I subsequently heard a number of similar stories of this nature and it became obvious that these literally fatal flutters were producing a far greater share of winning bets than any betting system I'd ever previously come across.

When another racing man, Derek Plunton, died in 1998 his grieving family actually put a death notice in their local paper on the eve of the Classic race, the 2,000 Guineas – including in it a tip for the horse Derek had been raving about for weeks – King Of Kings.

The retired British Rail fitter from Winchester in Hampshire had told son Michael how much he fancied the horse, but died six days before the Newmarket race. So the family passed on the information in the Hampshire Chronicle:

'Derek, dear Dad of Dave, Mick, Sal and Chris, and loved grandfather died suddenly Sunday.

Sadly missed and loved.

He would not have wanted flowers or donations but he did tip a horse, King of Kings, in the 2,000 Guineas.

So, stick a few quid on it and have a drink on Derek if it wins – his final tip, from the Great Beyond!'

The next day, scores of friends, family – together with readers of the paper who had taken the tip – plunged cash on the horse. It won at odds of 7/2. The local bookie was dead annoyed.

After the race, son Mick declared, 'I don't often bet but I felt I had to follow Dad's tip.' He won £70. 'I've had people – many complete strangers – coming up and thanking me.'

In February 2002, keen gambler Ronald Stonehill, 77, died in Morayshire. His betting pals raised £54 at his wake, and staked it on two horses running at Newbury, which both won, at 13/2 and 5/4 – they handed over £337 in winnings to his widow, Chrissie, to fund a plaque to be placed on the retired forester's grave, commemorating the 'last bet'.

The fatally successful system paid off yet again in 2004, when relatives of lifelong punter Jack Ross from Durham, who died aged 80, raised £52 to bet on any horse with the name Jack running that day. They were a little doubtful about the idea when they saw that Paxton Jack, running at Towcester, was a complete outsider, hadn't run for two years, and was offered at no-hoper odds of 40/1.

Nevertheless, Jack's grandson, John Durant, stuck the £52 on the nose, and watched in astonishment as the horse surged to victory. The £2,080 winnings were donated to the Durham hospital where Jack had been looked after in his final days.

It may well be worth making an enquiry about whether the person whose funeral you are next attending had any interest in racing!

Obviously buying into this system, during the 80s the Sunday Sport newspaper introduced a racing tipster who had assistance from beyond the grave. Doris Balwark, a self-proclaimed 'psychic', claimed to channel her selections via the spirit of legendary late 19th-century, 13-time champion jockey Fred Archer.

Presumably Archer, who shot himself fatally, aged 29, in 1886, got the job as it fitted in with his existing role, carrying out haunting stints on Newmarket Heath, which resulted in a famous print of him on a grey horse, galloping across the Heath, under which image is a verse:

'Across the heath, along the course, 'Tis said upon a phantom horse,
The greatest jockey of our days, Rides nightly in the moonlight rays.'

SUPERNATURAL RACING AND BETTING MATTERS

There are a number of stories of racehorses being buried on racetracks where they have been successful, but when keen racing punter Sam Baxter, from Brampton in Cambridgeshire, whose best winners had won at Huntingdon racecourse, died during 1986, he had his ashes scattered at the course's winning post.

There's a twist to a similar story, though.

Racehorse trainer Alex Whitting's Uncle Cyril, himself a trainer, predicted with his dying breath that no descendant of his would ever win a race at Nottingham – presumably so that they should not achieve what he had failed to do. His ashes were subsequently scattered on the course.

Determined to prove his relative wrong, Alex Whitting persisted in sending runners to the course – over 30 of his charges tried but failed. He called in a local priest to exorcise uncle's ghost from the track – but apparently to no avail.

Finally convinced he had broken the curse, on Friday, 21 November 1986, and beginning to breathe a sigh of relief, Whitting saw his runner, Taylor's Renovation, which had been made 7/4 favourite to win the Lake Hurdle, approaching the winning post well clear, with literally just five yards to run – only for his rookie jockey Kevin Sims to tumble off the horse before passing the post, thus being disqualified.

Whilst writing a book called *Amazing Bets* I heard of an astonishing court battle which, it seemed, had broken out in Austria – over the custody of a ghost that tipped winners. Helmut Flann and his ex-wife, I read in 1988, had sought legal advice to decide which of them should have custody of Helmut's deceased aunt, claiming that 'she' was 'my sole means of support. I earn something like £150,000 a year (originally quoted in local currency) at horse tracks throughout Europe, and a lot of my best tips come from my aunt. By actively encouraging my dear dead aunt to stay with her, my ex-wife is trying to deprive me of her company and my livelihood.'

The former Frau Flann disagreed: 'I don't want to exploit Helmut's aunt but I feel she's very disturbed and needs help and understanding so that she can find peace in the world beyond.'

The judge hearing the case was reported as saying: 'I'm taking this very seriously. By the power vested in me and the courts, one of these two is going to take legal custody of a ghost.' Frustratingly, I could find no UK media report of the outcome of the case.

Probably the UK's premier racecourse, Ascot was much frequented by popular thespian and British film star of his day Wilfrid Hyde-White, born in 1903, who, in 1935, went for a stroll around the Ascot track a short while before the Royal meeting there was due to take place.

As they walked, he and a friend accompanying him began to experience the apparition of a race meeting actually taking place. They heard the sounds of a racecourse going on around them, and listened, stunned, as a voice began to announce runners and riders for the afternoon – a system which had yet to be introduced.

While the astonished pair wondered what was going on, they even heard the names of winning horses being announced. Despite being an enthusiastic racing man, Hyde-White did not recognise any of the names of the phantom winners but made a note of them.

For years after, he made a point of regularly checking racecards for the names of the Ascot 'winners' but he sadly never had the ghost of a chance of backing any of them before he died in 1991.

Ascot was also the scene of an amazing feat by the horse Brown Jack who, in the 1930s, won six consecutive runnings of the Queen Alexandra Stakes, becoming a hugely popular figure in the process.

When Brown Jack died he was buried on an estate close to Ascot racecourse, which subsequently became the home of Mill Ride Golf Club – whose patrons the horse clearly did not take to.

During the 1990s, members of the club were startled by a phantom horse appearing on the putting green. Some other golfers on the course heard neighing and galloping sounds while others reported being mysteriously knocked over on the greens.

Managing director of the time, Dickie Freemantle, explained their theory: 'Brown Jack was buried under the 170-acre estate. The master greenkeeper has seen a horse twice while setting off the sprinklers at night.'

Ghostly goings-on affected Epsom racecourse in April 1996, when course sales manager Marilyn Wilkinson reported seeing a lady in black whilst working alone late one night: 'She appeared to me in the 1914 building, part of the racecourse offices which used to be a hospital during the Second World War. It suddenly felt very cold ... then, she appeared in the room, wearing a long gown. I really was rather scared.'

GHOSTLY GAMBLING

Betting shops are, of course, where a great many gamblers go to place their wagers. Regular gamblers spend many hours a day in them, so perhaps it is not that unusual that some are happy to remain there in spirit when they die.

When I worked for William Hill, Alan French, manager of a betting shop in Merton, London, told me that his shop had a phantom gambler who was regularly spotted. In a branch in Knaresborough, North Yorkshire, staff member Julie Addle recalled: 'I have been prodded in the back several times when there's been no one behind me. A clock flew off the wall one day for no reason and on another occasion I felt a hand skim over the top of my head.'

In Birmingham, Peter Casson recalled the time two members of staff were at the bus stop opposite the shop, having locked up for the day, when 'they saw a lad inside the shop.

They rushed over, thinking he must have been in the toilets when they locked up – but when they checked there was nobody inside.'

Doors, drawers and a loft opened and closed upstairs at a branch in Benchill, Manchester, while in Edinburgh manager Lyndsay McGregor's shop had a cellar 'with lots of dark nooks and crannies. A few years back a body was found wrapped in a carpet just outside the back door. Not long after, one of the shop employees heard his name being shouted and felt a cold breath down his neck. He ran out of the shop in fright.'

'Little Sue' is the name given to the resident shop ghost in Rhyl, North Wales – in honour of a staff member killed close to the premises. Customers have reported being pinched, while a cleaner reported that after hoovering thoroughly she turned round to see a trail of sugar running along the floor she'd just cleaned.

In Launceston, Cornwall, staff were so unnerved at goings-on in the staff area that they refused to use the toilets after 'my assistant manager was mysteriously locked in the cubicle, and another member of staff found the toilet door being held shut on her, from the outside,' confirmed boss Jane Whitaker. 'When a photograph was taken in the shop there was a ghostly apparition in the background.'

A racing dream he had turned into a nightmare – so the father of top Australian jockey Jimmy Duncan went to his son, shortly before he was due to race at Randwick racecourse in Sydney, in September 1946, and warned him that in his sleep he had seen him catapulted from his mount and killed.

Duncan junior told his anxious parent not to be concerned and went out to partner Lord Dundee in the First Novice Handicap. Minutes later the lightweight rider was dead – thrown from his horse, just as his father had dreamed.

On a similar theme, Walter Craig, owner of a hotel in Ballarat in Australia called Craig's Hotel, was owner of a horse due to line up in the Melbourne Cup, still the biggest Aussie race of all today, in 1870.

Like perhaps many other optimistic owners of runners in big races, Craig dreamed his horse won the big race in a close finish, but awoke pleased but a little spooked, as he had 'seen' Nimblefoot's jockey wearing a black armband – which could surely only mean that if the dream were to prove true, Craig would not be alive to see it happen.

Craig told his bookie, Jeremiah Slack, of the dream – and was promptly offered a bet of potential winnings of £1,000 to a stake of just four drinks or cigars. The bet was duly struck – but shortly afterwards Craig was struck down with pneumonia and died.

Recording the death, the *Melbourne Age* newspaper reported the story of the dream, which sparked a gamble on the horse, slashing the odds from 25/1 to 12/1 to beat his 27 rivals. Come the day of the race, Nimblefoot did indeed win, by the smallest of margins, from favourite

STRANGE STUFF

Lapdog, partnered by teenage jockey Johnny Day who, out of respect to the deceased owner, wore a black armband.

Many such stories can be dismissed when the facts around them are examined closely, and respected Melbourne Cup historian Maurice Cavanagh set out to do so – only to report: 'In some quarters the story is dismissed as legend, but contemporary sources indicate that, strange as it is, the story is true.'

Finally, a tale from Australia's Kiwi neighbours. The Riccarton Racecourse Hotel is considered to be one of the most haunted places in New Zealand. It is said that the ghost of former licensee Donald Fraser walks the corridors of the hotel looking for his killer.

According to *The Encyclopedia of New Zealand*, in 1933 Fraser was killed in the middle of the night in his bedroom, where his wife was asleep, by two blasts from a double-barrelled shotgun. The movements and circumstances of everyone in the hotel at the time, and of guests at a party held in the hotel earlier in the evening, were checked and rechecked but no one was ever found guilty of the murder.

UNEXPECTED RACING CONNECTIONS

LONG JOHN BALDRY (1941–2005) AND DENNIS O'KELLY (1725–87)
The lanky hit-making singer ('Mexico', 'Let The Heartaches Begin' etc) and the slightly dodgy wheeler and dealer who owned the first superstar racehorse are both buried at an Edgware church, north-west London. Born in Connacht in Ireland, O'Kelly owned the unbeaten Eclipse, the pre-eminent sire of the breed and ancestor of 95 per cent of modern thoroughbreds, and from him bred horses including Derby winners Young Eclipse and Serjeant.

KING CHARLES II AND KYLIE MINOGUE
According to the About Newmarket Racecourses website list of 15 key events in the Newmarket calendar, in which the pair both figure, in 1671 King Charles II competed in a race at Newmarket, and in 2015 Kylie topped the bill at the Newmarket Nights concerts.

CONRAD ALLEN AND THE AUTHOR OF THIS BOOK
Conrad – a man who appeared in TV adverts for Smarties and Jaffa Cakes as a child actor, trained Niklas Angel, who won the first-ever official all-weather race in Britain, run at Lingfield, in October 1989, and the presentation for the race was made by your author, Graham Sharpe, then a public relations man for sponsors of the meeting William Hill.

PETE TOWNSHEND AND THE 1855 DERBY WINNER
In 2013 The Who's guitarist and songwriter (including of 'You Better, You Bet') Pete Townshend reportedly purchased a 41-year lease on Lambourn's Ashdown House – the property from which Wild Dayrell – named after a 16th-century landowner who reportedly once threw a newborn baby on to a fire – was trained to win the 1855 Derby.

DICK FRANCIS AND PAIGNTON
Champion jump jockey Dick rode Hornblower, who was beaten at Devon. Owner Michael Joseph nonetheless invited Dick and wife Mary to the Paignton hotel where he was staying, and that meeting led to the arrangement that Joseph's company would publish Dick's novels.

STRANGE STUFF

The Queen greets Estimate after winning the Gold Cup at Royal Ascot in 2013.

CIEREN FALLON AND TURF

'I represented North Wales in cross-country,' boasts jockey Cieren Fallon, who also reveals, 'I whistle at horses, like Dad [Kieren Fallon].'

LEE MACK AND RED RUM

Although he'd never ridden a horse before, as a youngster comedian Lee Mack quite fancied becoming a jockey because 'how hard can it be when the horse is doing all the work?' He got a job, aged 16, as a stable hand at Ginger McCain's yard, and, although he never got much further than shovelling horse manure, he did have his very first riding lesson on future triple Grand National winner Red Rum.

RACING CELEBS

WHAT A BERK?
During a 2013 race meeting in Turkmenistan, the president, Gurbanguly Berdimuhamedov partnered his racehorse Berkar or Berkarar (translation – 'Mighty' or 'Powerful') to an impressive victory in a 1,000-metre race, seeing off six opponents.

The president announced that he would be donating the 11 million dollar prize to the state-run company that finances the breeding of such horses in the country.

A large crowd reportedly cheered the president, born in 1957, to victory as he emphasised his sporting credentials. Film of the victory was broadcast by the state media. However, rumours began to circulate that all was not quite as it seemed.

There were suggestions that the large crowd of presidential and racing fans had, in fact, been ordered to attend the meeting – or lose their jobs if they didn't show up. Then a video surfaced online showing an unexpected postscript to the race – which had not been reported. It showed the president, author of a book entitled The Flight Of Celestial Racehorses about his favourite Akhal-Teke breed (for which he also holds regular equine beauty contests), actually taking a punishing fall from his mount shortly after they had passed the winning post. Footage leaked to the internet showed people rushing to the president's aid, while he stayed on the track for some while.

A former dentist, the president was the subject of an impressive statue two years after the fall, the golden image depicting him riding one of his favourite steeds.

ROYAL RUMPUS
The Queen was delighted when her mare Estimate, trained by Sir Michael Stoute, finished second in the 2014 Ascot Gold Cup – only to be later disqualified after testing positive for morphine. It transpired the positive test came about as a result of a batch of contaminated feed.

STRANGE STUFF

THOMMO'S ON FIRE
Racing commentator and broadcaster Derek 'Thommo' Thompson felt the heat as he held court in the bar of the Boat House restaurant in Tewkesbury during the 2014 Cheltenham Festival.

Explained Charles Sale of the *Daily Mail*: 'He leant on a candle and found his jacket and jumper in flames.'

AWAY WITH THE FAIRIES?
Trainer Charlie Brooks, whose Suny Bay was twice a Grand National runner-up, appeared in court in April 2014 for non-racing related reasons. A character witness, Sara Bradstock, daughter of jockey and racing writer Lord Oaksey, gave a statement about Brooks, during which she said, 'I remember finding him frothing at the mouth and close to death one morning. He had not been bitten by a rabid dog, but had drunk a pint of Fairy Liquid to try and rid himself of the excesses of the night before.'

KING HYPOCRITE?
Former Bank of England governor Mervyn King raised eyebrows during his December 2014 'guest editor' stint on BBC Radio 4's *Today* programme by refusing to allow sport correspondent Rob Bonnet to read out the traditional two racing tips of the day – provided by racing correspondent Cornelius Lysaght – who later reported that one of them was a 13/2 winner.

Bonnet was literally at the point of announcing the selections when King interrupted: 'The editor is intervening here, we're not going to have any racing tips, we don't want to encourage people to spend their money by betting.'

Lysaght was evidently not best pleased, telling the *Racing Post*, 'The feeling on Twitter was that it was perhaps a bit rich of Mervyn King, who earlier in the programme had raised eyebrows by saying that being part of the financial crisis was fun. I think people might be taken aback he wasn't keen on people having a little bit of genuine fun with a couple of tips.'

Two years previously, when listeners were asked about the feature, they voted to retain it by a factor of around four to one.

TRUMPED
Baroness Trumpington, a Conservative politician who died in 2018 aged 96, had been 'to my absolute joy' a steward at Folkestone Racecourse. However, she recalled that, 'I didn't cover myself in glory at my first meet. When the senior steward told me to go to the first fence I knew I wouldn't make it, so I hid behind a fence. Before the next race, I went to the Starter's car and said, "I am Lady Trumpington, would you please give me a lift?" He said, "Certainly not, you're far too heavy, you'll ruin the going."'

She must have done okay eventually, though, as she was presented with a clock on her retirement from the role, 'one of my most treasured possessions.'

NO ANSWER TO THAT

'I once took her to Towcester races, where she met all the jockeys lined up before the race. She asked them: "How do you decide who is going to win?"' Her former private secretary, Charles Powell, recalling a day at the races with Baroness Thatcher.

HARRY REDFACED

In his 2013 autobiography, *Always Managing*, Harry Redknapp claimed he'd been conned for three years by a man pretending to be jockey Lee Topliss, providing the man with free tickets to Spurs games, taking him out for meals, and bankrolling him with money which was never repaid.

The man was finally rumbled when his agent met the real Topliss – and didn't recognise him as the one he and Harry 'knew'.

'He'd ring up, give me a few tips – they usually got beat. He was a conman preying on the racing scene and the little rogue had us all,' admitted Redknapp.

HARRY RED-NAP?

'Nan would collect all the bets and lay 'em out along the mantelpiece, then put them in a little bag,' remembered Harry Redknapp about his grandmother's betting habits in the days before legal betting shops, adding, 'Having a bet was part of life. She'd write out a bet for three tuppenny doubles and rub the bit of paper on me head – ginger for luck!' Redknapp also recalled how, during his days as a top football manager, he liked to take on players 'with a Timeform squiggle!' He recalled one player who was 'doing £50,000 greyhound forecasts' and another who was '£1.5m up at the end of an afternoon', but 'ended the night a million and a half down.' (*Racing Post*, 16 September 2012)

SUBO SETBACK

It was reported in 2014 that despite her untold riches and stardom, singing phenomenon Susan Boyle was planning to start working in a local betting shop. According to *The Sun* in their 26 January edition, Subo had 'stunned punters at her local betting shop (a branch of Ladbrokes) when she strolled in and applied for a cashier's job on the minimum wage.'

The branch was in Blackburn, West Lothian, in Scotland and deputy shop manager David Corr confirmed: 'Susan walked into the shop and enquired about the job (offering pay of £6.31 per hour) advertised in our window.'

There is no record of her making an official job application to Ladbrokes.

STRANGE STUFF

SWIFT CHANGE OF MIND

Singer Taylor Swift cancelled her scheduled performance at the 2019 Melbourne Cup, just six weeks before the race date of 5 November, with her team claiming that 'changes to [her] schedule made it logistically impossible' for her to be in Australia.

The Cup had announced Swift as its headline act, only for the American to be criticised by animal rights groups, who accused her of 'endorsing animal abuse' due to the race's record of six equine deaths since 2013.

A petition by the Coalition for the Protection of Racehorses said that Swift was 'either completely unaware of the cruel reality of horse racing or she has put money before compassion by agreeing to perform' at the races. It has since stated that it is 'absolutely delighted with the news' of the 29-year-old's withdrawal.

Victoria Racing Club's CEO Neil Wilson said Swift's cancellation would be 'disappointing for everyone'.

RACING AMBITION STUMPED

Having once declared that he'd like to 'get into [racehorse] breeding', former Middlesex bowler Chris Silverwood went on to become the England cricket team's head coach during 2019. But as a lifelong racing fan who grew up near Pontefract racecourse, Silverwood introduced a racing theme into his wedding to Victoria via a horse's head, sculpted in ice which had a slide behind the ears, down which vodka was poured, emerging chilled from the horse's mouth:

'I've never seen so many cricketers lining up to snog a horse,' said Silverwood, apparently suggesting that he HAD seen a fewer number doing so!

NATIONAL NEWS – THAT'S GRAND

NATIONAL'S GRAND PROBLEMS

The powers that be at Aintree racecourse introduced a bizarre rule for the 2015 running of the race – warning that photographers were banned from taking pictures of badly dressed women behaving in a risqué manner.'

John Baker, managing director of the racecourse, apparently hoped the ban would put an end to what he claimed was unfair coverage of customers getting drunk or flashing too much flesh at the event: 'We want to overwhelm the negativity, to push the positivity to the front. Our event is full of character, it's fun, and that's generated by the personality of the Liverpool people.'

However, he was roundly mocked for the impossible-to-police idea – 'silliest photo-finish in history of horse racing,' declared London's *Evening Standard* paper, calling it a 'spectacular public relations cock-up.' The paper added: 'Image censorship doesn't work in North Korea, and it won't work here.'

There was one supportive voice, with a *Guardian* writer concluding, 'This is a major victory for women.'

On a more serious note, however, the ongoing campaign to ban the race itself continued in 2019 as 'author and journalist' Chas Newkey, then 46, prolific writer of 'celebrity biographies', was given free rein to express his opinion in the *Metro* newspaper:

'This weekend is the Grand National, the biggest event in the horse racing calendar – and if I had my way, it would also be the last. According to racing regulatory body the British Horse racing Authority's (BHA) own statistics, 4,905 horses have died because of racing since 1994.

That means they have either died on the course, or have died or been put down later due to racing-linked injuries. And the number of deaths has risen: in 2018, 202 horses died as a result of racing in Great Britain – the highest number of deaths since 2014. According to Animal Aid's Racehorse Death Watch, who say they have confirmed every fatality, 52 horses have died this year alone on course. I believe drastic action is needed. We also have to consider the things that racing people prefer not to talk about at all – like what happens to horses when they are too old to race. Few horses enjoy a happy retirement. For many, their sad lives end in the slaughterhouse, with a bullet through the temple or a metal bolt fired into the brain. Their corpses are often driven to Europe to be sold as meat.

STRANGE STUFF

Ladies Day at Aintree 2017.

Racing bosses say that the sport is natural … but of course it only appears to be natural because racing horses have been conditioned into this behaviour from an early age. We only accept the current situation with horses because we've been manipulated into thinking different animals deserve different treatment. Don't bet on the Grand National. Give a tenner to a horse sanctuary instead.'

An addendum to the article said: 'The BHA responded to the figure that 52 horses have died this year by saying that they release statistics annually and so would not have access to this year's number.' They added that '99.58 per cent of runners in British racing complete their race without incurring any long-term injury. However, as with all elite sports and all activities involving horses, there is an element of risk. But as a consequence of British racing's investment in safety, welfare and health, the number of horses that have suffered fatal injuries has decreased by a third in the last 20 years.'

Another of the sport's opponents, Animal Aid, declared – in the process, revealing that the whole of horse racing is in its sights – 'At the root of the problem is racing's regulator, the

British Horse racing Authority (BHA). It is responsible for racehorse welfare but has failed to curb the number of fatalities in racing. 2018 saw a sharp increase in horse deaths in Britain, with the highest death rate since 2014.'

A Facebook page, 'Ban The Grand National', had 3,134 followers in October 2019 and by September 2021 had 5,600.

Confronting the fact that racing – both over jumps and on the Flat – will always have detractors, Dr Paul-Marie Gadot, France Galop's chief vet, commented before the 2019 Prix de l'Arc de Triomphe: 'The activists will ask for more, because their primary objection is that we simply use animals.'

RED RUMINDER OF CHIPPY McCAIN

Tiger Roll may have come closer than any other modern-day horse to threatening Red Rum's legacy as THE greatest horse ever to win the Grand National, and perhaps the only equine of the 20th century to exceed even the affection with which the grey superstar Desert 'Dessie' Orchid was regarded.

To illustrate his appeal, I went to the launch of a new William Hill betting shop in Manchester in the early 80s, to liaise with the media there to cover the story as Red Rum performed the opening ceremony. A tremendous crowd turned up to see Rummy. One lady asked me to arrange for her to present the horse with the cake she had brought along for him, and another – I am NOT joking here – spotted the camera I had with me to record the occasion, and asked me if, 'when you get close to him, can you get me his autograph, please?'

The great horse was seven years old when trainer Ginger McCain acquired him for 6,000 guineas on behalf of veteran owner Noel Le Mare, and he quickly won five chases in succession. He was aimed at the 1973 Grand National, which he won, only to take on the role of party-pooper, as charismatic sensational jumper, the Aussie-born 9/1 joint-favourite, Crisp, under Richard Pitman, led the field a merry dance only to be caught and overhauled close to the finish line by fast-finishing other joint-favourite, Rummy.

However, Rummy was out on his own as he won again in 1974, leaving hammered bookies, who had foolishly allowed him to start at 11/1 noticing that the name of the horse reversed spelt 'Murder'.

Amazingly, 40 years later, a Scottish punter called Bob Holmes contacted me to say he'd found an uncashed betting slip belong to his deceased father-in-law, of £1 on Red Rum to win the '74 National. To allow for inflation I paid him £130.

The bookies had learned their lesson by the time Red Rum lined up for the 1975 running of the National. This time he was a short-priced 7/2 favourite, but could only manage second place – which he again filled in 1976. Relieved bookies believed the horse's best days were now behind him.

STRANGE STUFF

Tiger Roll, ridden by Davy Russell, wins the 2019 Grand National.

However, aged 12, he was back at Aintree in 1977 – and incredibly, he won again, returning odds of 9/1.

He was favourite for a fourth triumph in 1978 only to be ruled out because of a hairline fracture of a bone in his foot – which didn't stop him leading the pre-race parade, launching a new tradition.

Rummy was so famous that his droppings were sold at 80p per bag, he was the first racehorse to be made into a limited company, he switched on the Blackpool illuminations, frequently appeared on TV – including once in the studio for the BBC TV *Sports Personality of the Year* show, during which his ears perked up as he recognised his jockey's voice.

A businessman's offer to buy him for one million dollars so that he could be used to promote his restaurant chain was swiftly rejected.

When Prime Minister John Major was under political pressure in September 1993, The *Sun* newspaper invited readers to vote on who they would prefer to run the country – Major or Rummy. Yes, Rummy polled nine times as many votes as Major.

As the Red Rum legend had blossomed, so had that of Donald 'Ginger' McCain – car dealer-cum-cabbie-turned-racehorse trainer, who exercised his stable star not on turf, but on the sands of Southport. McCain was also outspoken on almost any subject about which his opinion was sought by the media.

Political correctness was a concept he neither recognised nor respected.

Ginger had his say on animal rights protestors in April 1994 – 'I went on a TV programme and met these snotty-nosed, insignificant little girls and boys. These so-called do-gooders – cranks is a better word – got on the back of the National because they get publicity out of it. Never mind putting horses down, they should put these buggers down.'

Another of Ginger's old-fashioned prejudices loomed up when he was asked about female riders in the National – 'I expect that eventually a horse will be good enough to carry one round as a passenger to win.' Coursing had been one of Ginger's passions and wife Beryl said of his trips to see its main event the Waterloo Cup that 'he very rarely remembered coming home'.

Rummy died, aged 30, in 1995, shortly after Aintree had staged a meeting in his honour at which he received a 30-candle cake. He was laid to rest alongside the course's winning post. He was featured on an Isle of Man postage stamp, and in 2007 he won a poll to find the most famous horse ever – seeing off Black Beauty, Shergar and Desert Orchid in the process.

When Red Rum was retired, many felt McCain would slip back into obscurity, and indeed he sent out 14 National runners, none of which finished higher than 14th, until, in 2003, he had 11-year-old Amberleigh House running in the race – and he sent him out with a lock of Rummy's mane inserted in his headband. He ran a thoroughly decent race to finish third.

In 2004, with McCain now 73 years of age, and Amberleigh House a 16/1 shot, the magic touch returned and Ginger had his fourth National victory. Receiving the trophy from the Princess Royal, he told her: 'Not bad for a bloody taxi-driver.'

Now it was McCain's turn to be honoured by Aintree, when a plaque was unveiled on the stairs leading to the Queen Mother Stand, marking the spot where 'Ginger McCain traditionally watches the Grand National.'

The end of Ginger's training career was imminent and he bowed out, aged 75, retiring in favour of son Donald junior. But he didn't lose his ability to wind other members of the racing world up, and in 2005 when Carrie Ford partnered fancied runner Forest Gunner, he opined, 'Carrie is a grand lass, but she's a brood mare now, and having kids doesn't get you fit to ride Grand Nationals.'

When she finished a respectable fifth, Ginger told her he'd been out and bought the biggest pair of Y-fronts he could find, and had written 'Carrie Ford Rules OK' on them, insisting, said Carrie, that 'if I'd won he would have pulled them over his trousers and posed in them for the cameras.'

Ginger himself admitted, 'I stick my tongue in my cheek and wind them up. When they ask you bloody silly questions you tell them absolute crap and they take you seriously.'

I am, though, confident that he'd have been nothing but complimentary about Rachael Blackmore after she won the great race in 2021.

Beryl, Donald and Joanne McCain at the unveiling of the statue of their late father Ginger at Aintree in 2012.

Ginger, a former national serviceman in the RAF as a motorcycle despatch rider, and also a member of the RAF scrambling team, died two days before his 82nd birthday, on 19 September 2011.

On the opening day of the 2012 Grand National a bronze statue of McCain was unveiled at Aintree, looking down on the winning post where his victories unfolded.

CHOP, CHOP – FLYING DOC THINKS AHEAD

Realising in advance that even should his horse Pineau De Re somehow win the 2014 Grand National, he'd want to attend racing at Market Rasen the next day, trainer Dr Richard Newland made a provisional booking for a helicopter to take him, telling the company: 'I'd like to book the helicopter – but only want it if my horse wins the Grand National.'

They took the booking, asking for the name of the horse in the process. Pineau De Re duly obliged, and Dr Newland contacted the chopper boss, telling him he wanted the helicopter: 'Yes I know,' he was told, 'We all backed it.'

Dr Newland had two winners at Market Rasen.

FIRST LADY OF AINTREE

The first female clerk of the course at Aintree, 34-year-old Sulekha Varma, said of her tennis-playing friends when she started her new job: 'Most of them knew nothing about racing, but they knew what this job was. It meant something to them. That's the beauty of the race [the National] here. But it's a real challenge to create new fans for the sport. The battle for the leisure pound … for people's attention is probably one of the biggest [challenges]. The large majority of people who come are once-a-year racegoers.' (*The Times*, 2 March 2020)

SUPERSTITIONS

AIN'T SUPERSTITIOUS?
Henry Cecil told the *Sporting Life* racing paper, 'When I go racing I always fill the car with petrol on the way – if I don't fill it I don't win. Even if it's a question of just a quarter of a gallon I always stop at a garage, otherwise the whole day's racing is a disaster.'

Legendary trainer Cecil was also no fan of the colour green – 'I hate green,' he once said. 'Most of my family have died in green and I never wear anything of that colour. One ancestor fell down the stairs when wearing green, and another died eating watercress, which is green.'

FOOTNOTE
A superstition grew up about horses with white feet, resulting in the verse:
One white foot, buy a horse,
Two white feet, try a horse,
Three white feet look well about him,
Four white feet, do well without him.'
However, there are always exceptions to any rule – notably, in this case, 1977 Derby winner The Minstrel who boasted four white feet.

SUPER ... STITIONS
Sir Gordon Richards, champion Flat jockey, would always raise his hat to a chimney sweep on the way to the races, and wear the same tie and braces on big race days.

'I feel good about finding a penny heads up on the day of a race.' US trainer, Delmar William Carroll II.

'Don't pick up money if it's tails up.' US trainer Patrick Joseph Kelly.

'I was wearing a white summer suit – I was wearing that suit in the dead of winter.' US trainer Gary Contessa, who decided after his Owens Troupe won he needed to be wearing the same clothes for subsequent races – as the horse ran up a sequence.

'I used to not like it when someone brought peanuts into the barn.' US trainer Harry Allen Jerkens, backed up by fellow trainer John Joseph Len Jr – 'I don't eat peanuts at the track – and won't let anyone else if I see them.'

'I don't want to see a hat on a chair or bed.' US trainer Philip George Johnson.

US trainer Bill Mott, trainer of the great Cigar, admits to superstitions, but claimed, 'I'm too superstitious to talk about them.'

'I always keep my best horse in stall 13.' US trainer Ross Randolph Pearce.

'I never let anyone pull a horse's mane on the day or so before a race.' US trainer James Joseph Pascuma Jr.

'I have an owner who has to have on green socks. And if they don't match his outfit, he carries them in his pocket. He's been very lucky.' US trainer Robert Ribaudo.

'I never win if someone stands in my line of vision during the stretch run. It's the kiss of death, so I make sure I have an unobstructed view of the race.' US trainer, Michael C Sedlacek.

'I wear my underwear inside out for good luck.' Laffit Pincay, at one time US racing's all-time leading money-winning rider.

CATASTROPHIC IDEA?

American trainer Damon Pollard explained why his silks feature the image of a black cat on them: '[It is] because of my Uncle Ivan. He raced horses back in the 20s and 30s, and he thought that if you put a black cat on the back of your silks and you crossed in front of the rest of the field during a race you would give bad luck to the rest of the field.'

TUCK IN

During a 15-year riding career, Cheltenham Gold Cup-winning jockey Phil Tuck was so superstitious he would salute magpies to avoid bad luck – a superstition he had in common with Lord Oaksey, Ginger McCain, David Elsworth, Nicky Henderson and Jack Berry, to name just a few. He even called his house 'The Magpies'. Tuck became a stipendiary steward in Saudi Arabia after leaving his role as clerk of the course at Sedgefield several years ago.

Phil would also insist on wearing the same holey socks and tattered t-shirt to race in until one day declaring, 'It's all daftness,' and giving up the superstitions.

GINGERLY SUPERSTITIOUS

Owner and trainer Dan O'Brien, father of the great Vincent, had a superstition about ginger-haired women. 'He hated to see a ginger woman on his way to the races. If one then got beaten he would put it down to the ill-luck she brought,' said his daughter, Pauline.

INTRIGUINGLY INTERESTING RACEY CHARACTERS

FATHER OF RACING WAS NO HAS-BREEN

Explaining that until the early 1960s, bishops of the Irish Catholic church prohibited priests from attending race meetings, Father Sean Breen elaborated: 'The bishops thought it was wrong and evil for people to go racing, so they banned the priests from going.'

Father Breen was one of the first to take advantage when this stricture was relaxed – as a result he was able to see one of the greatest of all chasers, Arkle, winning the 1964 Cheltenham Gold Cup.

During the 70s, Father Breen, originally from Cavan, was parish priest in Glencullen near Leopardstown, where he rode out for local trainer Bill Durkan, and became friendly with another handler, Seamus McGrath – at whose yard future trainer Joanna Morgan was apprenticed. He then moved to a parish at Templeogue, and thence to Eadestown. He was becoming ever better known, and trainer Arthur Moore named winning hurdler, The Breener, after him in the 80s.

By 1993 he had made enough of a name for himself to be invited to offer Cheltenham Festival tips to *Daily Mail* readers. None of his nine selections won, leading to concerns that his ultimate boss may not approve.

In 1994, Breen told *The Guardian*, 'This is my 28th Cheltenham. A friend of mine once lost all his money at cards on the boat over and had to turn back for home without setting foot in England.'

He kept adding to his attendance record and creating a name for himself as racing's priest. Sadly, he was the victim of a vicious attack in 2004, and subsequently suffered chest problems – quite probably related to the tuberculosis from which he had suffered as a child.

Father Breen also became known for blessing race meetings, as befitted the man whose parish in County Kildare contained both Punchestown and Naas racecourses, the former of which boasts a hillock just outside the track, known as Priests' Hill – from where the excluded clergy would once watch the racing without entering the track.

In 2005 Breen celebrated Mass pre-Festival for some 200 racegoers at the Thistle – formerly Golden Valley – Hotel, prior to Cheltenham, telling them: 'We pray for winners, because they are so hard to get no matter what part of the country they come from.' Behind Breen were two glasses of red wine on the altar.

Also in 2005 Breen blessed the horse Kicking King, which went on to win the Gold Cup, and Breen collapsed after the race. He would also say Mass on the final day of the Galway Festival and at Cheltenham when the Festival included St Patrick's Day.

The Father's tipping column for the *Kildare Post* yielded Grand National winners Hedgehunter and Numbersixvalverde, and he also had a tipster spot on radio station Kildare FM. He owned horses himself – one in conjunction with another gentleman of the cloth, which, because of the secrecy concerning their involvement, they named Nobody Knows. Asked what his horse was called, 'I'd just whisper Nobody Knows, to which the response was always, 'Yes, yes, but what's his name?'

Nobody Knows was a six-time winner, while another of his, One Won One, was also a prolific winner, collecting £300,000 in prize money, and Portant Fella won 15 races, Raise Your Heart won over jumps as well as the Flat, and Show Blessed was first to finish five times.

The cleric had his disapproving critics, but declared, 'There is nothing in the Bible that says you can't gamble. We have to lighten up a bit. I'm not a big gambler. I can go to a race meeting and enjoy it without having a bet. I'm not anti-gambling or anti-drinking.'

Breen was well known to many racegoers, and once had to come to the rescue of The Sun's respected racing correspondent Claude Duval, who found himself unable to convince the powers that-be at Leopardstown of his bona fides, until Breen appeared, telling the lady minding the gate, 'I can vouch for him – it's the very devil himself.'

In April 2005, taking a detour from his racing tips, Breen told the BBC's Frank Keogh that he urged people to back Cardinal Joseph Ratzinger to become Pope: 'A few of the lads got on at 13/2, but I did not back him myself out of reverence.'

Breen was always keen to advise: 'If you have a bet, stick to your first choice. And always gamble only what you can afford to lose.'

Featured in Bill Barich's book *A Fine Place To Daydream*, Breen told the author that he first became interested in turf topics as a young priest in North County Dublin, and that his favourite meeting was Galway's seven-day July meeting: 'It's tremendous fun, everybody's there, even the politicians have caught on … the first three men I ran into one summer were the ministers for Justice, Finance and Agriculture.'

Attending Cheltenham on so many occasions meant that there would be absentees from previous years – 'A lot of people die. You don't see them there. You say to yourself, he isn't at Cheltenham, he must be dead. The Festival's a sort of check on who's still alive.'

Breen himself finally became an absentee from the Festival when he died aged 72 on 15 January 2009. He was buried in Glencullen cemetery, County Dublin. A huge congregation attended the funeral, and there was a two-hour Mass with a reported 37 priests in attendance.

His long-time friend, trainer Joanna Morgan, reflected: 'I knew him for 35 years. He was a great friend, and was so lucky you would almost give him a share in a horse. One morning at Phoenix Park Sean was riding out a half-bred I had stabled there. He was wearing a big black mac, and the horse took off with him, and went full gallop, with Sean only a passenger, and the mac flapping behind him. Unfortunately he got thrown off and broke his leg.'

'He was everybody's friend, everybody's priest and he touched the lives of all who knew him,' said trainer Arthur Moore's wife, Mary.

On the night Breen died one of Morgan's horses, Garcia, had won at 25/1 in Dubai earlier in the day.

CHURCHILL THE WINNIER

His never-to-be-forgotten exploits as his country's war leader are legendary – his racecourse triumphs less so. Winston Churchill's propensity for both racing and betting did not, though, impress wife Clementine, who in 1951 wrote to a friend about her husband's horse, Colonist II – 'I do think this is a queer new facet in Winston's variegated life. Before he bought the horse – I can't think why – he had hardly been on a racecourse in his life. I must say I don't find it madly amusing,'

But he had indeed not only been on racecourses, he had ridden on them – and as chancellor of the exchequer had been responsible for a far-reaching change in racecourse betting. Winston's maternal grandfather was active on the turf in the US, even building his own racecourse. His father, Lord Randolph, was a leading owner and turf figure between 1889–93, having bought a black filly, L'Abbesse de Jouarre – quickly renamed 'Abscess on the Jaw' by the racing public – which won the 1889 Oaks – only for the owner to decide that at 20/1 he'd be better off spending his time fishing instead.

The teenage Winston probably backed her, though, writing from school at Harrow: 'I have been congratulated on account of the flukey filly. I drank the Abbesse's health in lemon squash, and we ate her luck in strawberry mash.'

In March 1895 Winston contested a steeplechase, but 'the animal refused and swerved – very nearly did he break my leg.' Undeterred he tackled the 4th Hussars Subalterns' Cup, finishing third – a race that resulted in controversy when it was declared void, following allegations that the winner was a 'ringer' and that 'all those in the race must have been in on the plot'.

A publication named Truth alleged, 'The coup resulted in the defeat of a hot favourite by the last outsider in the betting.' Churchill was outraged at the aspersions and urged his mother to take legal action, but the matter was allowed to drop.

Churchill took part in pony races in India, but there was a lull in his racing exploits when he became an MP. As Chancellor he imposed a betting tax in 1926, and soon after was instrumental in the introduction of the Tote, which he claimed would mean 'the rowdy rascal element so prominent on our racecourses is eliminated.'

Aged 74, in 1949 Churchill became owner of French three-year-old Colonist II, once again prompting criticism from Clementine that his reputation could suffer. Colonist II won at Salisbury in August 1949 – his son-in-law Christopher Soames reported that, 'the crowd surged forward to see him come in and gave him [Churchill] a wonderful reception.' In 1951 the horse, who ended up with 13 victories and £120,000 prize money, won the Winston Churchill Stakes, then he landed the Jockey Club Cup and was runner-up in the Ascot Gold Cup.

When the horse was retired to stud, Winston suggested, tongue in cheek, that it might result in allegations that 'the Prime Minister is living on the immoral earnings of a horse.'

Winston owned a good number of other horses with trainer Walter Nightingall, who sent out 70 winners for him. In 1955 his Dark Issue gave him a Classic victory in the Irish 1,000 Guineas. His 33/1 shot Auroy ran fourth in the 1960 Derby, but his other intended runner, Vienna, rated a better prospect, had to be withdrawn when he was pricked by the blacksmith plating him, but went on to be third in the St Leger.

Winston became a member of the Jockey Club in 1950, but finally ended his association with the turf in 1964, the year before he died, explaining that 'my health does not allow me to attend race meetings any more.'

FRANKLY, WE ALL GIVE A DAMN ABOUT DETTORI

FRANKIE Dettori has long ago become an honorary Brit, despite being both Italian and, as an Arsenal fan, a 'Gooner'. His effortless charisma has enraptured not only racegoers, and he has transcended his sport to become universally known even by those who have never been racing or backed a horse.

His trademark flying dismount after riding yet another big-race winner helped him jump into people's affections – and his acceptance as a mainstream personality was enhanced when he became a team captain on the hugely popular TV show *A Question of Sport*.

But it was the incredible Magnificent Seven day on 28 September 1996 that made him a global racing superstar as he won all seven races run at Ascot that day, at accumulative odds of over 25,000/1. It cost Britain's bookies some £50 million – and individuals like Darren Yates of Morecambe won £550,000 by backing him to go through the card. I remember phoning the stunned Darren to tell him just how much he'd won. The win changed his life and he has gone on to become a prominent racehorse owner.

Frankie's ability runs in the family – Dad Gianfranco had made his impression as a jockey when he rode successive 2,000 Guineas winners on Bolkonski in 1975 and Wollow in 1976, both for Henry Cecil.

Son Lanfranco was born on 15 December 1970 and his parents split up before his first birthday – he stayed with his mother, Iris Maria – formerly a trapeze artist – until he was five, after which he moved in with his father and stepmother.

Frankie's early obsession was football, until he was 'forced' to ride at the age of six. At the age of nine he contested his first race, a Pony Derby at San Siro racecourse, on his own pony, Sylvia. He was unseated into a water jump – which may have ensured he wouldn't become a jump jockey. By the age of 11 he was betting – 'That's when I really got the love of horse racing,' he wrote in the book *A Year in the Life of Frankie Dettori*. His instinctive understanding of the integral relationship between racing and betting gave him an innate connection with the hopes and aspirations of the punters and racegoers following him.

Despite Dad warning son that 'only one in a thousand makes it as a jockey', Frankie started a six-month stint with Newmarket-based Luca Cumani, whose belief was that 'nobody is born a jockey'.

Frankie was 14 when he arrived in England with a million lire to his name – worth at that time £366.

'I didn't learn English, I just picked it up as I went along. I think the first word I learned was "Goodbye."'

With 16 winners under his belt in Turin and Naples, Frankie scored his first English win on Lizzie Hare at Goodwood in June 1987.

By 1989 he was champion apprentice, and in 1990 he became first-choice jockey for Cumani, becoming the first teenager since Lester Piggott in 1955 to ride a century of winners.

In 1993 Frankie's first setback came when he was cautioned by police who found drugs on him – an incident that resulted in the Hong Kong authorities revoking their offer to ride there for a year.

Luca Cumani was not best pleased and for the first time the public weren't on his side. 'I was at my lowest ebb,' reflected Frankie, and help arrived from an unexpected source when controversial trainer and punter Barney Curley took time out to give him excellent advice – 'He made me understand that I had too much, too early in my life.'

1993 saw Frankie ride his first four-timer, as he finished runner-up to champion jockey Pat Eddery, and by the next year he was riding regularly for John Gosden. Frankie's ploy of riding at winter all-weather meetings, where winners counted towards the title race in those days, gave him a flying start in the 1994 title race, and he duly ended up as champion with 233 winners.

He went to the USA and won the Breeders' Cup Mile on Cumani's Barathea – using the trademark flying dismount he'd copied from his hero, showman Puerto Rican rider Angel Cordero.

On 12 June 1996 Frankie rode six winners in total, at Kempton and Yarmouth – but a day later he broke his elbow in a fall in the Newbury paddock and was out until August – turning up for Royal Ascot in morning suit, top hat, multi-coloured tie, red rose buttonhole and arm in a sling.

Then came the miraculous seven and Frankie achieved legendary status – he presented TV's *Top of the Pops*, appeared on Clive Anderson's chat show, *TFI Friday* with Chris Evans!

He was third in the *BBC Sports Personality of the Year*. 'Frankie has been officially declared Good for Racing,' wrote anthropologist Kate Fox, 'and has accordingly been granted a sort of diplomatic immunity from traditionalist culture.'

A rare riding misjudgement came during the 1998 Breeders' Cup Classic, at the time the world's richest-ever race, with a $5.12m purse. Frankie, riding Swain for Godolphin, seemed to lose control of the horse, allowing him to swing out wide on the track, and having to give the horse an uncharacteristically hard ride under the whip, as they were beaten into third place. The Italian was harshly criticised as a result – 'his reputation was subsequently lynched in the American media,' wrote Richard Edmondson.

Nor did he get an easy ride in the UK, but, despite the visual evidence, Frankie grimly refused to accept he'd done wrong. He would later say, 'In racing it helps to be a good bullshi**er – you must have the ability to make excuses.' And he soon courted trouble again, admitting to have taken diuretic drugs in the past to keep his weight down.

When Frankie won the Breeders' Cup Turf the next year, in 1999, he clearly felt vindicated and released from purgatory, yelling in triumph at the crowd and leaping off his mount looking 'like a prisoner suddenly set free,' observed *Sports Illustrated's* William Nack.

Frankie declared: 'Revenge is a plate you eat cold, and mine was freezing. Everybody tried to kill me last year. OK, I made a mistake, but don't judge me on one ride.'

Frankie's next misadventure could have had literally fatal consequences. On 1 June 2000 he and fellow jockey Ray Cochrane set off to fly from Newmarket to Goodwood racecourse in a Piper Seneca light aircraft which nose-dived and crashed shortly after take-off, killing pilot Patrick Mackey. Frankie had been resigned to death – 'Before the impact I didn't scream, because I knew that I was going to die.'

But Cochrane rescued Frankie and was later awarded a Silver Medal by the Royal Humane Society.

They were both treated in hospital, Frankie for a broken ankle, damaged ribs and facial injuries, Cochrane for back, arm and face injuries.

STRANGE STUFF

A masked Frankie gives a flying dismount after winning the St James' Palace Stakes on Palace Pier at Royal Ascot in 2020.

Cochrane was riding again within seven weeks, only to announce his retirement – and Frankie came back on 5 August 2000 at Newmarket – completing a 10/1 double on his first two rides. But he was a changed man – 'Life for me was like being in an empty room looking for an exit that was never there,' he reflected starkly in October 2008, looking back to that day. He changed his professional priorities and they no longer included the aim of becoming champion jockey.

Frankie was awarded an honorary MBE in 2001, presented to him by racing fan and Foreign Secretary Robin Cook at Sandown. In the same year he botched his flying dismount for the first time – toppling over in Dubai.

Three winners at the Dubai World Cup meeting in 2003 earned him 'around a third of a million pounds', but Godolphin's firepower was failing, and Frankie found that 'it was the start of a summer of despair that left me feeling more depressed than at any other stage of my career.'

He'd cheered up by the time Italy won the 2006 World Cup, though, turning up for racing at Newmarket with his country's flag painted on his cheeks, even missing out on a winner thanks to his wife who had a share in a horse running in a race in which he was scheduled to be riding – a potential conflict of interests, said the rules.

In 2007 he filled the notable gap in his CV by winning the Derby on Authorized, then around a year later Alan Fraser of the *Daily Mail* decided to ask Frankie's wife, Catherine, about her husband, and produced one or two unexpected intimate details about him – such as his sleeping habits: 'We have got the darkest curtains. It is like the blackout. He gets into bed. It is already pitch black and he puts patches on his eyes. Then he covers his winkie with his hand. It's a habit.' When he does fall asleep he 'dreams in English.' He is also very tidy – 'It doesn't matter where he is, he always hangs up his clothes.'

Frankie is also apparently very prone to panic attacks, like his mother – 'Suddenly, he just overheats, and says "get me out of here". It happened on a ski lift, in a helicopter, in a jet during a dodgy landing, and in a taxi.'

He claims to be virtually English: 'I'm part of the furniture, an honorary Brit. I'm as English as anybody so I'm claiming dual nationality, my Arsenal shirt is my passport.'

But however famous anyone becomes, there will always be someone who doesn't know who they are – as Frankie discovered ...

Rushing to catch a Ryanair flight from Stansted to Scotland to ride Redford in the Ayr Gold Cup in September 2010, Frankie was refused permission to board the flight as he'd forgotten his passport.

Even though it was a domestic flight, airline rules would allow neither Frankie's driving licence, nor his face, to be regarded as proof of identity, so he had to return home, buy another ticket, find his passport then rush back in time to arrive for the race, winning on the David Nicholls-trained 14/1 shot.

STRANGE STUFF

Frankie teamed up with great filly Enable to two consecutive Prix de l'Arc de Triomphe, but many felt that his retirement might come when they were beaten in the bid for a hat-trick of wins in that great race in 2020. However, at the time of writing he was still showing few signs of losing his enthusiasm for the game, let alone quitting. When it does happen he will be greatly missed for his ability to appeal outside of the sometimes insular world of racing.

RICHARD DUNGOODY

Most champion jump jockeys are driven characters, obsessed by their winner-hunting objective, with little or no interest in the world outside of racing. One or two are somewhat different – John Francome, for example, who went out at the top when he quit on a random whim, and, perhaps, an even more notable example – Richard Dunwoody.

Dunwoody was one of the toughest of all riders, never giving his opponents an inch in the battle to be first to reach the finishing post. But when he retired – admittedly being forced to do so – almost literally, he walked as far away from the sport from which he'd acquired his living and his reputation as possible.

'Like all the other great sportspeople – whether you're talking about Tiger Woods, Mike Tyson or Zinedine Zidane – he had an element of madness in him,' said another great racing champion, AP McCoy.

And as if to prove McCoy right, Richard's autobiography, published in 2009, was called *Method In My Madness*, and in it he revealed himself in his own words to be a complicated character, to say the least.

For example, on Grand National day, very shortly after he'd quit, Richard opted to be at Southampton FC watching a match.

At half-time virtually everyone around him headed for a TV screen to watch the big race, or grabbed a radio to listen to it. Richard sat stubbornly in his seat, reading the match programme, to all intents and purposes not remotely interested in what was happening at Aintree.

Clearly a very complex character, since his racing career ended he has walked to the North and South Poles, skiing some 700 miles on the latter expedition, walked 2,000+ miles in Japan to raise money for charity, taken part in Strictly Come Dancing, clambered up lofty peaks, and travelled the world-leading riding tours in far flung lands – photographing equine events, such as the Mongolian Derby.

I met Richard when he was the host of a racing tour to Merano racecourse, perhaps the most scenic track I've ever seen, which is situated on the borders of Germany and Italy. We were there to witness one of Europe's most valuable jump races, the then-380,000 euro Gran Premio Merano Forst, run over 5,000 metres and worth 161,500 euros to winning connections.

Wandering around Verona, which was our stop-off point for Merano, taking in the Romeo & Juliet balcony there, immortalised by William Shakespeare, we bumped into Richard – and his mum.

Richard was there to keep we racegoers together and informed during the trip.

Once in Merano – a confusing place, where all the street – and building – signs seemed to be in both German and Italian, but where German seemed to be by far the predominantly used language – we were shepherded together by Richard and driven off to the racecourse.

It is really spectacular. Santa Anita – described to me by no less an authority than the late Hugh McIlvanney and for which reason I visited that track for the Breeders' Cup – is in the foothills of mountains – but Merano is surrounded by huge, looming, dramatic peaks. It is little short of sensational.

We walked the course with Richard talking us through the different obstacles and fences, being allowed to touch, feel and interfere with them, and getting a feel for the sheer size and difficulty they present to racehorse and rider alike.

I discussed with Richard the question of why with so much cash on offer at a course readily reachable from the UK there was no sign of any British-trained runners in the event. We were both lost for an explanation.

Shown around the course's inner sanctums, we saw a room in which there were portraits of every horse to win the big race – one of which suggested that in 1963 it was won by a greyhound.

The race itself was full of action, accidents and pile-ups – both Richard and British jockey Jamie Moore, who had been riding in the race, were later very critical of the standard of care for riders and horses who were injured when unseated or falling.

James Reveley partnered French-trained Rigoureux to win the spectacular race.

Before the next, Richard gave us a nod and a wink that Jamie Moore and Maxwil were expected to go well – and they duly sloshed up at 6/1.

Writing about Dunwoody, the *Racing Post's* Lee Mottershead spoke to bloodstock agent Aiden Murphy, a long-standing friend of the jockey: 'Apart from his fearlessness, I think Richard's hands were what made him the jockey he was. Anyone who met him would tell you about his knuckle-crunching handshake, yet on horseback he rode with hands of silk. Richard also has the most ridiculously high pain barrier. It almost seemed like his mind was determined to see how much pain his body could take before it surrendered.

'I remember going with him to La Napoule in France. He arrived as a very amateur water-skier, so he befriended a top instructor. For the next few days he put his body through hell and by day seven he was mono-skiing on water, something most people couldn't achieve in a lifetime.'

In 2018 Richard, and Olivia McDonald, founded Dunwoody Web Design & Photography, to provide 'online marketing and photography services.' The contact address of the company is in Madrid.

STRANGE STUFF

KRONE ALONE

Few would contest the claim that Julie Krone is one of the all-time great jockeys and inarguably the greatest of female jockeys.

Born in Michigan in July 1963, with an accomplished equestrian, and somewhat pushy, mother, when the girl who would become the world's most successful female jockey sought her first job in racing as a backstretch galloper at Churchill Downs racetrack, her mother gave her a forged birth certificate – as she was only 15 at the time. She rode her first winner, Lord Farkle, when she was really 17, at Tampa Bay on 12 February 1981.

Having been riding from the age of two, winning prizes at five and subsequently determined to become a jockey, her attitude was to 'approach the sport like there wasn't a gender issue, and I wouldn't participate in the mindset of "she is just a girl."'

She didn't integrate easily into male-dominated race-rooms – in 1982 she shoved jockey Yves Turcotte off the scales after a bad-tempered race. In 1986 she was involved in a contretemps with Miguel Rujano during a Monmouth race, after which she walloped the rider with a right hook to the jaw, then later battered him over the head with a chair. They were fined $100 each.

Another dust-up over a race saw her whip jockey Joe Bravo at Meadowlands, New Jersey, resulting in a 15-day ban.

By March 1988 she was the most successful female jockey, racking up 1,205 winners. Heading for another win in January 1991 at Gulfstream Park, Florida, she unexpectedly had to jump a fox sunning himself on the back straight and ended up second in a race that produced a record 96,751/1 trifecta.

On her first visit to England in July 1992 she landed a treble at Redcar. Three years later she broke both hands in an accident at Gulfstream Park, resulting in a loss of nerve, potentially threatening her continued career.

She did come back but retired in April 1999 at Lone Star Park where the occasion was marked with a huge cake, laid on by fellow jockeys, who promptly thrust her face into it.

During 2000 she became the first woman inducted into the National Museum of Racing and Hall of Fame, declaring, 'I want this to be a lesson to all kids – if the stable gate is closed, climb the fence.'

A brief return to action ensued in harness racing, before she became part of the racing media, only to return to the saddle in November 2002 at Santa Anita. Within weeks she'd fractured two bones in her lower back, but capped her year by becoming the first woman to ride a Breeders' Cup winner, on Halfbridled, shortly before breaking several ribs in a fall at Hollywood Park.

Back she came again on Valentine's Day, again announcing in July that she'd stopped riding.

Not for good, she hadn't, but in September 2005 she became a mum to Lorelei Judith.

In September 2011 – just under three years after a similar one-off outing in one sanctioned betting race at Santa Anita Park competing against seven other retired Hall of Fame jockeys – and far from home, the American rider proved herself something of a living legend as she partnered Invincible Hero to a charity race win at Doncaster.

Krone, 48, and the only woman jockey in racing history to win a US Triple Crown race, partnered the 4/1 favourite in the Clipper Logistics Leger Legends Classified Stakes. She rode 3,704 winners during her career, and showed 15 rival stars from the past the way home as she brought Invincible Hero home by three and a half lengths. 'A furlong out I gave him two token swats – "please keep me going to the wire!" – and I tried not to bounce around too much.'

Explaining her fitness regime in the run-up to her comeback, Krone said, 'I went out 40 days in a row and I breezed horses for Eoin Harty and Richard Mandella, who had me on every horse in the world and they got me fit.'

Amongst other things, Julie is now a motivational speaker.

In October 2013 Julie was inducted into the National Women's Hall of Fame in New York, then in 2018 the National Museum of Racing and Hall of Fame acquired a full-length bronze statue depicting Julie's image, created by artists Linda and Michael Stinson.

POOR LITTLE RICH GIRL PAGET'S LONELY DEATH

She was, by a considerable degree, the wealthiest, most eccentric but also perhaps the most successful owner on the turf. Dorothy Paget, born in 1950, owner of five-time Cheltenham Gold Cup winner Golden Miller, who also won the Grand National, was such an honest punter that William Hill himself permitted her to place bets on races already run.

On 8 February 1960 Dorothy, who surrounded herself with staff to supply her every need, whatever time of day or night, ate a large meal, despite complaining of feeling unwell. She rang her trainer, Sir Gordon Richards, at 7.30pm to ask him about her yearlings stabled with him. He was optimistic about her prospects, which delighted her. She began to read one of her favourite publications, the Racing Calendar, perhaps also thinking ahead to her 55th birthday celebrations, just under a fortnight away.

It was nothing unusual for Dorothy to stay awake all night and sleep all day. At 4.30am her secretary, Miss Williams, looked in on her to check all was well. Dorothy looked up from her reading matter – 'We must get these entries off first thing,' she told her.

An hour later her maid looked in and found Dorothy had died.

The death certificate confirmed the cause of death as 'coronary thrombosis and arteriosclerosis'.

Her chaser Cannobie Lee, due to run later that day at Newbury, was withdrawn.

STRANGE STUFF

Writing Dorothy's biography, published in 2017, I discovered that it had not taken long for rumours to surface that Dorothy had not died a natural death. One or two credible sources suggested that perhaps her demise had been 'encouraged' or 'hastened.'

A particular member of Dorothy's household, so the story goes, had been given to understand that her employer had made arrangements for her and others to become substantial beneficiaries of her will.

'I know that pressure had been put upon [Dorothy] by a certain individual to make a will,' claimed her first biographer, Quintin Gilbey, 'and she is alleged to have said that she was giving it her consideration.'

Impatient to collect on that deal, runs the theory, this individual spotted an opportunity to bring forward her reward when Dorothy suffered her heart attack that night. Rather than calling for immediate medical assistance, the perpetrator instead ensured there would be no possibility of that arriving, by smothering the source of the potential windfall.

Amongst the 'evidence' purportedly substantiating this seemingly unlikely allegation is the 'fact' that when Dorothy's body was eventually discovered, all the drawers in the room had been turned out, shelves clearly searched, papers disturbed, in an effort to find the will which the culprit feared might otherwise be discovered and disposed of in order to avoid any of the 'rogue' conditions being enacted.

No will was ever found. Or, at least, ever produced.

The other dramatic 'revelation' to emerge was the 'fact', at least according to him, that in High Wycombe there lives a man who was Dorothy's secret son.

In May 2017 I received a letter from a Surrey-based former jockey telling me, 'I would like to take up a little of your time by mentioning an incident, which was recounted to me free of hyperbole.

It occurred in the year of Miss Paget's death, when I was riding out for Peter Ashworth's stable at Epsom.

'Mr Ashworth had a quite heavy, mature "lad" working for him at the time, named Doug Holman, who had worked for Walter Nightingall, when the latter had horses of Miss P's. Doug got talking about his time there one day, and said he had been in the trainer's office in the house one evening, when the phone rang and one of Miss P's secretaries said her boss wanted to speak to him.

The trainer mentioned to Doug that their discussion would have to wait for another time, and as he left the room, Doug observed the trainer reaching for a bucket, which he placed below his chair, whilst undoing the front of his trousers.

Apparently, he had suffered these long phone calls on so many previous occasions that he was armed and ready, so to speak, to deal with the likelihood of a 'call of nature', instead of sitting in some discomfort for who knows how long!'

PIPE OPENER FOR THE CAROL SINGER

It is often forgotten that master trainer Martin Pipe was also a jockey. When he rode at Taunton in 1972 he broke his thigh when coming to grief at the last whilst riding a horse called Lorac – his wife Carol's name spelled backwards. Three years later he retired from the saddle, commenting: 'I was a pretend jockey. I was determined not to become a pretend trainer.'

A perfectionist, and aware of a reputation for his attitude, he sponsored a race at Taunton, and named it 'The Martin Pipe Am I That Difficult? Handicap'.

A TV programme accused him of blood doping his horses. He would tell *Sun* racing writer Claude Duval that as a result, 'I even thought of committing suicide.'

As his career continued to flourish and his attention to detail resulted in ever more winners from his yard, the racing world realised that Martin's success was down to determination, innovation and hard work.

I met him when I was writing a biography of the previously mentioned, eccentric, mega-wealthy owner and gambler Dorothy Paget – who fascinated Martin, to the extent that he has spent thousands tracking down memorabilia related to her. I was grateful to be picked up in his car from the station to whisk me to the stables – until I read his autobiography, in which he writes, 'By the time I was twenty I'd smashed up three VW Beetles, a Mini van, a Triumph GT6 and the first of three Triumph Stags.'

Martin told me he was not interested in reading, and disliked holidays, but that when Carol insisted on a break from the yard they went off to a remote Scottish island for a few days. 'There was nothing to do, but I found a dusty book there, which turned out to be about Dorothy Paget – I was hooked.'

Martin and son David, who took over as trainer when Martin officially retired, although it is clear that he has no objection to making the occasional 'suggestion' to his son, love to spring a small surprise to visitors to the yard – making them take a turn on the 'Equicizer' machine on which rookie jockeys learn how to ride properly.

Martin wrote the foreword for my book, and on my trips to research amongst his Paget archives, the fantastic bond between Carol and he became very obvious, leading me to the conclusion that it is very unlikely to be coincidental that Martin's favourite record is one of Neil Sedaka's hits, 'Oh, Carol.'

Martin loved a tilt at the bookies, and, as he explained to *Racing Post* readers in December 2015, his 'best bet' happened in a humble selling hurdle race at Haydock on 5 January 1980: 'I drove the Range Rover and trailer [containing his horse, Carrie Ann] to Haydock. It was the second time [his assistant] Chester Barnes had been racing with me.

'Chester backed the horse with bookmaker Pat Whelan – £3,300 to £100. He never even altered the odds, so I told Chester to go in again. He had another £100 on. I had gone around all the other bookmakers on the track – 30-plus in those days – backing the horse.

STRANGE STUFF

Martin Pipe; like the author also got hooked on Dorothy Paget.

'Meanwhile, my father had backed Carrie Ann in betting shops and with every credit firm in England on the Tote.

'Carrie Ann won comfortably under Rod Millman. I still remember my wife Carol greeting us when we returned home – and filled up lots of buckets with cash.'

Sadly, Chester died, aged 74, in March 2021.

Eighteen years later, another even more powerful Pipe bomb was aimed at bookies – this time partnered by equally legendary jockey, AP McCoy. In October 2012, the *Racing Post's* Tom Kerr described the knock-out blow Pipe sent in the bookies' direction under the heading: 'The Biggest Ever Certainty To Race At Cheltenham.'

'March 17, 1998, and at Cheltenham the gloom was gathering for its nightly conference. Beneath the darkening sky a chill settled on the betting ring, yet it was not just the falling mercury that was sending shivers down the layers' spines. Martin Pipe had the favourite in the last, and the money was coming.

The gamble was on a horse named Unsinkable Boxer, no spring chicken at nine but in the form of his life, and the trainer was the master Martin Pipe. The race: the usually highly competitive Unicoin Homes Gold Card Handicap Hurdle Final (now the Pertemps Final).

Unsinkable Boxer had begun his career four and a half years earlier in a bumper at Mallow racecourse, now Cork. Few who saw the horse that October day would have had any cause to suspect he would one day send tens of thousands into raptures. He came home sixth, 26 lengths behind Callisoe Bay, who in 1995 would finish fifth in the Supreme Novices' and never troubled such exalted company again.

After a difficult start to life in Britain, Unsinkable Boxer was transferred at the beginning of the 1997-98 season to champion trainer Pipe, who saw potential lurking within the horse's bulky frame. Pipe recalls: 'Mr [Philip] Green sent him to me and he was a lovely big, strong horse. He didn't have too much form but he had size and scope.

'We'd had him about three months and we took him to Plumpton. He was going well at home and working well and we were trying to keep him sound. He won at Plumpton, which was very impressive and very good, then he went off after that and won at Fontwell, then again easily at Donny.'

Unsinkable Boxer was rated 94 when he won that race at Plumpton on 7 December 1997. By the time he won less than two months later at Doncaster – his last race before Cheltenham – he had progressed 34lb in the eyes of the handicapper.

Along the way he'd also been withdrawn with a vet's certificate on the morning of his Cheltenham qualifier at Warwick, yet remained eligible for the race having been declared overnight.

Heading to Cheltenham and the Gold Card Handicap Hurdle Final, a choice of race confirmed at the last moment as the Coral Cup had also been touted as an option, connections knew the nine-year-old had plenty in hand. 'We were very confident,' says Pipe. 'He'd been working well and improving. We were over-confident.'

By the time of the race the Pipe camp had been buoyed and made carefree by the earlier success of Champleve, but still their confidence in the beast was extraordinarily absolute. Tony McCoy, writing in his autobiography, recalls a conversation with Pipe as the pair headed down the chute towards the racecourse: 'He [Pipe] looked up at me. I'll never forget it. He looked me straight in the eye without breaking stride, and he lowered his voice. "This horse," he said in a measured even tone, "is the biggest certainty that will ever walk out onto this racecourse."'

In the betting ring the punters too seemed to share Pipe's unshakable confidence. It didn't require a PhD in advanced mathematics to spot a looming Pipe plot and punters latched onto the gamble, forming long queues before the layers. On offer at 9/2 in the morning, they pummelled the price into 5/2.

STRANGE STUFF

'Everyone backed Unsinkable Boxer,' says layer Geoff Banks, who was working with his father John on the rail. 'Everybody wanted to back it to the exclusion of everything else. The whole world was on Unsinkable Boxer. You couldn't avoid it. You had to shut your eyes and go for it.'

Across the straight in the silver ring identical scenes were played out. Neil Channing, who has since traded the bookies board for the poker table, remembers a day that had been going well. He had ducked Istabraq, but Unsinkable Boxer's left-right hook was impossible to dodge. 'Literally every single bet was for Unsinkable Boxer. £25-£10, £25-£10, £25-£10. We didn't lay big prices, we were never bigger than 3/1, but we didn't lay another horse in the race,' he says.

Circling before the start, McCoy was pondering Pipe's words. 'All I was thinking was that I'm riding something that Martin Pipe has told me is the greatest certainty that will ever walk out on to this racecourse, so the only way it's going to get beat is if I muck it up.'

That, it soon became clear, was not going to happen. McCoy and Unsinkable Boxer cruised through the race as if it were no more than a basic piece of work. With both rider and mount exuding confidence and barely restrained power, they sluiced through the field from their early position towards the rear, taking order with the leading group after the third-last.

The run-in was a triumphal canter. 'I hardly broke sweat, he hardly broke sweat, and we cruised up the hill,' recalls McCoy in his autobiography.

Amid the deafening roars of a jubilant crowd, AP turned to the grandstand and received his acclaim. Newspapers and hats were flung in the air like confetti. Only on the rail, recalls Banks, was there silence as the layers contemplated the magnitude of the thrashing they had received.

Over in the silver ring it took Channing a full hour to pay out the hundreds of punters who backed Unsinkable Boxer, while Banks estimated the rails layers alone had lost in the region of £1 million on the race.

'For years it was spoken about as one of the biggest handicap hits at Cheltenham – even now it is one of the biggest handicap gambles landed,' recalls Coral's director of communications Simon Clare. It was also one of the most public gambles ever landed, not a private plot but a public giveaway.

Now, many years later, what of Pipe's bold assessment that no horse would ever be such a shoo-in as Unsinkable Boxer? McCoy is in no doubt. 'He was the biggest certainty that ever walked out on to that racecourse,' he says with emphasis. 'In the gloom of that Cheltenham evening, Unsinkable Boxer really was unsinkable.'

'Mr Bean' – Martin Pipe's answer to the question, 'Who would play you in a film of your life?' in December 2015.

JENNY PITMAN'S KNICKER ELASTIC

Jennifer Susan Pitman was the first female trainer to win the Grand National – when Corbiere – named for Jersey's lighthouse in the days when Bergerac, the Jersey cop, was a big deal on TV, thus making it a popular choice for once-a-year punters – triumphed in 1983. He would run in the race five times in all – also finishing third twice, 12th, and falling once.

Jenny's patience with horses is illustrated by the fact that she took Corbiere on as a three-year-old.

Something of a plain-speaking character, to say the least, she rapidly became very popular with the public for her no-nonsense approach to racing and life.

She once gave *Sun* racing reporter Claude Duval a mounted toilet-roll 'for writing so much crap about me.'

He remembered, 'The individual sheets were even personally inscribed.' He also recalled her threatening another racing scribe 'with castration.'

Respected *Times* sportswriter Simon Barnes, said of her, in 2005, she was 'by a considerable margin, the rudest woman I have ever met.' Yet, she was devoted to her equine friends, causing Sue Mott of the *Daily Telegraph* to note; 'The only reason she banks with Lloyds is because of the black horse on their logo.'

Born the fourth of seven children in 1946, nee Harvey, Jenny worked at a stable in Bishop's Cleeve for two years. One day, returning from a workout on the local gallops, her horse was spooked by a cyclist travelling around a corner too fast and on the wrong side of the road. The cyclist in question was jockey Richard Pitman. Jenny's initial reaction to Richard was unfavourable, but later, when Richard obtained a job at top trainer Fred Winter's stables 50 miles from Bishop's Cleeve, Jenny was persuaded to apply for a job in Lambourn with Major Champneys at Church Farm Stables. She moved there in 1964, and soon after, in 1965, aged 19, she married Richard Pitman.

Jenny kept her married name after divorcing Richard, who once described the qualities he looked for in the ideal woman – 'Gentleness, firm contours and a sense of humour.'

Jenny riposted, 'I've had the greatest romances in my life with horses.'

After they broke up for the first time, Jenny considered working in a shoe shop, but instead opted for working on a shoestring, taking on the almost derelict Weathercock House stables in Upper Lambourn, sending out her first winner in 1975.

The strained relationship with Richard ended for good when he walked out at Christmas 1977.

Corbiere's 1982 Welsh National win brought her to prominence, and by 1984 she was also a Cheltenham Gold Cup-winning trainer, courtesy of Burrough Hill Lad, of whom she said, 'He's had more operations than Joan Collins – and maybe more men working on him.' She also won the Gold Cup with Garrison Savannah in 1991.

She would also train the winners of not only Aintree's National, but added the Welsh, Scottish and Irish versions to her glorious CV.

In April 1990, she was fined by stewards at Ayr after striking jockey Jamie Osborne in the face, after her horse, Run to Form, collided with the rails, for which she blamed Osborne, who was riding Dwadme.

She admitted that during their contretemps she asked the jockey, 'Why don't you f+++ing grow up, Osborne? I told you at Aintree, this job's dangerous enough without you being an arsehole.'

Her son Mark had ridden the affected horse and she had to pay up. 'That £1,000 fine was a bit harsh,' reflected Mark, who told Claude Duval, 'but Mum said "it was the best grand I ever spent!"'

John McCririck dubbed her 'The Cuddly One', but champion jockey John Francome declared her to be 'about as cuddly as a dead hedgehog.'

The 1992 Cheltenham Gold Cup saw La Pitman mired in controversy as her outsider, Golden Freeze, stayed very close to market leader Carvill's Hill, trained by Martin Pipe, whose jumping seemed to suffer as a result and dropped out of contention.

Mrs Pitman justified the tactics by saying, 'Golden Freeze's owner backed him at 200/1 to finish in the first four. I have done nothing wrong.'

BBC TV commentator Julian Wilson referred to her as 'the Winnie Mandela of Racing', while Lord Oaksey declared her to be 'the most balanced person I know. She's got a chip on both shoulders.'

Jenny threatened to sue Wilson, 'I would sooner kiss my horse Garrison Savannah's arse than speak to Julian Wilson.'

Jenny was distinctly unamused – as were many others – after her horse Esha Ness passed the post first in the 1993 Grand National, only for the race to be declared void, following the shambles of the botched false start.

Even as the 'race' was unfolding, Jenny invaded the weighing room in an effort to force stewards to stop the race, telling them, 'My bloody horse has already gone one circuit. I don't want to "win" the National like this.' Later she contemptuously described the National's malfunctioning starting tapes as 'knicker elastic'.

She did win the National again, this time for real, in 1995, with 40/1 shot Royal Athlete, cementing her reputation as the Queen of Aintree – even literally kissing and making up with Julian Wilson.

She married for the second time in 1997, after an 18-year engagement to David Stait, whose pet name for her was 'waggle bum'.

INTRIGUINGLY INTERESTING RACEY CHARACTERS

Plain-speaking Jenny Pitman became popular with the public.

A year later she received the OBE and on Christmas Eve 1998 heard that she was clear of the thyroid cancer with which she had been diagnosed.

Her final – 797th – winner was Scarlet Emperor at Huntingdon in May 1999. She did not settle for retiring into obscurity but wrote a bestselling autobiography and a stream of thrillers – also returning to training – but this time, of greyhounds.

Taking on her male counterparts was a significant feature of her career, and she recalled in her autobiography, 'I was the only woman at a function when a colleague came up to me and said, "You're looking bloody good, Jenny. Tell me, has your sex life improved?" I was taken aback by his rudeness, but I wasn't going to let him see it: "Yes, it certainly has," I said, "but I can see yours hasn't."'

Despite her controversies, Jenny was clearly valued by racing's leaders and in 2017 she was appointed to their disciplinary committee by the British Horse racing Authority – 'I shall add a bit of common sense,' she declared.

She and *Sun* writer Claude Duval had their fallings-out, but in his autobiography *Moments In The Sun* Claude reflected after relating that she had given him a framed photograph of Corbiere with the message: 'From one old handicapper to another.'

'Behind the battleaxe exterior perhaps there was a genuine heart of gold.'

MARK MY WORDS, SIR

Sir Mark Prescott's Heath House Stables in Newmarket are said to be haunted, although the maverick trainer has denied ever seeing the shades of the alleged spirits of multiple champion jockey Fred Archer, who shot himself aged 29 in 1886 (it was claimed that in 1993 a séance held by stable lads at his old Pegasus stables summoned up Archer's spirit), and trainer Mat Dawson (1820–1898), whose career lasted from 1840 until his death. He trained the winners of 28 British Classics.

Asked once whether he believed in the afterlife, Sir Mark replied, 'I'm not prepared to bet against it.' But there seems to be little chance of Sir Mark himself taking on an eternity of haunting others when he finally takes his leave of this life.

In an interview with *Observer* journalist Will Buckley, he spoke of his plans for when this happens, telling him: 'I wanted to find myself a nice plot with some agreeable people around. I had to contact the Parks and Recreation authority. And there was a very nice fellow, he showed me the graveyard and there was Fred Archer, Mr Dawson, Mr Waugh. I found a nice corner, and said, "I want three plots down there," and he said, "Would that be for Sir and Lady Prescott and your son and heir?" "Certainly not," replied resolutely single man Prescott, "It's so I don't have to have any f***er next to me!"'

A bet struck between fellow trainer Charlie Fellowes and Sir Mark was settled in September 2019 – the payout being the latter agreeing to open up his historic Heath House yard, his base since 1970, for the first time at the Henry Cecil open weekend in Newmarket.

The terms of the original wager seem to have been lost in the mists of time with Prescott, who is not happy about having to show anything to the public, insisting he had been 'put away' by open weekend chairman Fellowes, who had taken over organising the event in 2018.

The bet was originally thought to be that Fellowes, not averse to sporting the odd five o'clock shadow on the gallops, would remain clean shaven on Newmarket Heath for a specified time in order to win.

Prescott said he would follow Fellowes around the heath 'like a labrador' to check if his face had made contact with a razor blade, and duly caught Fellowes out, only for the latter to insist the bet was just for six months, but Prescott disagrees.

He told the *Racing Post*: 'My good name has been exploited by Mr Fellowes, who has put me away and reneged on the terms of the bet. The original wager was that if I found him unshaven on any morning over the past 12 months I would not have to open the yard, but this seems to have morphed into having shaved once a day only for six months. To keep my good name, I decided to open between 9am and midday on September 22 on a strictly one-off basis.'

Prescott personally escorted many visitors round the historic stables, giving an excellent impersonation of a man pretending to be grumpily disgruntled by doing something he was thoroughly enjoying, by all accounts!

When it was all over, Sir Mark had allowed in over 1,000 visitors during the late September event, appearing to enjoy the occasion.

The determinedly non-pc, cigar-smoking Prescott broke his back at the age of 17 in a riding accident.

He told Simon Milham in a 2007 *Mail Online* interview: 'I couldn't speak, I couldn't swallow. I couldn't blink for nine weeks. It's the most terrible experience, being a prisoner inside your own body with your mind racing. You can't blink and if they don't remember to close your eyelids, they stick to your eyeballs.'

Sir Mark also explained to Milham: 'Because I firmly believe that no horse wants to go to a race meeting, I am grimly determined to make sure, and I appreciate how important it is, to never, ever run one that is not ready.'

Along with TV celebrity chef Clarissa Dickson-Wright, Sir Mark received an absolute discharge from Scarborough Magistrates Court in September 2009 after pleading guilty to hare coursing whilst attending an event organised by the Yorkshire Greyhound Field Trialling Club in March 2007.

When asked by journalist Peter Oborne whether he'd rather train the winner of The Derby or of coursing's main event, the Waterloo Cup, Sir Mark was in no doubt – 'I'd rather win the Waterloo Cup.'

He has also been known to support bull-fighting ('no other sport is life or death'), and Charlie Brooks wrote in a 2004 interview with Sir Mark: 'Cock fighting may now be illegal but the trainer has a copy of every book ever written about it.'

Sir Mark also noted in 2011: 'Newmarket moving the July Cup to the Saturday is a complete nightmare. They have paid absolutely no attention to the bullfighting calendar.'

Brooks, a former racehorse trainer, concluded his *Telegraph* article by suggesting: 'When his time comes, I just hope someone stuffs him and sticks him in his conservatory with his bulls, because I think he would like that very much.'

When he goes to meet his maker, Sir Mark told Simon Milham: 'When I die, there won't be one hare, one fox, one horse that I will be afraid of meeting – there will be a lot of people I don't want to meet – but there won't be one animal. I believe that.'

STRANGE STUFF

I will always have a soft spot for Sir Mark and his exploits, since the occasion when I was on a racing jaunt to Cagnes-sur-Mer in France. En route to the course, the word was passed around those present that a source close to the Prescott stable suggested that his horse, Humoreuse, would run well. Ensconced in the course's restaurant with friends, we enjoyed a fine afternoon's dining and drinking, cheering to the rafters as Humoreuse romped home at 7/1.

Only later did we wonder why other members of our party, elsewhere in the restaurant, seemed gloomy. It transpired that a late message had come through, advising us all not to back the horse, maybe because of the going, the draw … the reason wasn't clear, but it would certainly have stopped us backing the very welcome winner, so we raised another glass to Sir Mark!

PAGE TURNER HAYLEY RECOMMENDED

Hayley Turner is widely regarded as the first woman to achieve a sustained, day-in, day-out, successful career as a professional jockey in the UK. Even if it wasn't the reason she began riding, there is little doubt that her success resulted in an enormous increase in the number of female apprentice jockeys riding in the UK in the second decade of the 21st century.

In December 2008 (the month in which she became the third female rider used by Sir Michael Stoute), when she was on the verge of reaching the age of 25, and also becoming the first UK female jockey to ride 100 winners in a calendar year, Claude Duval of *The Sun* wrote: 'If you had told me a few years ago a female rider would ride a century of winners, I would have called for the men in white coats to take you away.' He added: 'Her stylish displays make her indistinguishable from the boys.'

Hayley knew that already: 'The only difference between me and the boys is that I've got a different changing room.'

Her mother, Kate, was a riding instructor, so Hayley was in the saddle from the age of three. Her first ride in public ended in tragedy as the horse broke a leg during the race, but on 4 June 2000, at Pontefract, Generate, her eighth ride, was her first winner – and the last for some 18 months as she struggled to make the big breakthrough.

In 2005, she shared the champion apprentice title with Saleem Golam, with 44 winners.

She had faced a little sexism, with trainer Marcus Tregoning becoming irritated when an interviewer asked why he'd given her the ride on a 20/1 Newbury winner – calling the question 'unnecessary', and pointing out that he rated her amongst the top ten riders in the land.

When a photographer wanted Hayley to don leathers and sit astride a motorbike for a shot to accompany a profile, the shrift she gave him was of the minuscule variety.

Many of her early rides were on inmates of Michael Bell's stable, who admitted, 'There were a few doubters initially among my owners, but virtually all now would be more than happy to have Hayley ride their horses.'

INTRIGUINGLY INTERESTING RACEY CHARACTERS

Mullitovermaurice was a 7/1 winner at Wolverhampton on 30 December 2008, and brought up the century – but there was a sting in the tail, as she was found guilty of careless riding and suspended for two days. 'If you don't get an occasional ban, you can't be trying hard enough,' remarked Hayley, described by Alan Lee of *The Times* as 'the self-effacing suffragette of British racing.'

She was now being brought into racing's mainstream – she skippered the home team in the 2008 Shergar Cup and was voted as Channel 4's Racing Personality during the same year, then appointed 2009 'Face of the Derby' and an ambassador for the Prince's Trust.

One of the pioneers of female riders, jockey-turned-trainer Gay Kelleway said of Hayley, 'What she has done is remarkable. I'm proud I contributed some winners for her.'

However, Gay was less than happy with an interview in 2019 in which Hayley was reported as saying, 'It's really only in recent years that the girls have been that good.'

'I've always admired Hayley for what she's achieved,' said Kelleway. 'But to say what she did about women jockeys today – compared to my generation – was disrespectful and nonsensical.

'In the 80s, riders like me and Julie Fallon rode the horses that none of the men would get on.'

This had all been on the cards for a while – in 2004, trainer Alan King had told *Racing Post* readers that the 5ft 2in, 7st 10lb rider was 'as strong and invigorating as a double brandy'.

Of course, fate decided to take a hand, and in March 2009, Hayley was badly injured in an accident while putting a horse through starting stalls on the Newmarket gallops, which initially threatened to sideline her for the rest of the year. She made guest appearances as a pundit on Channel 4 during this time.

When fresh medical evidence allowed her to return to race-riding in mid-summer she was instantly back to riding successfully, ending the year on 60 winners, despite missing much of the season.

The 2010 Flat racing year continued to be successful for Turner; highlights included a first Group 1 ride, a Group 2 victory, a successful partnership with classy two-year-old Margot Did, which included two winners and second places in two Group 3s and a Group 2. Her agent Guy Jewell declared, 'When the boys say Hayley's got balls, they are paying her the highest compliment.'

In January 2011, she had her first race-rides at Meydan in Dubai, as part of its Dubai Racing Carnival.

In July 2011, she rode her first Group 1 winner, Dream Ahead, in Newmarket's July Cup.

2012 saw Turner ride 92 winners, at a strike rate of 12 per cent. She ended the year early to have surgery on an ankle.

On 31 March 2012, she became the first female jockey in history to ride on the Dubai World Cup night and on 2 June in the same year she became the second female jockey to ride in the Derby. But most significantly that year, Turner won the Beverly D Stakes in America, becoming the first UK-based female to ride an international Grade 1 winner.

At the end of the 2015 season she announced her retirement. She was awarded the OBE in the 2016 Birthday Honours for services to horse racing. She wasn't retired for long ...

In 2017 Hayley was suspended for three months after she breached BHA rules when she bet on races after she reapplied for her racing licence: *The Guardian* reported that Hayley 'described herself as living two lives, one as a broadcaster who could bet when she pleased and one as an occasional jockey who could not.'

A disciplinary panel said it would not 'reject that explanation out of hand', but still felt it necessary to suspend her from riding for three months.

In 2018 Turner came out of retirement after her suspension and began riding in France to take advantage of the female jockey weight allowance there. And in August 2019, in one of her favourite events, the annual team-based Shergar Cup at Ascot, Turner dominated, winning

Hayley Turner, the first woman to achieve a 'sustained' career as a professional jockey in Britian.

two of the six races and carrying off the Silver Saddle for top jockey, becoming the first to do so in consecutive years. Her enthusiasm for the Shergar Cup is no secret and in the build-up she referred to the day as being 'like Christmas for me'.

A month earlier, Hayley had become the first female rider to win at Royal Ascot since Gay Kelleway in 1987, when she partnered Thanks Be to victory. But trainer Charlie Fellowes was not happy, and insisted that his horse should have been disqualified.

In a *Racing Post* article he wrote:

'Thanks Be gave me a moment I'll cherish forever when winning the Sandringham Handicap at Royal Ascot. It may surprise you to learn I do not believe I should have won that race, however.

'British Racing's whip rules are wrong – and because they are wrong, I won the first Royal Ascot race of my career. Hayley Turner broke the sport's whip rules aboard Thanks Be. For that simple reason I believe our filly should have been disqualified.

'Hayley received a nine-day suspension and was fined £1,600. If you could rewind the clock and tell her she could still exceed the permitted whip quota but win and be punished, I am absolutely certain she would opt for the win-and-be-punished approach. In an important race any jockey would do the same. That's the problem.

'I don't think the threat of a bigger suspension would have made a difference. I don't think the threat of a bigger fine would have made a difference. The only thing that would make a difference is the knowledge that going just one strike above the seven-hit limit would lead to disqualification.'

'I feel bad for beating Her Majesty, but I'm sure she'll understand,' said Hayley, after winning the Sandringham on 33/1 Thanks Be, beating the Queen's Magnetic Charm into second.

Unmarried at the time of writing, Hayley revealed in an interview that her family once tried to persuade her that she was a married woman after she lost her memory for two weeks due to a fall. Hayley said, 'They told me all this stuff which I believed, including that my husband was on his way over to see me. I've never been married!'

She's had a dream career already, but has also reportedly revealed that she had once literally dreamed of something completely different – being married to Bruce Forsyth!

After the 2021 running of the Shergar Cup, when the Girls won again, skipper Hayley, the most successful rider in the event's history with eight winners, was given the original Shergar Cup trophy to keep – fully deserved!

IN THE OLDIE DAYS LADIES MANNED THE BETTING SHOPS

1 MAY 2021 was the 60th anniversary of legal betting shops being introduced to the UK High Street scene.

Not that there weren't already a substantial number of such establishments flouting the law and operating openly if not legally, back in 1961 when the first 'kosher' shops opened for business.

They attracted an overwhelmingly male clientele, partly due to the spartan surroundings they offered their customers – and when they did finally gain licensed status they were, if anything, even less attractive to potential female punters – as the television screens and the odd cup of tea with biscuits offered illegally to the customers were now officially illegal.

The idea was that the new shops should be purely functional and not remotely comfortable for those bold enough to be seen entering the establishments, whose very raison d'etre was only permitted to be gleaned via the name above the door. The windows could display no incentives to entice customers to enter.

The shops were staffed almost exclusively by males, even though those entering to wager were not remotely concerned whether they were backing colts, fillies or geldings. But despite this male domination a small number of females had already made an impact on bookmaking and betting shops, though sadly their names have become virtually unknown and these feisty characters languish in obscurity.

These female trailblazers deserve to be recalled and given their due recognition.

Towards the end of the First World War, Molly Dawson's husband, who ran a previously flourishing, but now floundering, printing business was drinking heavily enough that she feared for her future finances. Cannily, though, she had anticipated this course of events and taken unexpectedly prescient precautions.

By opening a betting shop, Molly was anticipating the legalisation of such premises by over half a century.

Molly discarded her drunken husband, cashed in her savings, and opened up a newsagents/tobacconists shop to alleviate the strain and boredom of mundane domestic life.

She had begun by accepting a few bets over the counter, only to find that demand rapidly increased from the illicit facility.

Now local bookmaker John Swain, noticing what was happening, asked Molly if 'she might like to earn a little extra on the side by taking bets over the counter' – effectively acting as an agent for him on a percentage of turnover.

She didn't need a second invitation, and when, eventually, her betting income overtook the newsagent earnings, Molly opted for the former on a full-time basis and opened a betting office in Hackney, advertising herself as 'London's only Lady Bookmaker' and collecting bets from punters on the street and over the telephone.

Before long, she was opening another branch in the more salubrious surrounds of the City of London.

Back from evacuation in the countryside at the end of the First World War, Molly's 13-year-old daughter, Elizabeth Dawson, returned to London, only to discover that 'Mother had embarked on a new career as, of all things, a Turf Commission Agent – to put it bluntly, she was now a lady bookie,' she would later write.

Remembered Elizabeth: 'With a bookmaker for a mother, life couldn't possibly be dull ... Pol Roger, Mumm or the "Widow" generally flowed pretty freely whenever a rank outsider turned up for the book. The toast was always the same – 'Here's to the punters – bless their little cotton socks.'

With business flourishing in the new office in London's Bishopsgate, Molly was now dealing with more upmarket clients, but had her own standards, to which she adhered.

No one was allowed more than two weeks' credit. If they didn't pay up at the first polite demand, she would cut her losses and cross them off the books forthwith.

She was not, though, beyond lecturing customers who appeared to be betting beyond their means on 'the evils of gambling.'

At first her business flourished, but as it was very dependent on personal contact to keep the wagers rolling in it became very time consuming and she cashed in some of her chips and sold the Bishopsgate office on, after 'a lucrative offer from a firm of West End bookmakers.'

As happens to all bookies occasionally, results went against her, and she found it increasingly difficult to survive on the Hackney shop earnings but by embracing street, telephone and postal betting she once again began to thrive.

Street betting, though, although tolerated to some extent, was still illegal and occasionally clamped down on. Molly soon employed some 20 'runners' to collect the bets for her, working on 10 per cent commission, and earning up to £30 a day – big money for the time.

They all had to take their turn to be made an example of when the police were looking for easy 'collars' by being arrested and hauled in front of local magistrates to be fined under the Betting and Gaming Act.

Molly paid their fines, and a little personal acquaintance with local bobbies kept such inconveniences to a minimum, as her profits once again boomed.

Recalled Elizabeth: 'Mother's daily winnings could amount to quite fantastic sums, and they often ran into several hundreds of pounds. No wonder she used to refer to her telephone business as "bread and butter". The humbler tanner (sixpence – two and a half new pence) each-way punters supplied a liberal spreading of jam.'

But during the 1930s business slowed as the country's financial health showed signs of recession, and to make matters worse the taxman finally caught up with Molly.

Nor could she shrug off increasing health problems, contracting jaundice with complications. Molly died in October 1938 on the day before her 50th birthday.

Daughter Elizabeth paid fitting tribute to her: 'I'll wager if it wasn't long before she was organising a Pearly Gates Handicap and laying odds against the angel with the shortest wings.'

Molly was not, though, the first of her sex to enter the betting business.

As early as 1900 Theresa Butcher, a greengrocer based in Hulme, Manchester, and despite being described as 'an elderly white-haired woman, respectably dressed', was fined £10 for taking bets at her shop.

In the same year, in August, a Mr Lister was reported by the *Manchester Evening News* to have been 'shocked' when he was called home following a police raid, to discover that his wife had been running a 'secret betting business' from the front room of their house in Collyhurst, also in Manchester. Not only that, she apparently 'did most of her trade with women and children.'

Ann Arabella Thomason, generally known as Bella, was born in 1874 at number 15 Walkin Lane, Nether Hallam, Yorkshire, the daughter of a steel smelter and his wife. In 1896 she married ironworks labourer Stephen Thomason, who supplemented his income by taking bets from fellow workers.

The couple saved hard before using their profits to buy a shop that nominally sold fruit, but was really a home for their betting business, which was strictly illegal at that time as the Betting Houses Act of 1853 had made it illegal to take cash for a bet other than at a racecourse.

They were rumbled in 1905, and Stephen was taken to court and fined. He was also told that he should take responsibility for any crimes committed by his wife. Stephen promised he would not take any more bets at his shop and paid a £25 fine. But he had no intention of sticking to his promise, and the betting continued. By 1924 their business was still illegal but now well established and trusted by its customers.

The business was disguised as a tobacconist, but it was an open secret that it sold no cigarettes. Women were not allowed to enter. The fine for offences of this nature was £100 in 1924, but all pretence was now gone, as they installed a ticker-tape machine to deliver results before their local competitors.

After the war, Bella, as she was widely known, reopened 'Bella's', having found another business partner, Albert Hampson.

Their betting shop was in the town centre, and its business was now even more obvious than before.

The partners had an employee who would read aloud the ticker tape as it arrived, creating a professional and very profitable betting shop atmosphere.

The resulting business would be considered a model for later (legal) betting shops. Bella dressed smartly and was known for her honesty in paying out on bets, even on one occasion, two years after the race they were placed on had finished.

Her biographer, Carl Chinn, considers it likely that the business was frequently paying the police to avoid prosecution.

Thomason died in Bolton in 1959, two years before off-course bookmaking was legalised in the UK.

Rose Pickering ran a pre-Second World War fish and chip shop in Birmingham – but it was a front for her real business of taking bets – which was hidden away in the room at the back of the premises where she stashed the betting slips.

In 1926 her shop was part of a trio of businesses in a yard also including a genuine barber, and a butcher with a fridge in the yard which was used, revealed Rose's daughter, Mrs Packer, as an excuse to have two 'great big doors put on the yard so that it was all private, and there was a little door cut in the big door – and of course they used to put their bets in there.

'You used to have a man on the door because of the police – it wasn't legal then. That's how they used to just give the man the bets behind the door and he used to put them in a bag, and we used to bring them in the house and Mum and Dad used to do 'em in the house.'

Today, bookie Bet365 founder and joint chief executive, the billionaire Denise Coates, is running one of the biggest bookies in the business – and women are once again more than making their mark on the world of betting.

THE FIRST LADIES OF RACING

Molly may have been the first woman closely involved with the world of horse racing. It is very difficult to know just when female humans joined fillies as integral parts of the racing world, but here's perhaps the earliest mention of such matters I've come across:

- In March 1691, on the 7th of that month, some 330 years ago, the Diarist of the *Chester Recorder* may have been recording history when he (I presume!) wrote:
  'We rode to Farne race, where I run against Sir Edmund Ashton, Mrs Morte, Mr Mackworth, and Capt Warburton …'
  Then, this bombshell news:
  'Mrs Morte won the race.'
  Whether these were the owners of the horses involved, and/or the riders/jockeys, is neither recorded nor clear.

- In the early 18th century, Queen Anne showed an interest in racing and in 1711 presented a gold challenge cup worth 100 guineas to be run for each year at York – where, on 28 July 1719, her bay colt, Star, lived up to his name, winning a £14 plate for her. She was very ill so not present – but a courier galloped off to carry the news to her, arriving shortly before her death on 1 August.

- By the year 1900, 81 female owners were registered with Weatherbys.

- Epsom's Derby which would become probably the most prestigious worldwide Flat race was first run in 1780, yet it was not until 1918, when the race took place at Newmarket because of the First World War, that the first winner of this Blue Riband owned by a woman was recorded when Lady James Douglas-owned Gainsborough landed this historic breakthrough. Bit worrying that she had to be identified via her husband's first name, though.

- Lady James was born in France, and was a daughter of Mr F Hennessy, a member of the Anglo-French family of brandy distillers and thus, presumably, a spirited person.
  She lived to be 87, and in 1910 had set about establishing a stud, a resident of which, Oaks winner Rosedrop, was mated with Bayardo in 1914, producing Gainsborough.

- The year before, another woman had made a big impact on the Derby – as militant suffragette, Emily Davison, was killed by one of the runners as she dashed on to the track.
- Lady J was the first female Derby-winning owner, but the first female breeder of a Derby winner, courtesy of Volodyovski in 1901, was Lady Meux.
- In 1915 Lady Nelson's Ally Sloper was the first Grand National winner owned by a woman.
- Around the time of the First World War the overwhelmingly male on-course bookmaking world was infiltrated by Helen Vernet, born in 1877, who had begun taking racecourse bets from friends on a private basis, only to attract protests from legitimate bookies that they were losing turnover to her.

  A Ladbrokes representative arranged a meeting with her and promptly offered her a position as an on-course bookie with the company, which she accepted, and ended up so respected and successful that in 1928 she became a partner in the company.
- The first female National Hunt trainer was probably Gladys 'Posy' Lewis, born in 1907, who owned and trained the dual Welsh Grand National winner, of 1959, and 1961, Limonali.
- Born in 1899, Norah, daughter of Flat trainer Sir Robert Wilmot, began to take over her father's workload as he aged, and he wrote to the Jockey Club, explaining to them that now, in 1930, she was basically running things herself and requesting that she be allowed to assume his licence to train.

  Surprise, surprise, the request was refused. The last winner from the Berkshire stable at Binfield Grove before the death of Sir Robert, was Winning Ways at Hurst Park on 24 July 1931.

  Ludicrously, Norah had to apply for a licence to train in the name of her head lad, T Martin. Two weeks later Norah sent out Bunch, a four-year-old, to win at Lewes, which should properly be considered the first winner trained by a woman in Great Britain.

  Norah's application to be licensed as a trainer was turned down in 1931, 1932, 1933, 1934, 1935, 1936 and 1937, by which time she gave up even asking. However, now she had been joined in the quest to train legitimately, by Mrs Florence Nagle, who began applying in the early 40s, only to be told, 'It would not be in the best interests of racing for women to be granted trainer's licences.'

  Eventually, Florence took her case to the High Court in 1966 – where Mr Justice Sachs ruled in her favour, and on 3 August 1966 the *Racing Calendar* carried the announcement that: 'Mrs Florence Nagle and Miss Norah Eleanor Wilmot have been granted licences under Rule 102 of the Rules of Racing for 1966.'

  The day after receiving her licence, the Norah-trained Pat, ridden by Scobie Breasley, won on the Flat at Brighton, making Wilmot the first officially licensed woman trainer to win a race.

STRANGE STUFF

- On 16 March 1966, Jackie Brutton was officially the first woman trainer to send out a winner over jumps, as Snowdra Queen won the United Hunts Challenge Cup at Cheltenham.
- Meriel Tufnell is renowned for being the first female licence holder to ride the winner of a Flat race, when she won the Goya Stakes – open only to women riders – at Kempton in May 1972, on her mother's horse, Scorched Earth. She ended the season as the first champion female jockey.
- Linda Goodwill won the first 'mixed' race, the Lads & Lassies Handicap at Nottingham, on Pee Mai, on 1 April 1974.
- On 30 January 1976 Muriel Naughton became the first woman to ride over fences in Britain, finishing sixth on Ballycasey at Ayr. But Diana Thorne was the first of her sex to ride a winner under NH rules, on Ben Ruler at Stratford, on 7 February 1976. A week later, on Valentine's Day, Val Greaves became the first of her sex to compete against professional jockeys over hurdles, when she was unplaced on Silver Gal at Catterick.
- Charlotte Brew really broke the mould as, on 2 April 1977, she became the first woman to ride in the Grand National, partnering 200/1 chance Barony Fort to the fourth from home where he refused, as Red Rum won. Five years later Geraldine Rees was the first female to get round in the National, finishing eighth on 66/1 Cheers.
- Corbiere won the 1983 Grand National – the first winner trained by a woman – Jenny Pitman, would do it again in 1995 with Royal Athlete, before, in 2009, Venetia Williams became the second woman to train the winner – 100/1 chance Mon Mome.
- In 1991 Alex Greaves was the first female to win a prestigious William Hill Golden Spurs Award – for Apprentice Jockey of the Year. She was also the first woman to win the Lincoln, in 1991, on 22/1 Amenable. In 1993 Lynda Ramsden was the first woman to train a Lincoln winner, 16/1 High Premium. And in the same year, on 1 April, 19-year-old Deborah Ryan became the youngest female to make a book at a racecourse, representing her father Pat, at Wetherby.
- The death occurred on 11 February 1994 of Ann Argyle, 76, who had been one of the first women permitted by the Jockey Club to work in racing – which she did, as a work-rider for trainer Capt Sir Cecil Boyd-Rochfort.
- In 1984 Jenny Pitman became the first woman to train a Cheltenham Gold Cup winner – Burrough Hill Lad – and on the same date Jacqui Oliver was the first female jockey to ride a treble over the sticks – doing so at Uttoxeter.
- Stepping out from her husband Lester's shadow, Susan Piggott sent out Raahim to win at Folkestone – her first as a trainer.

Of course there would be many more female firsts as the years rolled on, taking us through to the jump jockeys Katie Walsh and sister-in-law Nina Carberry generation, as these two superb riders booted home jump winners galore, creating the pathway down which Bryony Frost and Rachael Blackmore have stormed, alongside Flat colleagues like Hollie Doyle, ensuring that never again will females be grudgingly tolerated, but instead welcomed and treated as equals on and around racecourses ...

BIBLIOGRAPHY

Bernard, J. and Dodd, H., T*ales from the Turf* (W&N, 1991).

Bibblecombe, T., *Tales Of Racing and Chasing* (Stanley Paul, 1985).

Campbell, R., *All Bets Are Off* (Gomer, 2004).

Church, M., *Ripping Gambling Yarns* (Raceform, 2001).

DeArment, R. K., *Knights of the Green Cloth* (Oklahoma, 1982).

Ducal, C., *Moments In The Sun* (*Racing Post*, 2017).

Fieldes, Finnegan, Lee, *Racing With Pacific* (Radio Pacific, 2000).

Francis, D. and Lord, G., *A Racing Life* (Little, Brown and Company, 1999).

Mackenzie, I. and Selby, T., *MacKenzie & Selby's Hunter Chasers & Point To Pointers* (Chase, 1992).

McAlpine, B., *One Shot At Life* (JJG, 2012).

Pitt, C., *Pitchcroft: 300 Years Of Racing In Worcester* (Pitchcroft 300, 2018).

Shack, J., *Straight from the Horse's Mouth* (Oat Cuisine Press, 1986).

Slusar, J., *Racecourses; Here Today and Gone Tomorrow* – Volume 4/3 (Cardan Publishing, 2016).

Smith Eccles, S. and Lee A., *Tales From The Turf* (Partridge Press, 1988).

Walmsley, M. and Smith-Baranzini M., *Horse racing* (Bowtie, 2006).

Warner, G. B., *Racing Review Annual,* 1952 (Racing Review, 1952).